FOUR THOUSAND LIVES

FOUR THOUSAND LIVES

THE RESCUE OF GERMAN JEWISH MEN TO BRITAIN, 1939

CLARE UNGERSON

In loving memory of my grandmother, Lilli Jordan Gumbel,
and my mother, Annelis Lore Grete Ungerson.
Both got away and made a life in England.

Cover illustration: Kitchener Camp. (Mary Evans/Robert Hunt Collection)

First published 2014
This paperback edition published 2019

The History Press
97 St George's Place
Cheltenham, GL50 3QB
www.thehistorypress.co.uk

British Library Cataloguing in Publication Data.
A catalogue record for this book is available from the British Library.

ISBN 978 0 7509 9235 0

Typesetting and origination by The History Press
Printed and bound in Great Britain by TJ Books Ltd

CONTENTS

ACKNOWLEDGEMENTS

Many people have helped me with this project and I am grateful to all of them. Gaby Glassman introduced me to the Association of Jewish Refugees, and through the AJR I gave a number of talks at an early stage in the project and thereby met a number of widows and descendants of Kitchener men. The staff of the AJR have also been very helpful, especially Esther Rinkoff, Hazel Beiny, Tony Grenville and Howard Spier. Three archivists, Ray Harlow at Sandwich Guildhall, Howard Falksohn at the Wiener Library, London, and Hadassah Assouline at the Central Archives for the History of the Jewish People at the Hebrew University of Jerusalem all sought out material for me and, in the case of the Jerusalem archives, catalogued the Bentwich papers. Staff at the Wiener Library have always been exceptionally welcoming and helpful, especially Bridget McGing, Marek Jaros and Toby Simpson.

Helen Fry generously introduced me to Harry Rossney and the group of old comrades who still meet at the Imperial Café in the Golders Green Road in London. Harry's enthusiasm and support were invaluable. Helen Fry also put me in touch with Walter Marmorek when he was still, at age 98, practising as an architect in London, but who sadly died before I could complete this project, which was very dear to his heart. Adrienne Harris, Phineas May's daughter, gave me very useful information on Phineas and Jonas May's background and family history and took a positive interest in what I was doing, Joan Cromwell and Philip Stirups gave essential help with the translation of German documents, and Sam Warshaw ably transcribed Phineas May's rather difficult to read Kitchener camp diary.

Others who, through conversation, letter, or more formal interview, have helped me with this book include Nikki van der Zyl, Hilda Keen, Patrick Miles, Rosa Plotnek, Katherine Shock, Howard Kendal, Monica Reynolds, Hans Jackson, Allen Sternstein, Harry Brooks, Stella Curzon, Eva Mendelson, Andrew Kodin, Ivy Kum, Pat Pay, Robert Fraser, Michael Streat, James Bird. Many others have sent me emails, often with attachments of photos or memoirs, all of which convinced me that there was a story here, well worth remembering and telling. Anne Deighton and Jane Deighton, both with memories of Sandwich summers in the 1950s, filled me in with details about an earlier Sandwich, and made insightful comments as the project progressed.

A number of people read early and late drafts. Mary Evans, Judith Friedlaender, Bernard Harris, Tony Kushner, Esther Saraga, the late A.W.B. (Brian) Simpson, Grace Tonner, Jenny Uglow, all made significant comments at crucial stages. Jean Gaffin deserves a special mention for encouraging me when I was flagging and reading all the early chapters. Towards the end of the project, a group of retired colleagues centred around the University of Kent started meeting on a monthly basis and presenting their work in progress to each other. The constructive, friendly and often forensic critique of Sarah Carter, Judith Hattaway, Lyn Innes, Jan Pahl, and Janet Sayers introduced a rigour and a rhythm to the writing process that were essential for the book's completion.

Finally, at home, William Fortescue always believed in the project, and was endlessly supportive and patient. He was the mainstay and I could not have done this without him.

Clare Ungerson
Sandwich, Kent

1

TERROR IN GERMANY

On the morning of 10 November 1938, Fritz Mansbacher was woken by his alarm clock at 4.45 a.m. At age 16 he had recently left school and started a job at a local factory, and it was very important that he got to work on time. Many of his Jewish friends had recently lost their jobs, and he hoped that punctuality and reliability would help him keep his. Now that he was earning his own money he was almost an adult and he had moved into a separate flat at the top of his parents' house in Lübeck, Germany.

That morning he was still half asleep as he dressed himself and started to go downstairs to the floors below. Suddenly he stopped:

> I thought I had heard voices! Normally nobody would be up and awake at this hour. I listened. A second later I saw two Nazi stormtroopers come out of my parents' apartment door. Quickly I crouched into the shadow and clung as closely to the stairwell wall as possible so as not to be seen. There I stayed quietly, not daring to breathe. Now they tramped down the stairs in their heavy boots. Now they closed the front door. Now they walked down the driveway to the sidewalk. Shortly after I could hear a car motor start up, a car door slam and a car driving away.[1]

Once it was safe to move he ran down the stairs and into his parents' flat. His mother was standing behind their front door, still in her nightdress, shaking and angry. His father was in bed: Mr Mansbacher had been ill for years, struggling with an illness that Fritz only learnt years later was multiple sclerosis:

> In a stern voice, mingled with grim humour and sarcasm, my father related what had just taken place in our apartment. He said that the Nazis had come at that unearthly hour of the morning to take him away to a concentration camp. They were very rough at first. They told him that he was under arrest and

to get out of bed, get dressed and follow them. My father, strong in character and afraid of nothing, jestingly told them that he would love to go with them but that he could not do so at this time. They demanded to know why not. 'I am sick' he told them. 'Got a cold, I suppose,' said the Nazi. 'No,' answered my father, 'it's worse than that; I cannot walk.' Now the two got impatient with my father. 'Get out of that bed, you swine, and show us how well you can walk!'

Fritz's father was a rational man and he thought that reason and evidence might appeal to these two gentlemen. The only thing to do was to phone his doctor and get him to talk to them, but as Mr Mansbacher picked up the receiver to make the call the stormtroopers had snatched it from him and slammed it down. Perhaps they did not want others to know what was going on, perhaps they thought it was just too much bother to drag a sick man from his bed, get him dressed and push him into their car. Something had stopped them, and in compensation for their weakness in the face of Mr Mansbacher's disability they had set about wrecking the flat, searching – they said – for guns. Eventually they had left, just as Fritz had reached the top of the stairs.

The Mansbachers were horrified. The situation was bad for the Jews as they knew only too well, but this invasion of their house and the threat of arrest was something new. At least they were still intact as a family and they all thought it best to behave as if nothing had happened. Fritz should go to work as usual. As he rode his bicycle into town he was surprised by something else – 'an unusual number of police cars, filled with people, driving toward the railway station'. And then at the factory there was a very odd atmosphere: nobody spoke to him and everyone avoided his gaze. He began to wonder if somehow or other his workmates knew about that morning's incursion and that they felt guilty:

> Finally, a fellow worker whom I knew to be a decent fellow, in spite of the fact that he was a member of the Nazi party, took me aside and asked me why I was at work. Did I not know that all the Jewish stores in Lübeck had been smashed, broken into and ransacked and that many of the owners had been badly beaten before being shipped out? And had I not heard that the Synagogue, the Jewish house of worship, had been destroyed? Of course I had not heard about all these events! And at six o'clock in the morning?[2]

Suddenly Fritz's boss appeared and sacked him on the spot. Fritz remonstrated that he had a contract till January 1939 and it was only November 1938. 'The Nazi Party does not honour any agreements or promises. Goodbye!'

Thus Fritz learnt about *Kristallnacht*. The Mansbachers lived in a quiet Lübeck suburb so they had not heard the rioting, the smashing of shop windows, and the razing of their synagogue, which had taken place in the city centre the previous night. But by the time Fritz came home later that morning his parents had rung round their friends and relatives and discovered even worse news. Almost all the adult men of their acquaintance had been arrested, taken to the railway station and thence they knew not where. And even more serious for them personally was that their friends had added if the Gestapo couldn't find the man of the house they often took the oldest adult son. It was only the odd arrangement of the Mansbacher's house, and its separation into two distinct flats, that had saved Fritz. It would not take long for the Gestapo to realise there was a younger male Mansbacher and they would return. Driven by desperation, Fritz's parents began the process of getting him on a *Kindertransport* (a train for unaccompanied Jewish children up to the maximum age of 16) to England. They loved their son and that was why they needed to send him away.

Thirty thousand Jewish men from all over Greater Germany were arrested during those few days in November 1938. Most of them were taken to one of three concentration camps – Dachau near Munich, Buchenwald near Weimar, and Sachsenhausen near Berlin. All three camps had been in existence for some years. In fact Dachau was the very first such camp, built as soon as Hitler came to power and in operation from 1933 onwards. It was the first really large material indication of the nature of the Nazi regime. The term 'concentration' camp meant a 'concentration' of prisoners in very large numbers, guarded, as efficiently as possible, by a minimum of guards who were encouraged to undertake their work with extreme brutality, meting out severe punishments, including death, for minor infractions of camp regulations.[3] Dachau was the template for its successors: it was there that the term '*Arbeit macht frei*' (literally, 'Work brings freedom') was first used on concentration camp gates (a phrase now notoriously linked with the gates to the Auschwitz death camp) and it was at Dachau that the 'Kapo' system of control, whereby brutalised prisoners controlled other prisoners, was first put in place.

In one important respect these camps differed from what was to come a few years later. There were no gas chambers; these early camps were not designed for mass murder on an industrial scale. They were not death camps but there were many deaths. And in the years preceding *Kristallnacht* their inmates were not necessarily or predominantly Jewish, but rather were people who, in one way or another, had crossed the Nazi regime since its inception in 1933: many were Communists and wore a red badge on their prison uniform, others were homosexual, with a pink badge, and other 'anti socials' including gypsies, 'criminals', Catholics and Quakers wore green badges. The Jewish prisoners wore yellow badges.

Everyone in Germany knew about these camps and the horror of what happened in them. Indeed there was a jingle that had been around since 1935, which went: 'Dear God, make me dumb, that I may not to Dachau come'

('*Lieber Gott, mach mich dumm, damit ich nicht nach Dachau kumm*'). So the day after *Kristallnacht* all Jewish families in Greater Germany knew that if their men had escaped immediate arrest it was imperative they get them out of the country as quickly as possible. The Mansbachers had been lucky in a way – their son Fritz was, at age 16, still eligible for the *Kindertransport* – just.

Fred Pelikan was not so fortunate.[4] He lived with his mother the other side of Germany in Breslau near the German–Polish border and, at age 20, was well beyond the upper age limit for the children's trains. On the morning after *Kristallnacht* Fred had crept out of the house to see for himself what was going on, and when the Gestapo had called for him his mother was able to say genuinely that she did not know where he was. When Fred did eventually come home he knew the worst. He had seen the blazing synagogue and the laughing crowds, heard the uniformed gangs singing Nazi songs as they ransacked Jewish shops. On his way home he had called at his aunt and uncle's and discovered that his Uncle Martin had already been taken away.

As soon as he got home he threw some things in a bag, kissed his terrified mother goodbye, and made his way to the railway station. The only place he could think of going was Berlin, where an old schoolfriend, David, was now living; by all accounts David's parents were well off and might be able to put him up. The journey to Berlin was uneventful – fortunately nobody recognised him or denounced him as a Jew – but when he got to David's house, David's parents were 'in a state of frenzy', terrified that they were about to lose their only son. They were apparently much more stoical about David's father, who was equally at risk. They were kind and welcoming to Fred, gave him a bed in their large and comfortable flat and then they hunkered down, waiting for the worst. There they stayed for some days, living very quietly and hoping no one would notice them.

A few days later David's father somehow or other made contact with a people-smuggler, a certain 'Herr X', who promised that, for a large fee, he could get both Fred and David over the border to Belgium. It was not to be. Maybe Herr X was a charlatan and a double crosser, maybe the plans simply went wrong, but when the young men reached the village close to the Belgian border, where they were supposed to board a train from which they could – literally – jump into Belgium, they were arrested by the SS. After a rough and aggressive interrogation they were taken to the regular prison in Aachen, close to the German–Belgian border. To Fred and David's surprise, this prison was actually quite bearable – there was adequate food and they had decent sleeping facilities. But it did not last: after twelve days they were suddenly told that all the Jewish prisoners were leaving that evening. In the darkness about 200 of them were loaded onto lorries and driven to Aachen railway station. A special train was waiting for them – not cattle trucks but a train with seats. Once on board, they were told to be absolutely quiet and keep the blinds drawn: no one waiting at a station as they passed through was to know what human cargo this train contained.

All night and well into the next day the train rolled slowly across Germany. There was no food, they were not allowed to go to the toilet and they had absolutely no idea where they were going or how long this journey was going to take. At long last, sometime in the early afternoon, the train ground to a halt:

> We must have been waiting a good half an hour when the train was invaded by numerous SS personnel with strange-sounding dialects which some of us recognized as either Bavarian or Austrian. We were literally pushed out onto the platform and ordered to line up for a roll-call … We were surrounded by a maze of railway lines, an indication of being somewhere near a big city. The SS guards were given the order, 'Fix bayonets' and we marched off over several railway lines, climbing over another platform leading on to the main station. My eyes instantly noticed the name München (Munich) and at the very same time I realized what Munich conveyed: *Munich meant Dachau.*[5]

It was a chilling moment. And then a woman came out of the jeering crowd, shrieked 'Dirty Jew' and spat straight into his face. 'I can only describe my own feelings: devastated, agonized, humiliated, what on earth did I do to deserve such treatment?'

At age 74, when Fred Pelican (he changed the 'k' to the anglicised 'c' when he enlisted in the British Army in 1940) came to write his autobiography, he remembered his time in Dachau as though it were yesterday. An inmate of Room 4, Block 10, he found himself one young man among about 150 prisoners in his 'room'. He seemed to be younger than most of the others and that meant that he could struggle more effectively for space to move about in and, in particular, for a bunk bed.

He also came to know his 'Kapo' very well. This Kapo was a man in his late twenties who had already been in Dachau for four years, having been arrested for being a Communist. It was the Kapo's responsibility to see that all the 150 men under his 'care' obeyed. However useless the occupation and however cruel the treatment, the Kapo knew that if his men did not do as they were ordered, and at the double, then the Kapo would be punished. And the punishment at Dachau, as at all these concentration camps, was a form of torture – with hands bound tightly behind their backs, men were suspended by their bonds from a 'gallows' for up to three hours. At the same time the Kapo enjoyed certain privileges: 'he slept in a segregated area from the prisoners and was always well supplied with clothes, shoes and underwear taken from prisoners who had passed away'.[6]

Fred's experience at Dachau turned out to be rather unusual. For the first few days after his arrival there was nothing to do – evidently the camp authorities were at a loss as to what tasks to devise for this sudden influx, post-*Kristallnacht*, of large numbers of new inmates. Fred became bored and rather irritated by his fellow inmates, who 'sat around either brooding, lamenting or even crying'. So he went to the washroom (Dachau, being the first concentration camp, had reasonable washing facilities), found a bucket and a mop and set about cleaning the entire place. He did this all day for four days. The windows sparkled, the floors shone. He knew the Kapo had noticed but neither man acknowledged the other. On the fourth day the camp authorities took action – they invented a task for the new inmates that involved shovelling the heavy snow (which had fallen the previous few days) from one part of the camp to another. It was to be dreadful work, from which many, particularly the older men, would fall ill with frostbite and exertion and eventually die. But Fred, along with two others, was selected out by the Kapo – these three were to be 'Room Orderlies'. Fred's devotion to washroom cleanliness had been rewarded and in a very satisfactory manner. He would be relatively warm, autonomous, and, so long as he did the work properly, would not be beaten. Thus Fred became an observer of horror rather than a participant:

> To see the prisoners return from work was a dreadful sight. Most of the men had never done manual work, they may have been academics, teachers, some even doctors. As time went on, some of those going out to work looked more dead than alive, especially the sixty to seventy age group. I felt very sorry for them, I carried inside me a feeling of guilt, that, as a young strong person, I stayed indoors in relative comfort while old men began to die [...] the reality of Dachau became more evident by the day. We had men in our room lying down for a night's sleep and not getting up in the morning. They were dead, their bodies collected by a special commando every morning. Gradually their numbers increased.[7]

Sometimes the men tried to help each other. A Dr Klein from Vienna took to administering his tiny supply of Vaseline in a useless effort to ease his companions' frostbite. This had a disastrous consequence. Betrayed to the Kapo, presumably by someone trying to curry favour, Dr Klein was taken away for the 'gallows' treatment. 'When he returned to the room, he seemed to have aged by ten years. Both his arms were swollen and he was completely mute. For days one could not get a single word out of him, as if he had lost his voice completely.'

In his memoir, Fred describes himself as becoming progressively inured to brutality – 'we seemed to have lost our feelings, we were going through a process of dehumanization'. But this did not prevent him taking pity on one particular elderly man and agreeing to swap places with him 'for one day only'. Fred himself says that perhaps he was driven by curiosity as much as by sympathy – 'I was curious about what really went on outside the huts on the working parties. Was it really as bad as others described?' – and he thought that as a fit young man he would be capable of dealing with whatever hardship and brutality was in store. But he had underestimated the irrationality of the camp regime – a young man working instead of an old, sick man was not a legitimate exchange. No permission had been asked for or given – it was against orders. He was spotted, and the result was two dreadful beatings, one from the SS overseer who first identified him and then a far worse one from the Kapo, who told him that the next time he would kill him. The Kapo was sentenced to the relatively lenient sentence of one hour on the 'gallows'.

Despite his misdemeanour and the Kapo's suffering for it, Fred retained his privileged status. He never went on a working party again, and very surprisingly he and the Kapo became friends. December 1938 and January 1939 came and went and the nightmare for the other prisoners continued. In February 1939 someone killed himself by running at the electrified fence and later that same month another man escaped. In punishment, the entire camp was made to stand in nothing but their striped uniforms all night in the freezing cold while a 'roll call' was taken. The death rate, which was already high (Fred thought it to be between 15 and 20 per cent), really spiked that night.

They knew they were not forgotten; they could stay in touch with their families but only with the briefest of messages. But they had no reason to think that they would ever get away from the concentration camp. There probably were rumours in the camps that men could leave on condition that they would quit Germany within a very short time, but for most of these men the prospect of leaving Germany was a chimera. This was despite the fact that many had already got away. When the Third Reich had begun in 1933 there had been about half a million Jews living in Germany and in the first year of the Reich there had been a very rapid upturn in the number of Jews emigrating (about 37,000 left Germany that year), but thereafter emigration had declined to about 25,000 a year, leaving about 200,000 Jews still living in Germany, and a further 100,000 still living in Austria, after *Kristallnacht*.[8] Those Jews who had already managed to leave were the well resourced and well networked who could, for example, persuade the British authorities that they could support themselves in the United Kingdom or find a British citizen willing to support them. Some had managed to be accepted for emigration to Palestine but this opportunity had recently declined: after the 1936 Arab Revolt the British had introduced a strict annual quota of 25,000 migrants to mandate Palestine. If they preferred to emigrate to the United States, which many did, then they had to find a US citizen to provide them with an 'affidavit' of support for entry to the United States, and then manage to obtain a visa within the very strict national quotas that the United States operated. There were other countries that would take refugees, but at a price. Steep 'landing fees' were demanded by the countries of Latin America, and by the international port of Shanghai. Such opportunities for emigration, which were expensive and often depended on the support of individuals already living in the receiving countries, took place in a context where the Jewish populations of Germany and Austria were being systematically stripped of their assets, sacked from their jobs, and paying the extortionate taxes that the Germans had imposed on the Jews, particularly after *Kristallnacht*, including a tax that forced the Jews to pay for the reparations for that night of terror. These were forbidding prospects for ordinary German Jews and many, however desperate, knew they could never afford the costs of escape from Nazi persecution.

However, *Kristallnacht* itself shifted the politics of refugee policy a little – particularly in Britain. The pogrom had drawn the attention of the world to the *domestic* policies of Nazi Germany. Until late 1938 it had been German *foreign* policy that had largely transfixed international opinion. (An international conference held at Evian in Switzerland earlier in 1938 to discuss the refugee issue with the intention of persuading various nations, including the USA, to take more refugees, had been an almost complete failure.) In some countries, particularly in Britain, opinion and sympathy for the Jews of Germany and Austria changed after *Kristallnacht*. The British newspapers, including those that supported appeasement, ran the story of the attacks on German Jewry as front page news the following day. The story was powerful enough to move very large numbers of ordinary people into action and very quickly the idea that a fund should be established that would pay for the rescue of destitute Jewry, particularly children, took hold. Less than a month after *Kristallnacht*, the ex-prime minister, Stanley Baldwin, now Lord Baldwin, gave his name to a National Appeal. The Lord Baldwin Fund for Refugees, supported by many of the prominent dignitaries of the day including the Archbishop of Canterbury, was launched by a special broadcast on BBC radio on Thursday 8 December. Money started to pour in. Special events in aid of the appeal were held on a national basis. For example, all cinema and theatre tickets sold on 14 January 1939 included a 10 per cent levy for the Baldwin Fund, and a filmed appeal for the Fund by the Archbishop of Canterbury was included in the *Pathé News* for that day. Within three months, by March 1939, the Baldwin Fund had attracted donations from rich and poor such that it had raised the astonishing sum of £461,658 (equivalent to £13.2 million in present day values).[9] This was a very convincing and material indication that British public opinion had softened and shifted in relation to the plight of German Jewry.

Fred Pelican, trapped in Dachau, knew nothing of how his plight had caught the imagination of many British people. He was not a child, but he was a Jew in desperate circumstances and public sympathy across the English Channel had been triggered. There was a chink of light at the end of the dark tunnel he was in and it was about to grow larger.

Notes

1. Peter Mansbacher, *'Refugee from Nazi Oppression', An Autobiography*, unpublished manuscript held at the Wiener Library, copyright 1991, p. 68. Fritz Mansbacher changed his first name to Peter at some point during the Second World War.

2. Ibid., p. 69.

3. See for example, Michael Burleigh, *The Third Reich, a New History*, London, Pan Macmillan, 2001, pp. 198–205.

4. Fred Pelican, *From Dachau to Dunkirk*, London, Vallentine Mitchell, 1993.

5. Fred Pelican, ibid., p. 10.

6. Ibid., p. 14.

7. Ibid., p. 16.

8. Pamela Shatzkes, *Holocaust and Rescue: Impotent or Indifferent? Anglo–Jewry 1938–1945,* London, Vallentine Mitchell, 2004.

9. Richard A. Hawkins, 'The Lord Baldwin Fund for Refugees, 1938–39: A Case Study of Third Sector Marketing in Pre-World War II Britain', in Neilson, L.C. (Ed.), (2013), 'Varieties, Alternatives, and Deviations in Marketing History: Proceedings of the 16th Conference on Historical Analysis and Research in Marketing (CHARM)', CHARM Association, Copenhagen, Denmark, pp. 82–105.

2

THE BRITISH
RESPONSE

On 4 January 1939 Norman Bentwich was at his desk in the offices of the Central British Fund for German Jewry in central London well before his colleagues. This was not unusual – he was still, at age 55, a man of prodigious energy who loved nothing better than getting on top of his work before anyone else could come into his office and disturb him. Woburn House, where his office was located, was occupied by many Jewish organisations, including the United Synagogue, and he enjoyed being surrounded by people who shared his deep faith and, like him, were committed to the welfare of European and Anglo–Jewry. For years Bentwich had worked tirelessly, and often for no salary, on behalf of Jewish refugees desperate to leave Germany, and now, since the German annexation of Austria in March 1938, on behalf of Austrian Jewry as well.

That morning in early January 1939 he was waiting for a very important letter. He knew more or less what would be in it and hoped it would be the agreement, in writing, that he and his colleagues had reached with the Home Office the previous day. It had been a friendly meeting between himself, Sir Robert Waley Cohen and Otto Hirsch from the Jewish agency in Berlin on the one hand and with familiar civil servants whom he trusted and whom he knew trusted him, on the other. It looked as though they were about to make real progress with an idea the Fund had long nurtured – that of setting up a refugee camp, somewhere in Britain, which would temporarily house Jewish refugees while they waited, in safety, for emigration elsewhere.

There were at that time in early 1939 probably about 30,000 German–Jewish refugees resident in Britain but all these refugees had been able to enter because they could show, on an *individual* basis, that they would make no call on the British State – either they, or someone willing to sponsor them, had the resources to support them over the long term. Now there seemed to be some prospect that the British government would accept the sponsorship of the Fund on a *collective* basis and this would allow Jews with far fewer resources in terms of money and networks to enter Britain, if only on a temporary basis.

Bentwich had been Honorary Director of Emigration and Training of the Fund since 1935, and in that capacity he had spent a great deal of time in Greater Germany liaising with the German–Jewish agencies in Berlin and Vienna and other major German cities, so he had seen at first hand what the Nazi regime was capable of. He was probably not surprised by the extremism of *Kristallnacht*. But for others it had been a considerable shock: until that moment it had been possible to ignore the persecution of the Jews in Greater Germany since much of it had taken place behind closed doors in schools and universities, shops and offices and theatres and orchestras, and in the prisons of the Gestapo. Now that persecution was on the street, highly visible and very dramatic.

British Prime Minister Neville Chamberlain, who in September 1938 had signed the notorious Munich agreement apparently bringing 'Peace in Our Time', had been as shocked by these events as most ordinary British people; when a delegation from the Fund had asked to see him he had readily consented. Accordingly, on 15 November 1938, the elite of Anglo–Jewry had crowded into the prime minister's rooms at the House of Commons and pleaded with Chamberlain for practical help. Viscount Samuel, Chair of the Central British Fund for German Jewry, took the lead, supported by another Jewish peer Viscount Bearsted, the chief rabbi; Neville Laski, who was president of the Board of Deputies of British Jews; Lionel de Rothschild of the famous banking family; and Dr Chaim Weizmann, the leader of British Zionism and later the founding president of the State of Israel. The delegation was careful not to suggest that the government throw open its doors to the estimated 300,000 Jews still in Greater Germany. Indeed it is very unlikely that they would have welcomed such an influx of refugees themselves. Instead they asked for targeted permissions, particularly for children under 17 years of age. They were also desperate for help with the funding of the rescue effort they proposed. Chamberlain was sympathetic; on the day of the pogrom he had written to his sister, 'I am horrified by the German behaviour to the Jews' even though he was himself a casual, unfocussed anti-semite – 'no doubt Jews aren't lovable people, I don't care about them myself'.[1] He talked of the possibility of the permanent resettlement of German Jewry in British Guiana, but with some pessimism and only in the very long term; privately he decided to persuade his cabinet to consider ways in which Britain could alleviate the plight of the Jews by allowing them to come to Britain as 'transmigrants'.

A few days later the Fund grandees went to see Lord Winterton, the member of government directly concerned with refugee matters. Despite eloquent pleading particularly by Viscount Samuel for funding for a refugee camp where 'the intention was, first to put [the refugees] in safety, and then, while there, to train them for ultimate settlement in suitable places abroad' they had made little headway. The one chink of light was the statement by Lord Winterton that 'the Home Secretary Sir Samuel Hoare had authorised him to say on his behalf that he had no objection in principle to camps for transmigrants in this country, and he would be glad if the leaders of British Jewry would take the matter up with him'.[2]

It was at this point that their luck began to turn. This may have been because the Home Secretary was a scion of a distinguished Quaker family and the Quakers had worked very effectively with their own staff in Berlin and Vienna rescuing Jews and supporting destitute Jews.[3] Moreover, Sir Samuel Hoare's senior civil servants, particularly Sir Alexander Maxwell and Ernest Cooper, the Director of the Aliens Section at the Home Office, were known to be sympathetic to the plight of Jews in Germany. It was this team at the Home Office that had given the Fund its first real hope that something collective might be undertaken to save the masses of adult Jews still in Greater Germany and the idea of a rescue camp had first begun to gain some purchase.

The men of the Fund had had to wait for a final decision over Christmas and the New Year but as soon as the festive season was over the Home Office had set up the all-important meeting of 3 January. The letter that Bentwich had been waiting for duly arrived on 4 January 1939. Addressed to 'Professor Bentwich, MC, OBE, MA' and signed by Sir Alexander Maxwell, permanent under-secretary at the Home Office, its contents were more or less as expected, although Bentwich knew that it would not contain everything they had hoped for. The main point of the letter was that it laid out the terms and conditions for the establishment of a refugee transit camp somewhere in the UK. The tone was sympathetic:

> I am directed by the Secretary of State to say that if the Council for German Jewry establish a camp in England for refugees who have a prospect of 'migration within a reasonable period' he will be glad to facilitate arrangements to enable selected persons to come to this country with a view to their residing in this camp until arrangements can be made for their settlement.

But of course there were provisos, not least that the Central British Fund was on its own as far as the management and funding of the camp were concerned. There was definitely to be no money:

> He understands the Council will make themselves responsible for seeing that the camp is properly organised and that proper sanitary arrangements are made, and that provision will be available for the maintenance of the persons residing in this camp.

Moreover there was to be no possibility that the camp inmates would acquire rights of citizenship or permanent residence in Britain. Nor would they be able to work, except in exceptional circumstances:

> He understands further that the Council will give a collective guarantee that persons admitted to this country for the purpose of going to the camp would not take any employment in this country unless a special permit was obtained, and would not be a public charge and would, so far as possible, migrate within a year.

Two further points were made. At the meeting the previous day the delegation from the Fund, fully aware that the camp numbers would hardly scratch the surface as far as the numbers of Jews desperate to get out of Germany were concerned, had been anxious that the camp population should be continuously replenished as the refugees moved on to other countries. This the Home Office had conceded:

> The Secretary of State agrees with the suggestion made at the discussion that it would be desirable to select, as far as possible, persons who have a prospect of migration at a comparatively early date so that vacancies may be made in the camp as soon as possible and facilities thereby afforded for the admission of other selected refugees to fill such vacancies.

And the most satisfying point of all was that the vetting of applicants for the camp would be the responsibility not of the British consulates in Berlin and Vienna but rather of the Jewish agencies in Greater Germany. Moreover, there would be no need to sort out individual visas and individual payments for those visas:

> The Secretary of State would look to the responsible Jewry organisation in Germany acting as agents for the Council to make themselves responsible for selecting suitable people for admission to the camp. Provided that the Council satisfy the Department that due care is being taken in the selection of persons, there will be no difficulty in granting permits for their admission to the United Kingdom. Details as to the arrangements to be made for this purpose will be a matter for discussion between the Council and officials of this Department.[4]

In fact, what was being proposed was an identical operation to that of the *Kindertransport*. The transports of unaccompanied children from Berlin and Vienna to the United Kingdom had already started – the first one, with about 200 children, had arrived in England on 2 December 1938. The system of selection of the children for the transports by the Jewish agencies in Berlin and

Vienna, and their fast-tracked admission by the British Home Office, had already been tried and tested. Exactly the same system was being proposed for the adults who were to come to a transit camp somewhere in Britain. Set up within the same context of enhanced public sympathy, following the same procedures, conceived, as the *Kindertransporte* were originally, as only allowing temporary immigration into Britain, this rescue was to be, in every sense, a parallel rescue to the *Kindertransporte*.

The Home Office letter, filled with ifs and buts as it was, must have seemed a real turning point to the grandees of Anglo–Jewry who led the Central British Fund. These kinds of transit and training camps, on a small scale, had long been established on Continental Europe and they were subsidised by the Fund. In Germany itself, since the 1920s, local Jewish communities had set up training camps for their young people where they could learn the skills – predominantly agricultural skills – that would find them employment in the colonial world, particularly in Palestine.[5] And since the inception of the Third Reich and all that entailed for the Jews of Germany, a number of small camps had been established elsewhere in Europe which fulfilled the dual purpose of training *and* temporary rescue. Bentwich had particular reason to be delighted: since 1935 when he had taken on the unpaid post of Director of Emigration and Training he had spent many weeks away from home inspecting the training centres and agricultural enterprises, most of them in Germany, that the Fund subsidised. Now at least he could stay in England and oversee the strategy of combined rescue and training on his home ground.

There was a huge amount to be done and it had to be done at speed. The first thing the Fund had to do was find a large and usable camp. It must have seemed little short of a miracle when a member of the Fund Executive, the distinguished architect Ernest Joseph, remembered that there was a disused First World War camp along the coast from Dover, the port at which they expected the refugees to enter Britain, located on the edge of the little medieval town of Sandwich. Joseph – or 'EMJ' as he was known to his friends – had designed the NAAFI dining hall there when the camp had been built more than twenty years earlier. It was known as 'The Kitchener Camp at Richborough' and had been named after Field Marshal Lord Kitchener, who had been Secretary of State for War from 1914 to his death in 1916.

Coincidentally EMJ had a great interest in the Jewish Lads Brigade – an oddly militaristic but very popular organisation designed by the Anglo-Jewish gentry to inculcate order, discipline and a culture of British fair play into the lives of working-class Jewish 'lads' from the poorer parts of Britain's cities.[6] For many years between the wars EMJ went down to the brigade summer camp overlooking the White Cliffs at the nearby coastal town of Deal. When he took some of the lads along the coast to the long pebble beach of Sandwich Bay he would have seen that the Kitchener Camp, where he had designed the soldiers' mess, was empty and beginning to moulder away.

There was another minor miracle: the owners of this camp were now only too pleased to be approached by the Fund about the availability of the camp for rent, and although the Fund had at first assumed that these derelict huts would not command much more than £100 a year in rental, the owners finally made the entire camp available for the still affordable amount of £380 a year. The Jewish Lads Brigade turned out to be useful again when they declared themselves willing to second their secretary, Jonas May, to be director of the refugee camp for the duration of its existence (no doubt pressured by EMJ to do so). Jonas's brother, Phineas May, also became available, because his employers, the United Synagogue, decided to follow suit and second him as well. These two relatively young men had experience of running summer camps for boys so it was a sensible idea, at least on the surface, to appoint them to run a camp which the Fund expected to contain many thousands of refugees.

It was no accident that the Fund was able to exert such influence and get staff seconded to take on vital jobs at very short notice. As a group of men – and they were all men – they represented an extraordinary resource. Lord Samuel normally chaired their executive meetings. Very recently ennobled, he had been High Commissioner in Palestine in the 1920s and Home Secretary in the National Government of the early 1930s. Viscount Bearsted had inherited the title from his father, but was an important figure in his own right, having been Chair of Shell (a company which his father and uncle founded) and a close colleague of Sir Robert Waley Cohen who had been Shell's managing director and was also, at that time, vice president of the United Synagogue. Simon Marks was the son of the original founder of Marks and Spencer and currently Chair of the company, Harry Sacher was a director of Marks and Spencer. Frank Samuel had also been a colleague of Sir Robert Waley Cohen's both at the United Synagogue and in a commercial enterprise, and he was now managing director of Unilever. Chaim Weizmann was the leader of British Zionism and later founding president of the State of Israel, Anthony de Rothschild and his brother Leo were major figures in one of England's leading banking families, Neville Laski was the president of the Board of Deputies of British Jews. Amongst these huge fish, Norman Bentwich – who was always listed as 'also present' at the executive meetings – must have seemed a mere sprat, but he himself had been Attorney General in mandate Palestine, a Deputy Commissioner at the League of Nations with responsibility for refugees, and a founding Professor of the Hebrew University of Jerusalem.

One extraordinary feature of these gentlemen was that they were all related to each other, both by blood and by marriage. They were brothers-in-law, cousins, first, second and third, they went to each others' weddings and funerals. They were referred to as 'the cousinhood' and they perceived themselves as such.[7]

For example, Norman Bentwich's wife Helen was a niece of Viscount Samuel, the Chair of the Fund Executive, and whenever Norman wrote to Lord Samuel he addressed him, rather endearingly, as 'Dear Uncle Herbert'. These gentlemen were in one another's pockets all the time: if it wasn't family matters that brought them together, then it was their business and charitable lives, or their membership of the same synagogue in Bayswater or Hampstead. They could make joint organisational and institutional arrangements at any moment of their busy lives, including their 'family time'. The one issue that had the potential to drive them apart was Zionism – although all of them would have signed up to some kind of settlement by European Jews in Palestine. Numbers of them, including Norman Bentwich, were reluctant to argue for a Jewish state, and some of them were eager to maintain and promote good relations with the Arabs of Palestine.[8] Because of early arguments amomgst them when the Fund was first established they always took care to balance Zionists with 'non Zionists' (this latter phrase was the one preferred by Sir Robert Waley Cohen who said he was not an 'anti Zionist' but a 'non-Zionist').

It was probably not in any of these gentlemen's mind-sets to countenance failure. But nevertheless, in taking on the funding and organising of a refugee camp for an – as yet – unstated number of refugees (but which could run to many thousands), they were taking considerable risks. Over the years the Fund had been in operation they had raised vast sums to support their various rescue and training activities and most recently they had been called upon to fund the *Kindertransporte*. Those transports had only just begun and already the organisational and financial effort it was taking to put them in place was proving almost overwhelming.[9] It was just possible that the Anglo–Jewish community was 'philanthropied out' and that the money they needed for the parallel rescue of the refugee camp would not be forthcoming.

There was another reason to be worried: they were anxious about an upsurge in anti-Semitism provoked by a sudden influx of German Jews in one particular locality. Helen Bentwich, Norman's wife, was secretary of the Movement for the Care of Children from Germany, the administrative body overseeing the *Kindertransporte*, and she herself had 'advocated the spreading of "our children as far over the British Isles as possible. We do not want too great numbers of them in any one place."'[10] Adults could be even more problematic, particularly adults of working age during an era of economic depression. Indeed, only ten days before *Kristallnacht* one of their number, Otto Schiff, was minuted as saying to the head of the Aliens Section at the Home Office that the flow of refugees from Germany should be halted altogether:

> [he] feels that the time has come when his Committee must refuse to entertain
> any more applications. This is partly due to the physical impossibility of coping

with the work, but more especially because the Committee have no longer available the necessary financial resources; but more important than these, in Mr Schiff's opinion, which was also endorsed by Mr Davidson is the view that we have already received in this country a sufficient number of refugees from Germany and Austria, and Mr Schiff thinks it is time we closed down at any rate temporarily until those who have been already admitted have been assimilated or emigrated. Mr Schiff's Committee are at present spending £1,000 per week for emigration work. Mr Schiff also expressed his view that to admit many more refugees might evoke strong public feeling against refugees generally.[11]

Clearly once *Kristallnacht* had happened the Fund had taken the view that they could not continue to suggest to the Home Office that a moratorium be placed on the entry of refugees – but their worries about anti-Semitism were not likely to disappear.

At least one amongst their number was not the type to baulk at these anxieties. Sir Robert Waley Cohen had a supremely ebullient manner and he was no doubt of the opinion that obstacles could be overcome if the will was robust enough. Sir Robert saw himself as a natural leader: when asked what he wanted to be during the First World War he had said 'one of the higher sorts of General' and when asked 'to command what?' had simply replied 'other Generals'.[12] He was also very rich, very large (he was wont to write 'HUGE' when asked on a form to state his measurements) and very bad tempered.[13] Having retired early from being managing director of Shell, as the decade of the 1930s continued he became steadily more involved with philanthropy, including the Central British Fund for German Jewry. He was a committed Jew who was a vice president of the United Synagogue – notwithstanding a vitriolic relationship with the chief rabbi, whom he despised. He was clearly the sort of person whom it paid to keep on the right side of, but once his respect was gained he was loyal and helpful. And his single criterion of whether a project was or was not worth undertaking was whether it was 'constructive'. The rescue and training of a very large number of Jewish refugees temporarily residing in the country that he loved with a passionate patriotism must have seemed to Sir Robert about the most constructive thing he could possibly do at that stage in his life. The Executive decided to establish a 'Camp Committee' with Waley Cohen as Chair. He started the work of the committee on 12 December 1938.

Alongside Sir Robert, the Fund appointed Harry Sacher and Norman Bentwich. Harry Sacher was almost certainly there because he was a Zionist (he had helped draft the Balfour Declaration and always appeared at the Executive of the Fund as deputising for Chaim Weizmann) and would therefore balance the 'non-Zionism' of Robert Waley Cohen. Certainly, as the camp developed through 1939 there is no evidence at all of Sacher playing any part in it, although as a director of Marks and Spencer he must have been one of those making the decision that his company should continue to support the Fund to a very considerable extent.

Norman Bentwich, however, was to play a very important and ongoing role in the development of the refugee camp. At the start of the camp venture he and Sir Robert did not know each other very well – it was only in April 1939 that the procedurally careful Norman declared in a letter that he was now going to address Sir Robert as 'My dear Bob' rather than 'Dear Waley Cohen' at the top of letters since everyone else called him 'Bob'.[14] The two men were, no doubt, as all the 'cousinhood' were, somehow and complicatedly related. They were also neighbours. Sir Robert lived at the north end of Hampstead Heath in North London, in an enormous mansion called 'Caen Wood Towers', where, in the middle of London, he could effectively pretend that he lived in the depths of the countryside. Bentwich lived at the south end of the Heath in a Victorian development known as the Vale of Health; this community perceived itself as a 'village' and his neighbours were intellectuals, musicians, artists and poets.

Their London homes basically summed up the differences between them. Sir Robert saw himself as landed English gentry, albeit of the Jewish faith, and indeed he had bought himself a large estate on Exmoor where he liked nothing better than to ride to hounds with the local stag hunt and lord it over the local Rural District Council.[15] He enjoyed control – whether it was horse riding, running large corporations or managing local politics, it was the sense of power and the thought that he was getting things done efficiently and effectively that appealed.

Bentwich, in contrast, was an intellectual who, with a spare five minutes, would retreat to his study and pen yet another chapter in one of his many books, or write an article for *The Times*. He was an 'organisation man' through and through: he enjoyed the acts of reading and of writing, he always tried to answer letters by return, he understood the power of records and tended to keep every piece of paper that came his way. Although he disliked petty rules and regulations, he was deeply wedded to the ideas of the rule of law, of equity and of democracy, and he understood that none of these three deeply held values could proceed without an organisational hierarchy, without committees that reached consensus, and without written records of discussions held, decisions taken and precedent established. His highest value was order, and the word 'order' recurs not only in the many documents and papers he penned while working for the Central British Fund for German Jewry, but also in the books he wrote after the Second World War where he recounted his pre-war refugee work.[16] Nothing horrified Bentwich more than the thought of a disorderly refugee process, whereby Jews crossed international borders illegally and in unmanageable numbers. He wanted orderly queuing and rationing systems, based on legal rights and documented permissions to emigrate and immigrate.

Sir Robert was a widower, but Bentwich was married and he and his wife Helen led lives, together and separately, that combined bookishness with political activism. Norman and Helen shared a passion for Jerusalem – thirty years later, when Helen wrote a *History of Sandwich*, she compared the little medieval town to the ancient and historic city of Jerusalem, and through that odd comparison indicated that Jerusalem was never far from her thoughts. Rather like Beatrice and Sidney Webb, the Bentwiches were serious, devoted to each other, deeply embedded in the Labour Party, and childless. In his book on 'the cousinhood' Chaim Bermant says of Norman: 'He carried a constant sense of urgency even into his old age. One tended to think of him as Quick, Quick, Bentwich.'[17] As many devoted couples do, Norman and Helen died within one year of each other, and it must have been during that in-between year that Chaim Bermant caught sight of Helen:

> … with stick in hand, walking through the Whitechapel Art Gallery of which she is treasurer, grimacing here, beaming there, as she passes from exhibit to exhibit, a white-haired, pale-faced English lady, but hardly a frail, vague little soul. The chin juts out and the almost inevitable cigarette in her mouth gives her a mildly pugnacious appearance, which is not entirely out of keeping with her character.[18]

There is a wonderful photograph of Sir Robert, taken in 1948, of him standing on one of his Exmoor hills, scowling into the camera and apparently holding an enormous ram on a lead; the ram seems to be smiling benignly.[19] In contrast the studio photographs of Bentwich indicate a bespectacled and slight man, with a kindly expression. His affectionate obituaries, written by refugees he rescued, describe a man with a happy and optimistic disposition, always open to new experiences.[20] Bentwich did not yearn for the country life: he was an urbanite, at home in London, Berlin, Vienna and New York – all of them cities where he spent much time.

Bentwich and Sir Robert could hardly have been more different in personality and in values, but that year of 1939 they shared a passion: the rescue of Jews from Greater Germany. They were to develop a working relationship which resembled that of a minister (Sir Robert) and a permanent secretary (Bentwich) – and it was never clear who was in charge. But what is not in doubt is that together they managed to put together, at top speed, a remarkable rescue operation.

Notes

1. Cited in Louise London, *Whitehall and the Jews 1933–1948*, Cambridge, Cambridge University Press, 2000, p. 106.
2. National Archives, File PREM1/326.
3. It should be noted that Louise London argues that it was Chamberlain who was the more sympathetic to the plight of German Jewry after *Kristallnacht* and that Hoare was only a reluctant supporter of increased German–Jewish immigration and strictly on condition that the immigration was temporary. Louise London, op. cit. pp. 97–112.
4. 'Copy of a letter received by Professor Norman Bentwich from Mr H. Maxwell of the Home Office', CBF Archives, minutes of the Executive of the Council for German Jewry, January 1939. The letter is dated '3rd January 1939'. There is no doubt the original letter was from Sir Alexander Maxwell, permanent under-secretary at the Home Office.
5. Not all the German training camps were Zionist. There were also non-Zionist camps, notably one run by Dr Bondi, who was later recruited as a 'staff' member for the Kitchener Camp. But all the camps were intended to teach the young trainees skills that they could use in non-industrial settings.
6. Sharman Kadish, *'A Good Jew and a Good Englishman', The Jewish Lads' and Girls' Brigade 1895–1995*, Vallentine Mitchell, 1995.
7. Chaim Bermant, *The Cousinhood: the Anglo-Jewish Gentry*, London: Eyre and Spottiswoode, 1971.
8. Norman Bentwich wrote to Cyrus Adler, a prominent American jurist, as follows: 'I should say frankly that I do not object to the Jewish State in itself, and cannot go so far as to say that its establishment must be prevented at all costs. It seems to me hard to say whether the establishment of a Jewish State would help or prejudice the Jewish position as a whole. But what I feel certain about is that it would excite determined Arab hostility, give an opportunity for endless intrigue of the enemies of Great Britain and the Jews, and almost inevitably force the Jews in Palestine to become a military people. And I believe that if a genuine and serious effort were made to bring about a direct understanding between Jews and Arabs on the basis of an undivided independent Palestine, an agreement could be reached.' Letter to Dr Cyrus Adler from Norman Bentwich, dated 22 December, 1937, Bentwich papers, File P174/25a.
9. Amy Gottlieb, *Men of Vision: Anglo–Jewry's Aid to Victims of the Nazi Regime 1933–45*, Weidenfeld and Nicolson, 1998, *passim* and Chapters 9 and 10.
10. Pamela Shatzkes, op. cit., p. 35.

11. Minute of a meeting with Ernest Cooper, Director of the Home Office Aliens Section, 29 October 1938, National Archives, File HO213/1636.

12. Robert Henriques, *Sir Robert Waley Cohen 1877–1952*, Secker and Warburg, 1966.

13. Ibid.

14. Norman Bentwich to Robert Waley Cohen, 9 April 1939, BWP, File P174/13b.

15. Robert Henriques, op. cit., p. 298.

16. Norman Bentwich, *I Understand the Risks*, Victor Gollancz, 1950; Norman Bentwich, *They Found Refuge*, The Cresset Press, 1956; Norman Bentwich, *My 77 Years*, Philadelphia, The Jewish Publication Society of America, 1961.

17. Chaim Bermant, op. cit., p. 274.

18. Chaim Bermant, ibid.

19. Robert Henriques, op. cit., plate 7.

20. 'In Memory of Norman Bentwich, February 28, 1883–April 8, 1971', obituaries by Werner Rosenstock and Eva G. Reichmann, AJR Information, May 1971, pp. 6–7.

3

CHOICES AND RESOURCES

The 'Camp Committee', meeting for the first time over Christmas and New Year 1938–39, knew they faced huge difficulties. Only two weeks before they settled to work in mid-December 1938, their colleagues on the Fund Executive had been writing memoranda to government ministers arguing that it was impossible for voluntary organisations to take on the huge task of refugee rescue after *Kristallnacht* and that they needed government help with funding.[1] But the British government had offered them nothing material at all – not even a disused camp left over from the First World War. Now the Fund was going to have to make a complete *volte face*. Instead of pessimism about their own capacity they were going to have to develop optimism – even, some might say, foolhardiness. In this situation the ebullient bulk of the entrepreneurial Waley Cohen must have seemed the ideal reassuring presence, and the naturally quiet but also very optimistic Bentwich his perfect foil.

The first decision the Camp Committee had to make was about the scale of the enterprise they were about to launch. Various numbers had been mentioned. For example earlier that December, Dr Baeck, the president of the Jewish Agency in Berlin who frequently attended Fund executive meetings in London, had first raised the question of a 'transmigration' camp. He had mentioned a figure of 30,000 men and women at any one time in a camp or camps; and he thought they could be maintained at a cost of £2.10s per person per month. These huge numbers must have worried a lot of gentlemen at that meeting but Dr Baeck's speech to them was impassioned and alarming and the Executive were convinced by him that something drastic had to be done. Knowing that their own resources were already stretched to breaking point they fervently hoped that others might also come to the rescue. Later, at that same meeting, the Executive had discussed the possibility of spreading the 30,000 around other 'refugee countries such as

Holland, Belgium, Switzerland, France etc' and determined to enquire what steps were being taken in these countries to set up transmigration camps.[2] But nothing came of these enquiries and over Christmas they had realised that if anyone was going to do something it was up to them and them alone.

Fortunately for the worried members of the Fund rather more manageable numbers began to be discussed at an early stage in the deliberations of their Camp Committee. At some point over the Christmas period the General Manager of Dorman Pearson Long, the firm which owned the Kitchener Camp, was prevailed upon to come up to London and go through the plans of the camp with them. He explained to Waley Cohen and his colleagues that although the Kitchener Camp had originally been built for 40,000 troops in the First World War (it was about 100 square acres),[3] only one part of the camp was still in reasonable condition. In that section there were forty-eight huts 'each capable of holding forty-eight people' and 'one hut divided into cubicles which is capable of holding 24'. In addition there were two very large dining rooms, kitchens and 'other large buildings'.

There may have been some sense of relief when it became clear that the capacity of the camp would itself constitute a considerable restraint on numbers. The net result was that Sir Robert wrote a report on their deliberations which concluded that 'with a small expenditure on repairs, [the Kitchener Camp] would be capable of accommodating from 2,500 to 3,000 people' of whom some would be single men and others, given the huts with the cubicles, could be 'married people'. The money that was needed to do this was apparently manageable – 'certainly not more than £100,000 a year and probably a figure more nearly approaching £80,000'. In addition to the £5000 needed for the initial reconstruction they thought that a further £10,000 would cover the cost of 'the necessary equipment, such as furniture, cooking utensils, etc. less any that could be obtained by way of gifts from the trades concerned'.

These figures have the air of a back-of-the-envelope calculation but they do sound vaguely realistic. However, there was one dazzling certainty that was based entirely on guesswork. Sir Robert pronounced, 'At a very conservative estimate it is felt that it should be possible by the process of defiltration now being carried out in many different directions that the camp could be filled in total twice over during the course of a year.' 'Defiltration' was a technocratic way of talking about outflows and inflows of refugees; he expected that the camp would empty and refill again within the space of a year. It was a clumsy neologism that reflected the fact that the enforced mass movement of people in the twentieth century had been stripped of human meaning and it assumed that other countries would also be willing to take very large numbers of the refugees who had come as 'transmigrants' to the Kitchener Camp. Given international reluctance to that date this must have seemed, even then, a very optimistic objective. But

Sir Robert foresaw everything going smoothly, at top speed and with maximum efficiency. Not only was he claiming, *conservatively*, that 6,000 would be saved in any one year, he also stated that 'half of these could be received from Germany in the early days of February'. It was a typical Waley Cohen document and it was very persuasive.[4] They would get a great many rescues accomplished for a manageable amount of money. The Executive of the Fund received the report on 29 December and agreed to press ahead with the plan.[5]

The Executive had been told that they had to find £100,000 for the maintenance of the refugees and about £15,000 for capital renovations and equipment for the camp. Both were enormous sums (the equivalent of about £2.8 million and £431,000 today)[6] and the Executive's insouciance in the face of this funding mountain to climb is, with hindsight, astonishing. But Sir Robert and Bentwich had plans to deal with it. Their first thought was to turn to their American counterparts. In mid-December Bentwich had already made overtures to the American Joint Distribution Committee (the equivalent to the Fund with offices in Paris as well as New York and known as 'The Joint' or 'the JDC') by writing to his friend, Morris Troper, at the Paris office of the Joint. However, he clearly felt he had not had an adequate response because on 11 January 1939, after he had received the letter from the Home Office confirming that they could go ahead, he wrote directly to Paul Baerwald, chairman of the Joint in New York City.

Bentwich's letter to Paul Baerwald is couched in the language of risk – 'We have decided to take the plunge' – and there is a long paragraph listing all the other commitments that the Fund was also undertaking at the same time, including the *Kindertransporte* – 'the children of whom three thousand have been brought here during the last six weeks and more are to arrive soon' – and 'all kinds of training enterprises'. These activities based in the UK were of course above and beyond the large sums of money that the Fund was already sending the Jewish agencies in Greater Germany. The number of refugees the Fund expected to house in the camp at any one time had shifted upwards to 'four to five thousand persons' and the letter contains the first overt mention that the camp was, as he put it, 'in large part for young men'. In order to persuade the Joint that they had a moral obligation to help with the Kitchener Camp, Bentwich stressed that most of these young men would either already have visas for the United States or a 'definite prospect' of getting one – in other words they were Americans–in–the–making and hence the Joint was *de facto* closely concerned. He concluded, 'We should like to know as soon as possible what you can do, because the measure in which we can develop the camp will be largely determined by your action.'[7]

At this the Americans started to move. Two weeks later, and after many cables and phone calls, a letter went from Paris to New York. The Paris Joint were keen to see the camp succeed because they felt it would thereby set a good example for other such camps that might be established elsewhere in other countries.

However, Morris Troper, the author of the letter, knew there would be difficulties over and above the financial considerations: 'the carrying out of the plan is looked upon with some anxiety because it will surely create problems of psychological and social adjustment which will need constant attention.'[8] But at this stage it was money that the Americans were being asked to provide rather than psychologists and counsellors and Troper said it was a question of either promising enough money to make sure the camp worked effectively, or, he felt, a question of giving nothing at all.

A month later Morris Troper was in England and took the opportunity to go down to Sandwich and take a look at the embryonic Kitchener Camp. He very much liked what he saw. He thought the buildings were 'in marvellous shape' and had gathered that the building materials for the outstanding renovations had been 'given gratis'. Every comfort was possible: the hot water equipment was 'still in practically perfect condition' and there was already a plan for a 'moving picture theater', which was being gifted to the camp. There was lots of constructive training work to be done – 'the place has possibilities for truck farming, for the raising of poultry and sheep etc. and a number of small shops for mechanical training'. When he visited in mid-February 1939 there were only three refugees resident, one of whom was a rabbi and another an accountant, and he remarked with apparent approval that 'all three were acting as laborers, unloading supplies from a truck'. No doubt these supplies consisted of the ton of nails donated by a building firm and which he had seen being delivered. His report went to the New York office of the Joint.[9] They were convinced, and agreed to fund the Kitchener Camp to the tune of 20 per cent of the running costs for 1939, not exceeding $100,000.

It was a good start. And while the Americans were making up their minds to help, so too were many British companies. Ernest Joseph, the architect, used his contacts in the building trades to get free building materials – hence 'a ton of nails' – and other companies gave bunk beds, cooking utensils, stoves and ranges. Perhaps the most useful gift at this stage was a guarantee from Unilevers, no doubt prompted by Frank Samuel, a newly co-opted member of the Camp Committee and Unilevers' managing director, to provide the camp with all its dry foodstuffs – porridge oats for example, which came to be a dreaded comestible – and above all with soap.[10] Other essentials for the refugees' well-being were also put in place – on 20 January Sir Robert wrote to Edward Baron, a Jew and a director of Carreras Cigarettes, of which his philanthropic father was Chair, asking him to provide enough cigarettes for about 3,500 people to smoke 5 cigarettes a day 'for some months'. This was in effect asking for at least half a million cigarettes. In a handwritten note to Bentwich at the bottom of a copy of this letter, Sir Robert asked him to 'write something of this sort to chocolate manufacturers', adding that if he wrote to Cadbury's (a very well known chocolate firm of Quaker origins) he should 'leave out the reference to Jews and speak only of refugees'.[11] (It is interesting that Sir Robert wrote to the Jewish manufacturers and asked Norman to write to the Christians – judging from Norman's correspondence with other Christians he went out of his way to keep on very good terms with them, often sounding more polite to his avowed Christian correspondents than he was to his Jewish correspondents, with whom he could be quite direct and sharp when it suited him.) The request for cigarettes was successful – even those one-time Kitchener residents still alive today remember their five cigarettes a day and the brisk trade the non-smokers ran with their ration.

The Kitchener Camp was put in place with the most extraordinary speed. With Sir Robert at the helm – Norman has been quoted as saying of him, 'action follows suggestion as thunder, lightning'[12] – they had gone from scratch on 12 December 1938 to having everything arranged by 20 January 1939 to such an extent that they could, on that day, turn to the really pressing issue of cigarettes and chocolates. They had indeed 'taken the plunge' with eyes tight shut, noses held, and with, perhaps, at the back of their minds the thought that if things went really wrong they could always ask for yet another loan from the Rothschilds. They were lucky, risk takers, resourced and resourceful. And they were dealing with an extraordinarily generous Anglo–Jewish community.

But there was one major issue that they still had to settle and that was who, precisely, they were going to rescue? They knew the entry conditions of the British government. These meant that the refugees would have to have guarantees they would leave the UK within about a year and that the refugees could not normally be employed by anyone outside the camp. They knew, too, the circumstances that had driven the urgent need for such a transit camp – there were many thousands of men who had been incarcerated in concentration camps in Germany and there were terrible rumours about the conditions there; also at any moment the Nazis might manufacture yet another reason for some dreadful series of events that would make *Kristallnacht* look relatively mild. But by mid-January they also knew that the capacity of the Kitchener Camp and their resources as a whole could only rescue a few of the many thousands desperate to leave Greater Germany. The Camp Committee, and, more particularly, the Jewish agencies in Berlin and Vienna, were going to have to choose who could come to Sandwich.

When the Fund first turned to organising the rescue to Kitchener its members had been persuaded by Leo Baeck in early December that it was '30,000 men and women'[13] who needed to be removed from Germany urgently. The gender-neutral word of 'people' was used in many of the early documents concerning the camp so that it did seem possible that women might be included amongst those they rescued. Moreover, in Waley Cohen's original report on the Kitchener Camp to the Executive, he had mentioned the possibility of housing 'married couples'. Slowly but surely, over Christmas and New Year 1938–39, an image of the ideal refugee recruit to the Kitchener Camp entered the minds of the gentlemen of the Fund, such that by the end of January 1939 they knew who that person was. First and foremost, it was a *man* and, if possible, one not trammelled with the encumbrance of a wife. Men rather than women absolutely fitted the bill: men could undertake the hard physical work of putting the camp to rights, their labour would be free and their occupation as builders and builders' labourers would provide them, at one and the same time, with training and with occupational therapy. Moreover, men rather than women would be much more likely already to have the skills the camp would need – they would be the carpenters, the electricians, the doctors and the dentists of the camp, and these were all male-dominated professions in the 1930s. In addition, the really skilled craftsmen could take leadership roles in the training activities. And given the way in which the international migration processes worked, men were much more likely than women to have the chance to re-emigrate to the new nations and developing countries that were at that time seeking physically strong workers who would help them build their agricultural infrastructures. Those skilled in commerce could help construct their trading economies. Men also fitted the emerging ethos of the Kitchener Camp. They had, after all, recruited Jonas May, who was secretary of the Jewish Lads Brigade, to be director of the camp and Jonas's brother Phineas, who was also an experienced leader of brigade summer camps, was going to work alongside him at Kitchener. Jonas and Phineas knew about managing boys and young men in residential camps; they had absolutely no experience of managing lots of young women, let alone married couples.

There was one more important set of reasons for selecting men: the Fund was consistently clear that they were not going to undertake the selection of the refugees for the Kitchener Camp; that was to be the responsibility of the Jewish agencies in Berlin and in Vienna.[14] These agencies were very comfortable with the idea that men rather than women should be admitted to the camp. This was because the local Jewish agencies were under tremendous pressure from the families of the men who had been incarcerated in the three German concentration camps of Buchenwald, Dachau and Sachsenhausen immediately after *Kristallnacht*. The families were desperate to get their men out of these camps. The only way the Gestapo would release them was if there was documentary proof that the men, once out of the concentration camps, would leave Greater Germany within a few days. It was inevitable that the Jewish agencies on the spot would do what they could for these men, but in prioritising them for rescue the Jewish agencies were echoing the Nazi policy of arrest after *Kristallnacht*. Only men had been arrested after those events. This was a reflection of the gender ideology of National Socialism, which placed women firmly in the home and only men in the public domain. Even though the families of these men were in an extremely precarious position in Germany and Austria, it was still a few years before the Final Solution when *all* Jews, irrespective of their age or their sex, became the objects of murderous intent. It was clear that at that moment in 1938–39 the most powerful life-or-death threat applied to Jewish men rather than to Jewish women and children. For the moment, then, there was to be no provision for women in the transit camp at all. It was for men only.

Almost all these arguments could equally apply to the priority that was given to the selection of so-called 'young' men. They were likely to be fitter and more attractive as migrants to European colonies and to Palestine and hence they were the more obvious candidates for a transit camp. However, the question of urgency was not confined to 'young' men: the Nazis had not held back from arresting older men when it came to incarceration in the concentration camps and, indeed, it was known that the death rate – which in these camps was probably running at about 15 per cent – was certainly higher among the older prisoners. So the urgent need for rescue of older men was well established. However, the 'youth' policy of both the Fund and the Jewish agencies in Greater Germany reflected their long and traditional commitment to the coupling up of migration with training camps. Training camps were quite deliberately targeted at younger people who were regarded as the most likely migrants. Many members of the Fund, and this included the key players of Waley Cohen and Bentwich,[15] saw the Kitchener Camp as a training camp as much as a rescue camp. Youth and masculinity were part of their mind-set when it came to rescue, even though Norman Bentwich, who visited both Berlin and Vienna in 1939, would have been well aware of the consequences of that policy for the rapidly aging Jewish communities and families left behind in Greater Germany.

However, it is also clear that the question of what constituted the upper-age limit for the men in the Kitchener Camp was never properly settled. Sir Robert, for months after the camp was established, was convinced that the maximum age was 35, whereas Bentwich was consistent in applying an age limit of 45 – and all the data on the camp, some of which includes the ages of some of the men, indicates that 45 was indeed the upper-age limit. Many years later, however, when Bentwich came to write his memoirs and his books about his refugee experiences, he always said that the upper age for Kitchener was 40. He was wrong, but the fact that he was wrong is symptomatic – the camp was certainly not full of obviously 'young' men, although in their minds' eye Sir Robert and Bentwich thought it was. It was, rather, full of 'not old' men, and the huge disparity between 17-year-olds (the minimum age) and the 45-year-olds, who were easily old enough to be their fathers, was something neither man wanted to reflect upon.

Finally there was the question of Sandwich. How would these men be received? What would the local people make of so many Jews, and not just 'Jews', *German* Jews, concentrated in one spot on the edge of the little town and only twenty-two years since Britain had been at war with Germany? The heyday of British Fascism was apparently over by 1938–39 and what was left of it was most worrying in the cities, particularly the East End of London. But the gentlemen of the Fund knew two things. The first was that xenophobia and anti-Semitism were very close to the surface of British social life. Terms like 'Jew-boy' were used in commonplace language by all social classes, many clubs and societies banned Jewish membership (and Sandwich was *the* place for golf clubs, all of them grand and very exclusive), and Jews were generally thought to be suspect in their business dealings.

They also knew that there were organised Fascists in Sandwich. It was Sir Robert who would have been particularly aware of this since he was a member of the Board of Deputies of British Jews 'Defence Committee' and, as such, was privy to secret reports about Fascist activity from all over Britain. Amongst their network of infiltrators and observers was someone who sent regular reports to the Defence Committee about Fascists in the Ramsgate and Margate area (Ramsgate is 5 miles from Sandwich). Sir Robert would have seen the intelligence presented to a meeting of the Defence Committee in July 1938: '*Ramsgate and Margate* No signs of increased activity. Some meetings held in the area, but importance much exaggerated. Lady Pearson is the chief supporter of these activities, especially in Sandwich.'[16]

The Fund knew it was too late to change their minds about locating their refugees at the Kitchener Camp on the edge of Sandwich, but once again Sir Robert could afford to be confident and reassuring. There was really nothing worth worrying about going on in Sandwich and, anyway, being forewarned was forearmed. They would just have to be vigilant.

Hasty and possibly over-confident the decisions may have been but by the end of January 1939 everything was ready: the bunk beds were in the huts, the boilers were working, the basic 'staff' were in place, the dry foodstuffs and the soap, courtesy of Unilevers, had been delivered. The Jewish agencies in Berlin and Vienna were geared up for the business of selection for the Kitchener Camp and knew the criteria they were supposed to use. The Home Office officials in the Aliens Section were ready to work the new rapid permissions system. Sandwich, though it did not yet know it, was about to experience a large influx of German-speaking Jews.

Notes

1.   '… the voluntary organisations find themselves totally unable to accept the implication that the extent to which the rescue of thousands can be organised, temporary refuge provided, and large-scale migration for hundreds of thousands carried out must remain entirely dependent

on private effort'. Excerpt from long document entitled 'Action of Governments and of Private Organisations in Regard to Refugees', Memorandum drafted 25/11/38, marked 'Confidential' and unsigned; Document 63/88, CBF Archives.

2.   Minutes of the Meeting of the Executive of the Council for German Jewry, held on 12 December 1938, CBF Archives, document 2/268. Bentwich wrote to a M. Gottschalk at the Belgian Jewish Agency and to his old correspondent Mrs van Tijn at the Dutch Belgian Agency to ask them what their agencies and their governments could do to help but he doesn't seem to have had a reply to the substantive point from either. Letters dated 13 December 1938 found in the Archives of the American Joint Distribution Committee, Jerusalem.

3.   Information supplied by Mr James Bird, one-time chairman of Petbow Engineering, the company which took over the Kitchener Camp in 1947.

4.   'Establishment of Refugee Camps', memorandum to the Council for German Jewry, dated 28/12/1938; found in the Archives of the American JDC.

5.   Minutes of the Executive of the Council for German Jewry, 29 December 1938, Central British Fund Archives, document 2/278.

6.   UK National Archives online Currency Converter. These figures convert 1940 numbers into 2005 numbers. Currency converters are notoriously inaccurate and vary in their results. The National Archives converter has been used because it probably has the highest legitimacy.

7.   Copy of a letter from Norman Bentwich to Paul Baerwald, 11 January, 1939, JDC Archives.

8.   Morris Troper to Paul Baerwald, 27 January 1939, JDC Archives.

9.   'Memorandum re Kitchener Camp', on the notepaper of the American Joint Distribution Committee, Paris, unsigned but no doubt written by Morris Troper, dated 17 February 1939, JDC Archives.

10. 'Through the generosity of the Unilever company, Frank Samuel was able to provide all the food and toiletries needed in the camp.' From Amy Zahl Gottlieb, op. cit., p. 140.

11. BWP, File P174/12a. The full note from Waley Cohen to Bentwich reads: 'Do you think you should write something of this sort to chocolate manufacturers. If you are writing to Cadbury's it would probably be better to leave out the reference to Jews and speak only of refugees. It was decided after you left the meeting that this camp must definitely be regarded as a camp for all refugees in the sense of the Baldwin appeal that is to say, not confined entirely to Jews.'

12. Quoted by Amy Zahl Gottlieb, op. cit., p. 138.

13. Minutes of the meeting of the Executive of the Council for German Jewry, held on 12 December 1938; CBF Archives, 2/128.

14. See for example the minuted statement by Waley Cohen, CBF Executive Committee meeting, 5 January 1939: 'Sir Robert said that priority would be given to persons who could be emigrated from this country within a period of two years, and that the selection of those who came from abroad would be in the hands of the Reichsvertretung in Berlin and the Israelitische Kultusgemeinde in Vienna.' CBF Archives, File 2/289.

15. Bentwich's title, for the purposes of the Fund, was 'Honorary Director of Emigration and Training'.

16. Minutes of the Co-ordinating Committee (later changed name to Defence Committee); excerpt from 'Reports of Blackshirt Activities in the Provinces', dated July 1938. Archives of Board of Deputies of British Jews Defence Committee, held at the Wiener Library, London, File 1658/1/1/1, Folder 2 of two, p. 166.

4

AN ARRIVAL AND A PARTY

Phineas May travelled down to Sandwich from London on the last Sunday in January 1939. It was his first ever visit to the place that was about to become his home for a considerable time and he was going to join his older brother Jonas, who had travelled to Sandwich a few days earlier. Jonas had been appointed director of the Kitchener Camp and Phineas was going to act in some important capacity, as yet undefined, as his brother's second-in-command.

Phineas was 33 at the time, Jonas a couple of years older. They were the youngest of five siblings, born into an Orthodox Jewish family and brought up in a large family home in Cricklewood, an area with a substantial Jewish community, in North London. Their mother had been born a Franklin, one of the small number of families that regarded themselves as Jewish aristocracy known as 'the cousinhood' (Helen Bentwich was also née Franklin – of which more later), and Mrs May had the nineteenth-century manners and culture of the English urban upper middle class. In contrast, their father, Aaron May, was of German origin and very firmly 'in trade' – he was an importer of kitchen equipment from Germany. In certain respects it was a bifurcated household in its Jewish practice. Mrs May disliked what is sometimes called, with tongue firmly in cheek, 'culinary Judaism': she rejected Jewish traditional food such as gefilte fish and latkes and preferred instead the steak-and-kidney puddings, the kippers and thick soups of English cuisine. She was also determined that her children should not speak German, her husband's mother tongue, and that they should be 'English' in every possible way – apart, of course, from their religion.

Not surprisingly, in this context, Jonas and Phineas had been sent to public day school in North London, where they had been inculcated with the manners and culture of the English upper middle class. It was also a school with many other Jewish boys and there was no attempt to divert them from their Judaism.

Indeed, that would probably have been impossible – both Jonas and Phineas were steeped in their family's religion and Phineas, particularly, spent his subsequent life, until the day he died, working for and with Jewish causes. He also kept to the Orthodox path. Both Jonas and Phineas left school early, probably because the family business went into rapid decline in the 1930s, and they had to find their own way thereafter. But the world they entered for employment was the Jewish world, so that by the time they became involved in the Kitchener Camp, Jonas was in full-time employment as the secretary of the Jewish Lads Brigade and known as 'Major' Jonas May (because he had reached the rank of major within the brigade), and Phineas had become an administrator working for the United Synagogue (the Orthodox branch of Jewish practice and the branch that appoints the chief rabbi). Phineas too was involved with the brigade but on a voluntary basis, cycling across London from Cricklewood to a drill hall in Brixton every week to lead a group of 'lads' in the 'scouting for boys' activities promoted by the brigade and taking part in a summer camp which was held in Deal, very near Sandwich, every year.

They both spoke the clipped upper-class English of the 1930s, thought of themselves as 'English Jews', and maintained the habits of reticence about feelings often called the 'stiff upper lip'. In certain ways it was obvious that they were equipped to run a camp of thousands of men; in others it was much less clear – two youngish men steeped in the culture of the English upper middle class were going to have to deal with the less inhibited habits of German Jewry, and with the fact that so many of the men who were going to come to the Kitchener Camp would be traumatised by their experience of the Nazi regime. It was a major challenge, as Jonas and Phineas were about to discover.[1]

That January Sunday, Phineas travelled down to Sandwich in a little car driven by someone called Banks, who was always known as 'Banks' and never by his first name – even though his original surname, which he had recently changed, was Levy. (Banks remains a somewhat shadowy figure in this story; he clearly liked girls and a drink, and how this affected his ability to run the Kitchener Camp's physical fitness activities – which is what he had been appointed to do – is anyone's guess.) The weather was awful and their car struggled with headwinds over the 80 miles from London, such that the journey took much longer than expected – quite apart from having to pick up 'a fair friend' of Banks and drop her off in Canterbury, 12 miles west of Sandwich. However, it was a Sunday and the traffic was light and they reached Sandwich and the Bell Hotel, where Phineas was going to stay, just in time for lunch.

To his delight Phineas discovered The Bell had very recently been done up, there were roaring fires in every public room, the bedrooms had basins with hot and cold running water, and the staff treated their very few guests like royalty. He sat down to lunch with his brother Jonas who had already been in Sandwich for a couple of days, Ernest Joseph (EMJ) and his wife who had come down for the weekend, and a gentleman called Donald Woolf who, like EMJ, was a member of the Fund and very involved with the brigade. The meal may not have been up to much by today's standards (the next day Phineas recorded, apparently with strong approval, a lunch of 'boiled cod and vegetables, figs and cream and toast') but his companions were happy to tease him about how he had landed in the lap of luxury. Later that evening Phineas noted that he had 'promised to endeavour to tolerate this luxury on the condition that it is not for a longer period than one week'.

Once lunch was over the little party made their way to the Kitchener Camp. It was a ten-minute walk from the Bell, just the other side of the river from the medieval core of central Sandwich, crossed by an old swing bridge that charged a toll. Phineas' reaction to his first sight of the Kitchener Camp was mixed: on the one hand the camp looked like 'the perfect concentration camp or Dartmoor [prison] on one floor'; on the other hand, he 'was immediately struck by the amazing possibilities of the place and also considering it is 22 years since it was last occupied what an excellent condition the various huts were in'. His spirits were high: there were jolly larks when Donald Woolf was locked in the camp by accident and had to climb the gate to get out, whereupon the high wind blew his hat off and he had to climb back again to retrieve it; and although the huts looked grim Phineas knew that the men who were shortly to come from Germany would soon get them into shape.

Later that afternoon Phineas was told to expect about thirty refugees 'any day now' and that brought home to him that something important both for himself and for posterity was just around the corner. These were interesting times and he wanted to record them. When all the others had set off back to London he crept down the hotel stairs in the quiet of the evening to look for writing paper. Taking a stash of Bell Hotel notepaper back to his room he lay on his bed and began his 'Kitchener Camp Diary' on the thick and creamy pages. He was the Samuel Pepys of Sandwich and, after about twenty minutes covering two or three pages in his tiny writing, he wrote his last sentence of the day: 'and so to bed at 9.30.'[2]

The next day, Monday, work started in earnest. Phineas was at the camp at 8.30 a.m. and found that local workmen were already there 'busily engaged'. Their foreman – 'a fairly decent fellow' – was grumbling but then that was what foremen did. The main thing, though, was that other local businessmen were being drawn to the camp like bees to the honey pot. Two came to offer their services for camp laundry, another was a coal merchant who seemed to have no idea that they would need huge quantities of coal – 6 tons in the first instance – and he was sent away with a flea in his ear. Phineas had to get in supplies at speed – that evening Jonas rang to say that thirty refugees would probably be arriving the next day, and to his horror Phineas discovered that that day's *News Chronicle* had a paragraph saying there were 100 refugees at the camp already. No panic, but nevertheless he wrote at the end of the day that he would not be at all surprised if his brother phoned the next day 'to say the 3,500 are coming at once and have a meal ready for them within half an hour and all beds to be erected and well aired'.

The next morning there was confirmation that thirty refugees were indeed arriving that evening, so Phineas rushed round Sandwich arranging with 'the grocer, the baker and the milkman' for emergency supplies. He even ordered hay to fill palliasses for the refugees to sleep on, but fortunately for everyone concerned more conventional mattresses arrived during the day. He skipped lunch and fielded phone calls from an endless stream of local tradesmen by referring them 'to London'. By 6.45 p.m. when the refugees were expected, everything was ready: beds were 'fixed up', coal, paraffin, hurricane lanterns were in place, they had some non-perishable food, and there were tables and chairs in the dining area. He waited and waited and waited. Nobody came.

The rest of Phineas' first week proceeded in much the same way. Refugees were expected at any moment and there was still a great deal of work to do to prepare for their arrival. Huge crates of hundreds of plates arrived on Wednesday, 2,000 blankets in bales of twenty arrived on Thursday, lorry-loads of timber and chairs arrived on Friday. With all this coming and going of overladen lorries, the inevitable happened and one got stuck in the churned-up mud, and for the first time – but certainly not for the last – Phineas started yelling at whoever was within earshot, including the foreman and the brand new camp architect, Dr Walter Marmorek, who had arrived the day before. On the Friday Jonas arrived and later on EMJ, and, hoping for a contemplative evening at the start of Shabbat, they had a quiet supper at the Bell Hotel – only to be disturbed by the arrival of yet another lorry just as they had finished. It was all go. Phineas wrote that he was 'sure the Almighty will forgive my working so hard on this occasion' but he was very pleased to note that on the Saturday no more lorries arrived. Instead, Norman and Helen Bentwich put in their first ever appearance in Sandwich and Phineas was delighted to be told by Helen that they were cousins – of course!

Amidst all this frenzied activity the brothers were beginning to embed the local network of the Kitchener Camp. Local farmers came round to offer training positions for the refugees (if they ever arrived), the Divisional and Local police sergeants came to visit Jonas and 'were most charming', and on the Sunday the brothers renewed contacts they already had with the large Jewish community that lived in Cliftonville, a suburb of Margate, about half an hour's drive away. Word had got round very quickly that there were business opportunities suddenly available at the Kitchener Camp and not surprisingly the Sandwich Chamber of

Commerce was quick to respond. On Monday 6 February the chairman and the secretary of the Chamber of Commerce called round to see Jonas in his office at the Camp and invited him to be the guest of honour at their annual dinner–dance on the following Thursday. He graciously accepted and agreed to respond to the toast of 'The Visitors'. Later that evening he and Phineas and the Chamber of Commerce all bumped into each other again in the bar of the Bell Hotel and 'this necessitated drinks all round'.

The Sandwich Chamber of Commerce annual dinner–dance set the tone of many things to come. It is, with hindsight, rather odd that Jonas was invited at such short notice to play such a major part in it, but then they *were* 'visitors' and the new Kitchener campers were already providing excellent opportunities for traders in the town. Maybe someone was tactfully asked to stand down so that these new gentlemen from the camp could play a part.

One curious aspect of the Sandwich Chamber of Commerce was that its retiring president was the prominent local fascist, Lady Grace Pearson. Lady Pearson had been born into an aristocratic family, the Page Crofts, who had a castle and estates in Herefordshire. Her brother, Henry Page Croft, was a very right-wing Conservative MP who, later on in the Second World War, became Minister of Aviation. Marriage to an industrialist, Sir Edward Pearson, had added to her wealth but she was now a widower of about 60 years of age. She was the prospective parliamentary candidate for the British Union of Fascists (BUF) for the nearby cathedral city of Canterbury. Oswald Mosley, the leader of the BUF, had addressed meetings in Canterbury through her auspices[3] and is known to have visited her home in Sandwich, where she held small Fascist soirées for him in her beautiful house and garden. A local Sandwich resident whose father was Lady Pearson's butler is certain that she and Mosley were lovers. Mosley was twenty years her junior, but she is said by another Sandwich resident to have been 'utterly charming' and he was a notorious womaniser, so anything is possible.

However, she was not always 'utterly charming', particularly towards Jews. It is an interesting fact that her niece Diana, a daughter of Henry Page Croft, had married, in 1936, a German–Jewish refugee, Fred Uhlman. The whole Page Croft family had recoiled in horror at the prospect of this marriage, and Uhlman, in his fascinating memoir published in 1960, recalls, in a cool tone and over several pages, the manifold ways in which the Page Croft family proceeded to insult him – although they never severed complete contact with him and Diana. Lady Pearson was one of the worst:

A few weeks after my arrival in England I became engaged to Diana and the problem was how to break the news to her family. We could not postpone it too long because a first cousin had already informed my wife's aunt that she had seen Diana about 'with a little Jew in Kew Gardens' – which made the aunt remark that she knew always when a Jew was in her room because she had an uncanny feeling, 'just like touching a grass-snake'.[4]

Pearson was a Fascist for all the reasons some aristocratic women were – the BUF, unlike many Continental Fascist parties, was keen to involve women in the mainstream of the party, not just as appendages to male Fascists, Mosley himself was a powerful pull for aristocratic women who found him personally fascinating, and, above all, the party appealed to very rich and bigoted people in its anti-democratic, anti-communist and anti-Semitic stance.[5]

Lady Pearson had taken advantage of Sandwich's depressed state during the 1930s and acquired a great deal of Sandwich property. In one of the town's ancient medieval houses, in the main street leading into the town and very close to the Bell Hotel, she had housed the Fascist headquarters complete with a large shop front. Phineas, on his first walk into town, had noticed the shop and, at least in his diary, he had treated this with a certain lightheartedness. He wrote that he was sure the local fascists 'will reap a rich harvest from the Camp' and that he hoped 'our 3,500 will keep them well "occupied"'.

Whether the two brothers knew that Lady Pearson would be at the dinner–dance, or indeed if Lady Pearson knew beforehand that she would be in Jewish company, is not recorded. However, as Phineas recorded, the evening started well when, as guests of honour, the brothers were collected by car from their camp quarters and taken to the Sandwich Guildhall, a striking building in the middle of the little town that consisted, mainly, of medieval rooms panelled in oak and mullioned windows. Phineas found all this hospitality from, as he put it, 'the commencement of the function … amazing'. About ninety gentlemen and their ladies sat down to an excellent meal and while they ate, Mr Bert French played popular tunes on the piano and Mrs Evelyn Yeadon played the violin. Then the company settled down to hear the speeches, of which there were a great number. Lady Pearson gave the first, saying, amongst other things, that the Chamber of Commerce 'must think out new ideals and visions for the future' and that while she regretted the absence of the Mayor of Sandwich (who had taken himself off to the rather grander affair of the Canterbury Chamber of Commerce which, through some catastrophic piece of mismanagement was being held on the same evening) she did particularly welcome Alderman Martin as one of 'the oldest, truest and best friends of Sandwich'. (The Martin family had demonstrated this friendship by doing the catering for the dinner.) In response Alderman Martin mentioned 'saucy letters' received from the Chamber of Commerce (their precise nature left unspecified in the lengthy press report), and once he had sat down, the rector began *his* speech, followed by a 'Captain Lewin', a 'Mr Pittock' and a 'Mr Little'.

All this must have taken hours, so that by the time Jonas May stood up to make his speech the company would have been more than a little merry. But he had something very important to say, and he was clearly a man who had taken the measure of his audience and what would hold their attention:

> Major May said he could not stress too sincerely or deeply what the temporary rest from persecution meant to the poor men who were coming to the refugee camp at Stonar. They would find, as he had found already, an unbelievably generous welcome. They were going to be the town's guests for some time and they would be welcome ones. They were very ordinary people and he appealed to everyone, even those who had some doubt as to the wisdom of having large numbers of refugees near the town, to extend to them the helping hand they needed so badly.
>
> Naturally the Chamber of Commerce is interested in the camp, not only from the heart, but from the pocket. There is no doubt that a camp of this size (accommodating about 3,500 people) can bring a very large volume of business to the town and the surrounding district. I want you to be assured it is the declared policy of the committee which is organising the camp that as much of the business as it is possible to place here will be placed in Sandwich and district. Naturally it will be impossible for every tradesman to benefit directly by the camp. I have to look after the funds which have been given by charitable people like yourselves and you would not wish that money to be spent otherwise than wisely and carefully. In considering this matter the committee has said that even if the goods cost a little more by buying in this district we are to do so. That will help those who cannot compete with the larger people in London and elsewhere.[6]

The applause at the end of this speech must have been considerable. It wasn't just that at long last the speechifying was over, it was also that what Jonas had said would have been music to the ears of the traders of Sandwich, who, in 1930s Britain, like everyone else apart from the very rich, had been going through very lean times. We do not know what Lady Pearson thought but she must have seen the headline in the local paper two days later – 'Sandwich Chamber of Commerce: Traders to Benefit from Stonar Refugee Camp; Good News at Annual Dinner' – and realised that she was going to have to tread carefully. There was little point in making speeches about hating Jews and blaming them for the nation's ills if it was trading with Jews that was going to bring some prosperity to Sandwich.

Phineas had no desire to be cautious about anything – he was determined to enjoy himself, which he did. Impressed by the catering, he arranged with Alderman Martin (and his 'charming daughter in law') that they would provide 'the Camp with Bread – a very nice order', and he had a long conversation with 'a jolly small balded man' who reminded him of someone called Polak who used to be in the Jewish Lads Brigade. The small balded man turned out to be a well disposed local vicar who offered Phineas the use of an empty vicarage with eight bedrooms for any purpose they wanted – which was graciously accepted. The dancing, to the music of Twyman's Band from Deal, continued till midnight and at the witching hour the vicar drove Jonas and Phineas home. It had been, as Phineas noted just before he finally went to bed, 'a most enjoyable evening and one I shall long remember'.

But someone else, almost certainly Jonas, was thinking somewhat less positive thoughts about the evening. Phineas had thought the juxtaposition of Lady Pearson's speech at the beginning of the proceedings with Jonas's speech at the end 'amusing', but to someone with a more sceptical frame of mind the whole evening had demonstrated that Lady Pearson was a force to be reckoned with and, as an important figure in Sandwich, could not and should not be treated lightheartedly.

It cannot be a coincidence that on 13 February 1939 a 'special meeting' of the Defence Committee of the Board of Deputies of British Jews was held in London, at Woburn House. This was four days after the Sandwich dinner–dance and the gentlemen of the Defence Committee had before them, among a very limited number of papers, a document entitled 'Report of Investigation into B.U.F. Activities in Sandwich and Surrounding Districts'.[7] Such reports were not, in themselves, unusual; indeed, it was part of the Defence Committee's remit to consider reports from their extensive and secret network of infiltrators and observers. They made it their business to observe any form of anti-Semitic activity and particularly any activity of the BUF. What was unusual about this particular report was, firstly, its length – normally such reports were no more than a sentence or two and this was three pages – and secondly the place it was observing. Most of these reports were of BUF meetings in the major metropolitan areas of London, Manchester and Leeds and here was one – a long one – describing the Fascist activities in the little backwater of Sandwich and East Kent. After the dinner–dance Jonas had probably spoken to Robert Waley Cohen, a member of the Defence Committee, who in turn had asked someone from the Margate Jewish community to make a foray to Sandwich and Canterbury and report back as a matter of urgency.

Whoever they sent from Margate, he had a certain wry take on Sandwich and he wrote well. He was also determined to reassure. His first description, of the BUF bookshop in Strand Street which, later in the report, he correctly indicated was in property owned by Lady Pearson, suggested a practically moribund commercial enterprise:

The shop itself is devoid of stock, and has a window display consisting of only *Action* and *Tomorrow We Live*. There is seldom anyone in attendance, the place being used as a headquarters only, and when a meeting is in progress the persons present are hid from public view by a heavy curtain, below the edge of which wisps of light escape, but there is no attempt at window illumination, and the shop is by no means open for business.

The secret investigator then took himself round the Sandwich pubs and settled in for some good conversations. According to Phineas there were twenty-seven pubs in Sandwich at the time so this visitor presumably only took in a sample. He discovered that a few active Fascists tried to sell the weekly newspaper, *The Blackshirt*, in the town of a Saturday but that they got short shrift: "'I'd sooner give tuppence to a Jew-boy any day than buy a copy of *The Blackshirt*," said one working man, and his witticism was appreciated and endorsed by several others.' Eventually the investigator did encounter a member of the BUF but he was unconcerned: he was 'a mild old labourer of seventy-five years of age'. The old man wore what the special correspondent described as 'the flash in the pan badge' but seemed to want to hide it, even though he defended his membership of the BUF by saying that 'we must give the rising generation a chance'. The special correspondent thought this a 'very laudable' reason but the old man's 'own section of the rising generation, a son of some thirty summers, grinned sheepishly and later confessed that if he was anything, he was a Bolshevik'. The special investigator soon discovered the true reason for the older man's BUF membership: 'Upon the departure of both father and son I learned that the old man's real reason for being a blackshirt was that his bread and butter depended upon it, he being Lady Pearson's gardener and man-of-all-work.'

In fact the message that this observer began to pick up loud and clear was that Lady Pearson was widely disliked amongst Sandwich's working-class pub goers. She was rich – she lived in one of the most beautiful houses in Sandwich, Manwood Court, in a town which boasted many beautiful houses – she owned a large car and had a chauffeur, and she was the *rentier* of a great deal of property in Sandwich for which she charged high rents and refused to do repairs. Nor was there much sympathy for her and her ilk in other more upper-class establishments. The observer paid a visit to The Pilgrim's House, which he described as 'a very up-stage and County teashop where the local well-to-do residents from surrounding big houses stroll in':

These people, who might reasonably be impressed by Mosley's Eton, Oxford, and the Guards History, are not interested in him – regard him as a turncoat, and not a fellow to be trusted. His matrimonial adventure seems to have gone against him somehow. This Pilgrim's House is the property of, and is run by, Lady Pearson, but that did not seem to affect the opinions of the habitués.

Of course not all was completely well. The observer heard the usual kind of anti-Semitism widely current at the time (and, some might say, still widely current), but it did not seem to him to have worsened over the past ten years. Jews ran the country's finances, none worked with their hands, all Jews were money lenders of some kind; however, when it came to who was to blame for the depression and mass poverty, it was not the Jews who were in the firing line: 'it's the "government" that they are after.' When he broached the subject of refugees they seemed 'in the main kindly disposed' but at that moment they were hardly likely to have encountered any. It was the shopkeepers who began to express views based on a little experience:

> Most of them do not expect 'the Jews' camp' to bring a ha'penny worth of trade to the town. Some of them are quite content with this and consider it only reasonable that such business should be done by wholesale, but others seem affronted ('that fraternity hang together – look after each other – only trade with each other … etc.') The few who have already benefited by Jewish people connected with the camp making small purchases are very pleased about it, and generally speaking, pleasantly surprised to find Jews so 'affable and polite'.

The whole tone of the report was reassuring and there is nothing to indicate in the minutes of the meeting that received it that any discussion of further action took place. Both the Board of Deputies and the Kitchener camp staff were comfortable with the level of anti-Semitic opinion in Sandwich, so comfortable in fact that Norman and Helen Bentwich very shortly afterwards started to look for a holiday home in the town. The Bentwiches did not expect to see Fascists marching in Sandwich or past the Kitchener Camp, and those that sold *The Blackshirt* in the Market Square could be correctly dismissed as one or two crackpots or, most likely, Lady Pearson's employees. As to being disliked socially for their ethnicity and their religion, the Bentwiches had known that all their lives and knew how to handle it.

However, what none of them knew was that set apart from the centre of Sandwich but only about twenty minutes walk away, in a gated community based on the Royal St George's Golf course known as 'The Sandwich Bay Estate', there was a coterie of high powered politicos, some of them permanent residents and others, such as Waldorf and Nancy Astor, and Harold and Dorothy Macmillan, weekenders and holiday makers. The section of the British Secret Service known as MI5 was aware of some of these people: in particular they knew about a certain

Captain Robert Gordon Canning, old Etonian, graduate of the University of Oxford, and late of the 10th Hussars, gentleman farmer and permanent resident of a large house called 'Sandilands' on the Sandwich Bay Estate. He was a close friend of Oswald Mosley and had, in 1936, spent three months with Mosley in Rome where they had probably arranged with Mussolini and his henchmen for the Italian subsidy to the BUF. He had also visited Berlin in the same year to go to Mosley's wedding to Diana Guinness (née Mitford) and at the wedding he had met Adolf Hitler who was a fellow guest. He had met Hitler on at least two other occasions. He was a golfing pal of Ribbentrop's (the one time German ambassador to Britain, fervent anti-semite and enthusiast for an Anglo–German alliance) and he funded the Fascist newspaper, *Action*, and chaired its board. He was fiercely anti-Semitic largely arising out of his strongly pro-Arab sympathies, and MI5, much more worried about his activities in the Palestine Mandate than any concerns about his anti-Semitism, had started a file on him as far back as 1924. By February 1939, his MI5 file was many inches thick.[8] He was a big fish in national Fascist circles, and he was very close by.

Notes

1. I am grateful to Adrienne Harris, daughter of Phineas May, for talking to me on a number of occasions about her father and her uncle and for giving me permission to use this information.
2. All quotes, unless otherwise indicated, are taken from the unpublished diary of Phineas May, held at the Wiener Library. The diary starts on 29 January 1939 and contains a daily entry, apart from ten days in August when Phineas was away from the Kitchener Camp in order to run the Jewish Lads Brigade summer camp at Deal, until the last entry on 30 August 1939. The diary is written – in tiny handwriting – on Bell Hotel stationery. It occasionally contains drawings – Phineas May was an accomplished cartoonist. The diary was kindly transcribed for me by Sam Warshaw.
3. Mosley addressed a packed meeting in Canterbury on 10 July 1937, which was organised to support Lady Pearson's Canterbury nomination as a candidate for the parliamentary seat. He spoke for an hour and a half, mainly on agriculture, and the meeting was frequently in uproar, silenced only by the arrival of the police. I am grateful to Fred Whitemore for the loan of his research on the *Kentish Gazette* of the period.
4. Fred Uhlman, *The Making of an Englishman*, London, Victor Gollancz, 1960, p. 204. Fred Uhlman became a painter and writer (his novel *Reunion* was recast as a play by Harold Pinter) and his naïve-style paintings now sell for decent sums at the London auction galleries. He was a family friend of

the present author, having been a school contemporary of her uncle's in Stuttgart.

5.   Julie Gottlieb, *Feminine Fascism: Women in Britain's Fascist Movement, 1923–1945*, I.B. Tauris, 2000.

6.   *East Kent Mercury*, 11 February 1939, pp. 8–10.

7.   'B.U.F.' were the initials of the British Union of Fascists, led by Oswald Mosley. The full report is taken from the 'Jewish Defence Committee Minute of Special Meeting', 13 February 1939, archives of the Defence Committee of the Board of Deputies of British Jews, held at the Wiener Library, and accessed by kind permission of the Board of Deputies of British Jews.

8.   National Archives, File KV2/877: Captain Robert Cecil Gordon Canning, 29 August 1924 – 7 November 1943.

5

MORE ARRIVALS AND A FRACAS

By the middle of February, a few of the huts were ready for occupation. They had been reconstructed and refurbished by local workmen, swept and polished by local ladies whose raucous manners Phineas much enjoyed: 'the charwomen by the way – there are four of them – are real characters, and if they did their job as present performed on the Palladium stage, they would be a riot.' An ex-Royal Marine cook had been employed for the canteen, and the kitchens were well stocked. However, the number of refugees who had arrived at the camp was hardly more than on the fingers of one hand – this despite the fact that almost daily Phineas received notice that there would be large numbers of refugees arriving that very evening. A typical entry in his diary for 16 February reads, 'phone call this morning to say that the odd 20 Refugees are coming tomorrow – as tomorrow never comes, may be it will be the same with them'.

Moreover, the refugees who had arrived were not of the kind that had been expected. The first to come – rather unfortunately called Adolf but thereafter always referred to as 'Refugee Number One' – had been in Britain for some time and had volunteered to come to live in the camp and work as an electrician. Similarly a Mr Sonneberg, a refugee accountant, at age 58 much older than the maximum age for refugees to the camp, arrived, with an assistant, to be the camp's Chief Cashier. He was delighted to be regarded as 'staff' and hence eligible to eat at the 'staff' table in the dining room but he may have been less pleased, given his name and his age, to be promptly rechristened 'Sonny Boy'. Dr Walter Marmorek, also a refugee who had come from Vienna a few months earlier and who had been working in Ernest Joseph's London office, had arrived to be the resident architect. Phineas, who could never spell Marmorek's name correctly, spelling and syntax not being his strong suits, gave up and renamed him 'Marmalade'. The only 'proper' refugees, who had come straight from Germany, were four who had arrived on 10 February – all of them carpenters described by Phineas as 'typical Germans with black top boots'.

It was a good few days for this little group. Although the refugees occasionally complained of being 'freessing' they also said they appreciated the food – 'they looked upon the white bread almost as delicatessen'. On one evening they were given the money (6d each) to visit the Empire Cinema in the town where they encountered a Mr Goodman, the cinema manager, who was extremely well disposed towards them and ushered them to the best seats. Finally, on 17 February, the first large group of refugees arrived: there were eighteen of them, all 'looking very forlorn and downcast', although they soon cheered up after a meal of fried fish. Later Phineas had to show them the intricacies of making an 'English bed'. Again all these men were skilled craftsmen, being either carpenters or bricklayers, and they went to work willingly the next day even though it was a Saturday – formally, of course, their day of rest.

Phineas arranged all sorts of activities to keep them amused in the long evenings, including table tennis, chess, darts, and something called 'Russian billiards', and he began the Kitchener Camp Library with some gifts of books which included 'an amazing collection of rubbish', mostly in German. 'The cream of the whole collection of books sent to this Camp of 3,500 Refugees – males – was a German version of "When a Baby Comes".' Phineas was really beginning to get rather fed up. The problem was, as he rightly identified, that they were ready to 'receive a large number' and yet hardly anyone had arrived.

This had not gone unnoticed by the members of the Kitchener Camp Committee who, throughout February, made it their business to come down to Sandwich every weekend. Amongst them was Robert Waley Cohen, whom Phineas could not resist referring to in his diary as '*Sir* Robert Waley Cohen' with the 'Sir' very firmly underlined. Sir Robert was no doubt unhappy about the empty camp – he had after all told the Executive Committee of the Fund the previous December that, given the very great urgency of the refugee problem, he expected the camp to be half full by the middle of February. Here was the camp, leeching money, with huts prepared – but empty.

Sir Robert was not a man to twiddle his thumbs and wait for something – or someone – to turn up. Norman Bentwich, whose wife Helen was the secretary of the *Kindertransport* organisation, would have told him that there was a group of young men, already living in the UK, who might be suitable as residents of the Kitchener Camp and provide much needed additional labour. These young men had travelled to Britain on the *Kindertransport* trains in December 1938 and January 1939. While many of the children arriving on these trains had been rapidly fostered in families all over the country, there were a few hundred who had proved more difficult to place largely because they were in their teens, and they had been housed in a Butlins holiday camp at Dovercourt, near the port of

Harwich. This camp was not really suitable for them – there was nothing worse than spending a winter in a place built for the warmth of summer. Moreover, the year was advancing and eventually the Butlins family would want the children to make way for proper holiday makers. With no time to lose, Waley Cohen proposed to the Fund Executive on 20 February[1] that the older boys at Dovercourt be invited to volunteer to come to the Kitchener Camp and help with its refurbishment (the girls at Dovercourt were not given a second thought since by now it had been very firmly established that the Kitchener Camp was only for men).

Amongst the Dovercourt boys was Fritz Mansbacher. Ever since the shock of *Kristallnacht* his parents, in Lübeck, had worked to get him on a *Kindertransport* and he had arrived in England on 15 December 1938.[2] Fritz was not unhappy at Dovercourt but he felt rather aimless there, so when a 'lady and gentleman from London'[3] arrived to tell the young people about the Kitchener Camp he listened carefully. 'The purpose of their coming, they told us, was to recruit volunteers all over England to come and help rebuild the Kitchener Camp and provide a safe heaven [*sic*] for those released from the concentration camps.' This visit prompted much discussion at supper that evening – 'what if our visa for the United States should arrive while we were in the Kitchener Camp? Would they let us go to the United States? Would it be possible to continue our efforts to help our parents out of Germany while at the Kitchener Camp? Should we leave this nice life at Dovercourt for the uncertain life at Lord Kitchener [*sic*]?' These were very difficult decisions for these youngsters who until recently could have consulted their parents but now were entirely without family support. But Fritz eventually came to a decision and put himself forward: it was 'the idea of helping others [that] won out over all other considerations'.

The next few days were spent making preparations including getting their clothes into reasonable shape – apparently they washed their socks and shirts by wearing them in the bath and some of them attempted a bit of darning. Then one morning in early March they said their farewells to their Dovercourt friends and travelled together to London.

They arrived at Liverpool Street station and took a bus through the City of London, down Fleet Street and along the Strand to Trafalgar Square. These young men came from two of Europe's great cities – Berlin and Vienna – but here they were at the hub of the British Empire and they found it fantastically exciting. They couldn't believe their eyes when they saw the City gents in their extraordinary bowler hats, the huge buildings in the City of London, many of them for banks in far flung outposts of the British Empire, Nelson on his column and Big Ben and the Houses of Parliament. 'The more we looked the more we saw. We fell over each other trying to show our friends what we had just discovered ourselves.' They walked down Whitehall past the incongruously modest Downing Street and went inside Westminster Abbey, where they sat quietly for a few minutes. And then they hurried back to Charing Cross station and boarded the train for Sandwich. Quite quickly the city gave way to the suburbs and thence to the wide open countryside dotted with farms and Kentish oast houses and eventually, near Dover, to the White Cliffs and the sea. At Sandwich station there was a moment of panic: 'My God, are they going to dump us in an open field?' And then an old bus appeared to take them to the Kitchener Camp.

It was 3 March 1939 and Phineas simply recorded in his diary that sixty-nine boys had arrived from Dovercourt that afternoon. If Phineas had thought the camp was ready, the boys were really not so sure. In fact they were appalled by the sight that greeted them:

All around us was mud and dirt and stone [sic] huts without windows or roofs.[4] As our courage sank, several men who had arrived some time earlier came to greet us. We all plodded through the mud [...] after our journey we were eager to use the toilet and wash up before dinner, but neither was yet available.

After a somewhat inadequate supper they were given their new work clothes of overalls and 'Wellingtons' and ushered to their hut. They were moderately impressed by its new roof, floor and windows, but they soon discovered the heating hardly existed so they slept that first night in their clothes; if they needed the toilet it was 'almost a five minutes trudge through the mud and cold and it was not fun going there. At night, most guys just opened the door and let it go at that'. At 6 a.m. the next morning they were rudely awoken by a certain 'Mr Phineas' who barged into their hut banging a large gong. Somewhat dozy, they made their way to the dining room where they were given their first of very many breakfasts of porridge, white bread and marmalade, and 'English tea'. At least it was filling, if a little strange.

In the dining hall they discovered fifty or sixty other refugees. Life at the camp had moved on since Phineas's frustration in mid-February and in the preceding fortnight the camp had begun to fill up a little, some men coming straight from Greater Germany and others persuaded to move there by the Jewish Refugees Committee in London as a way of providing support for destitute refugees already in Britain. Breakfast over, they were assembled into work gangs headed by the craftsmen and skilled refugees and dispersed throughout the camp to build roads, dig drains, and refurbish huts. That was to be the pattern of their days for many weeks to come, day in day out, with very little time off, not even on Saturdays – to the dismay of the more observant Jews. Only Saturday afternoons – devoted to sports – and a slight lie in on Sunday mornings were conceded to leisure. There was so much to be done and so many men back 'home' waiting to be rescued.

Despite the bleakness of the camp – everyone who has ever written about it has always remarked on how awful it looked – there was still a sense of excitement and novelty about it. Phineas was in his element. It was just like the Jewish Lads Brigade: lots of youngish men to organise, dragoon into entertainments, lead on walks across the golf course down to the beach (they got lost coming back) and conduct in sing-songs. Ivy, Jonas' wife, had written a 'Kitchener Camp Song' sung to the tune of the Lambeth Walk, which must have struck these cosmopolitan young men as very odd indeed. Phineas recruited two football teams, one for Germany, the other for Austria. Unfortunately, in their first match, Germany thrashed Austria by 10 goals to 3, which can't have done much for international relations. Deutschland was yet again 'über alles' even if it was in a far flung corner of a rough-and-ready foreign football field.

The other aspect of camp life that Phineas really enjoyed was the increasing presence of more Orthodox Jews. He himself was a seriously observant man which was reflected in the fact that he had been seconded to the Kitchener Camp from an administrative post working for the United Synagogue. His Friday evenings and Saturday mornings at this time were taken up with leading Orthodox style readings and discussion groups, although he was pleased when a Liberal rabbi, called van der Zyl, arrived in early March from Vienna with his wife and baby daughter and took over the spiritual leadership of the camp. In addition, the presence of the more observant Jews meant that life in the kitchens and in the dining room began to be more complicated because of the need to provide for kosher diets and Orthodox dining rituals. This Phineas clearly did not mind at all, although much later on in the life of the camp it was to cause real difficulty. He also started giving English lessons: 'I gave one myself for an hour and a quarter, although I say it myself, I think they enjoyed it very much and learnt quite a lot'; however, judging by his diary, Phineas' own spelling and syntax often left something to be desired. He was extremely busy, and very happy: 'As anticipated I am on the go from very early morning until 10pm, when I see them all to bed and switch the lights out. They are, however, such a fine lot that they are well worth working for.'

There were two major events in early March that were 'firsts', and, like the Chamber of Commerce dinner–dance at the Sandwich Guildhall in early February, set the tone of the Camp for some months to come. Someone, probably Jonas, took the decision that, at the Camp gate, the Union Flag should fly. This had considerable significance. It would give the men, from the moment of their arrival, a sense that there was something official about this camp (which was, of course, not the case), but far more important, it would show them that Britain still had a national flag and not a party political one – for the Swastika, the symbol of National Socialism, had long since replaced the national flags, first of Germany, and after the *Anschluss* of March 1938, of Austria. The Union Flag was raised for the first time at 10 a.m. on the morning of 1 March. Jonas May gave a short speech:

> We know what this flag means to you: it means FREEDOM! Freedom that I hope will never be taken away from you again, freedom that I hope will now be yours to the end of your days ... when we have sent the flag up, we shall sing 'God Save the King' – and I want you to sing it with 'all you have got in you' and with all your heart, because our King represents the freedom which is so important to us all.[5]

Then this little group of Germans and Austrians, for whom British citizenship was a very distant reality (most of them did not get British citizenship until 1947 at the earliest), gathered round the flagpole and sang the National Anthem. They had sung it a few days before, at the end of a camp sing-song, and Phineas had explained then 'that we must stand to attention when we sing it and remove our hats. They then sang it and I have never heard it with much more feeling'. A photo was taken of the flag raising ceremony and someone had a postcard made of the image. Many years later the postcard was deposited in the Imperial War Museum. Addressed to a 'Mr Fritz Sonneberg' – quite possibly a relative of 'Sonny Boy' the camp cashier – and sent in May 1939, it has a wonderfully telling caption typed below the image: 'Hoistening the "UNION JACK" over Kitchener Camp on the 1st March 39. Speech delivered from Director May.' English lessons there may have been but the idiosyncracies of the language were just too hard – if it's 'moist' and 'moisten', what's wrong with 'hoist' and 'hoisten'? And as for prepositions, just take a guess.

The other 'first' at this time in the camp's history was the appearance of the first issue of the *Kitchener Camp Review*. This was to be the camp newspaper and Phineas was its editor, a responsibility he took very seriously and which he worried about month in, month out. There were eventually nine issues of the paper, on a monthly basis, and each issue had up to sixteen pages. Phineas was determined to get the refugees to write the articles and he had some success in gathering around him a small coterie of men who contributed regularly. Almost all the articles were published anonymously, the contributors only identified by their initials, and, judging by the style and by the subject matter which often closely resembled his diary, Phineas was usually the main contributor. It is not clear that the men of the camp actually read it. It was written almost entirely in English (though often somewhat Germanic in style) and none of the men I have interviewed remember ever having seen it. It is fairly obvious that the journal was really for outside consumption – there was a notice in every issue that readers could subscribe at the cost of 10s a year, and it is highly likely that copies were given away to the more distinguished of the Kitchener Camp visitors. A copy seems to have been sent to the *Jewish Chronicle* every month, and that paper sometimes used stories from the *Review*. Jonas, in the first issue, stated explicitly that the *Review* should be a *memorial*:

> This little Magazine is started at this early period in the Kitchener Camp's history so that a brief record can be kept of the various incidents that occur that those who stay here for a while may take away with them, as a souvenir, what must inevitably be a memorable period of their lives.

In every issue Jonas wrote a short and always exhortatory introduction, suggesting, for example, that the camp motto should be 'Do it With a Smile!' and always using a metaphor for camp life that referred to 'family'. This was not necessarily the most sensitive of metaphors since almost all of these men had left their families behind in Greater Germany, and many of them forever (although they would have had no certainty of this). The first issue of the *Kitchener Camp Review* contained most of the elements of the magazine throughout its nine issues. There was an introductory exhortation from the camp director and an enthusiastic article by 'Sonny Boy' (Mr Sonneberg, the camp cashier, had been designated 'Foreign Editor' of the *Review*) on how amazed he was by the 'Humanity' and 'Gentlemanliness' of all 'representatives of the British character' whom he had so far encountered. An unnamed refugee wrote of how hard the 'Quartermaster' worked (the writer was almost certainly the 'Quartermaster' himself), and another wrote about the raising, for the first time, of the camp Union Flag: 'Today we ourselves honour this flag under which we receive shelter, and, whilst standing to attention, our thoughts flew back to our home countries which are no more our homes.' Camp officialdom was also present in the first issue: the brand new camp doctor (an Italian) wrote about the health care of the camp, the resident architect (Dr Marmorek, otherwise known as 'Marmalade') described his daily work, and the camp cook published a week's temporary menus – all of it rather unappetising. Monday's menu, for example, consisted of 'Stew. Veg. Plum Duff' for lunch, and 'Macaroni Cheese. Bread and Butter. Cocoa' for supper.[6]

The camp was taking shape and in an entirely satisfactory way. Phineas described himself and the camp, more than once, as 'happy' or even, after a successful Friday evening meal and service led by the new camp rabbi, 'extremely happy'. And on Thursday 9 March it was this beguiling atmosphere that greeted another large group of young men who arrived at lunchtime. These youngsters came straight from Germany and, like the Dovercourt boys, they already knew each other because they had been living together in a residential training camp for Jewish youths at a place called Niederschönhausen, very close to Berlin. As at Dovercourt, one hundred young men had been invited to volunteer to come to help rebuild the Kitchener Camp. Norman Bentwich had had a hand in this – in 1937 he had visited the Niederschönhausen camp as part of his duties as Director of Emigration and Training for the CBF and had been very impressed, particularly by its young leader:

> I cannot speak too highly of the way the place was run, or of the spirit which is being imbued into the students by Mr. Kuh, who, while himself a man of only 32 years of age, has been able to control, with such excellent results, students of ages from 16 up to 50.[7]

Two years later Norman remembered young Mr Kuh and his well disciplined charges, so it is no surprise at all that Poldi Kuh was also recruited to Kitchener. He was going to be 'staff' and in charge of training so, like the camp rabbi, he was able to bring his wife with him – a very rare privilege and one that, much later, became a focus for resentment amongst the other refugees. Poldi and 'Marmalade' (Walter Marmorek) became inseparable at the Kitchener Camp and their strong friendship was lifelong.

Amongst the Niederschönhausen boys was one Helmut Rosettenstein, who, as 'Harry Rossney', the name he took in 1940, was destined to become one of the keepers of the Kitchener Camp collective memory.[8] Harry was 19 at the time and exceptionally among the Niederschönhausen boys he had actually been resident at a hostel for Jewish youth in Berlin itself rather than at the camp. But he was being trained at this hostel by one of the carpenters at Niederschönhausen so when it came to recruiting volunteers for Kitchener he just happened to be invited, along with one other young man at the hostel, to volunteer. Harry was only half Jewish and had been defined, under the 1935 Nuremberg Laws, by the Nazi term of 'Mischling', which meant that he still had some freedoms compared to his full Jewish companions. But he lived in a Jewish milieu and found life increasingly unbearable. His best friend at school had joined the 'Brownshirts' early on and now ignored him in the street; and around his eighteenth birthday he was summoned by the Gestapo and told to get out of the country or be called up for military service. He knew what army service for a 'Mischling' would entail and the invitation to go to the Kitchener Camp was his golden opportunity to get away. The offer to go to England had come to him by a roundabout route: as he was the first to claim, luck was always on Harry's side.

Harry left Berlin on 8 March 1939. His Jewish father had died many years before so when he came to say goodbye to his mother, who was in Nazi parlance an 'aryan', he was fairly confident that she would be all right. He was the last of her children to leave Germany and at Berlin railway station she stood on the long platform, a lonely figure waving a long goodbye.

It was an anxious journey: they were delayed at Aachen on the German–Belgian frontier for an interminable two hours, 'inspection after inspection. Dreaded police and Gestapo in their long leathercoats, hardfaced and ruthless'. At last the train lurched forward and they crossed the border: 'we rolled into Belgium. "FREE! FREE!" We could hardly believe our luck. The accumulated weight of six years of oppression and fear lifted at last. We could breathe and laugh again.' They reached the ferry port of Ostend in the very early hours of the morning and boarded the first of that day's ferries to Dover. The crossing was rough – it was the second week of March – and took about two hours, but when Harry saw the white cliffs of Dover it was 'the most beautiful sight of my life'.[9] It is no surprise that Harry often, in later years, likened this journey to 'being born again' and this sense of rebirth is echoed in a poem he wrote many decades later. The last two lines read:

> but above all I bless fate for letting me see,
> almost too late, twilight at Dover … the making of me.[10]

Harry and his companions finally arrived at the Kitchener Camp. Shabby huts, muddy fields, hard bunk beds, and boring food were not enough to dampen his enthusiasm. The main point was that he was with friends and he was *welcome*. As a group of young men they were kept together in their huts, one of which came to be called the 'Jugend Hütte'. A good friend of Harry was designated hut leader, a post that Harry himself took on a few months later and fulfilled with pride. Just as with the Dovercourt boys, they were plunged into really hard work as soon as they arrived and Poldi Kuh, a familiar face to all of them and no doubt a surrogate father for some of them, kept them going in their well disciplined teams. Harry, who was a trained signwriter, was kept busy writing signs for the camp – for the new first-aid station, for the post office, for the library ('Keep Quiet Please') and even for the huts: 'England Expects Every Man To Do His Duty: You Are Not Englishmen But You Must Do Your Duty.'[11]

It had been a happy time for the Kitchener Camp, but it was a honeymoon. In the second half of March, life there suddenly became less tractable and both Phineas and Jonas realised that they had taken a great deal on, some of which might prove very difficult indeed. Many of the refugees were troubled and anxious and the May brothers were ill equipped to deal with this, having, as Phineas' own daughter has said to me, a 'stiff upper lip' and a 'buck up and put up' attitude to emotional problems. Despite this, Phineas thought of himself as 'soft', so when men started to come to him to find comfort through talk, it did not really surprise him. His frustration was that there was so little he could do. He did listen though, at least in the early days, and he did agree to the designation of his job in the camp as 'Entertainments and Welfare Officer'.

Judging by the emphasis in his diary, it was the entertainment side that really engaged him.

There had been, in the second part of March, a drip-drip of visitors to Phineas' office, including one very upset Dovercourt boy who was missing his first love whom he had met in the Butlins holiday camp. Phineas gave him a cigarette and he apparently cheered up. But the first event that really brought Jonas and Phineas up with a jolt was a terrible row. On the night of 13 March Phineas had already written up his diary for the day and was just beginning to lock up when a boy rushed up to him: 'it was raining, the ground was wet and muddy – he had no boots on, his socks were covered with mud, he could hardly speak for want of breath'. Phineas pushed him into a spare pair of boots and the two of them ran to the other side of the camp:

> When I arrived I found the occupants of his hut some 70 boys (the lot from Dovercourt) standing round a table and making an awful uproar. A middle-aged man from another hut was shouting and fuming at them and to put it bluntly there was a hell of a din. When they saw me they indicated by 'heres [sic] Mr Phineas' as if the Saviour from heavan [sic] had come. They started to shout all their troubles at me. I first made them be quiet and told them I would not listen unless they told me as quietly and quickly as possible what was the matter. They did, and apparently some of them had been disrespectful to the older men. I gave them a lecture about an Englishman not doing this and that and other fatherly twaddle which went home however for every word was interpreted and I told those who had any complaints to see me in the morning. All being quiet I switched the lights off and got them all to bed. It was a case of 'a stitch in time'.

This was the first sign that there were divisions in the camp and that a common experience of persecution and shared identity as Jews was not enough to hold it together. As on a varnished painting small cracks were appearing, between, for example, the Orthodox, the not-so-Orthodox, and the secular; between young and old; between Austrians and Germans (encouraged by the separate football teams); between social classes. One elderly surviving resident has told me how he found the swapping of titles – 'Dr' this and 'Herr Professor' that – quite unbearable and caused another row and was threatened, by Jonas, with expulsion back to Vienna. Jonas and Phineas were faced with an awkward mixture of men from a culture they were not themselves personally at ease with, and men from a very wide variety of backgrounds, many of them traumatised, bitter and unhappy. It was going to be a very big challenge to hold it together. Small wonder that the following Sunday a staff meeting was called and the decision taken to tighten up on camp discipline.

There was one more blow that late March in 1939 and in every respect this was far more important than a minor fracas between boys and men, and it was also to have a profound effect on Kitchener. On 18 March German troops marched into Bohemia and Moravia, Prague fell without a shot fired in its defence, and the whole of Czechoslovakia came into the hands of the Nazi regime of the Third Reich. For the first time in his diary Phineas used the word 'depressed'. He was of course not the only one that day who saw the writing on the wall. The Munich agreement of the previous year, in which Hitler had promised there would be no more incursions and invasions, had been blown apart and the whole world knew it. Neville Chamberlain had spoken then of 'Peace in our Time' and many had believed him. It was now practically certain there would be no 'peace', and as far as getting Jews out of Greater Germany was concerned, there was hardly any 'time'.

Notes

1. Minutes of the meeting of the Executive of the Central British Fund, 20 February 1939, CBF Archives.
2. Memoir of Peter Mansbacher, op. cit.
3. This may well have been Norman and Helen Bentwich.
4. The huts were made of concrete.
5. *Kitchener Camp Review*, Issue One, March 1939; copies held at Sandwich Guildhall Archives and the Wiener Library.
6. *Kitchener Camp Review*, Issue No. 1.
7. Report by Norman Bentwich to the CBF, 24 May 1937, CBF Archive, File 65/123
8. Harry H. Rossney, *Grey Dawns*, edited by Dr Helen Fry, History Web Limited; H.H. Rossney, *Grey Dawns*, Illustrated Poems, unpublished mimeo; Harry Rossney, *Kitchener Camp, March 1939 to May 1940, The Second World War Recollections*, unpublished mimeo. Harry Rossney, until very recently, organised monthly reunions of ex-British Army colleagues (all of them German–Jewish refugees) in the Imperial Café in the Golders Green Road in North West London.
9. All quotes from Harry Rossney, *Kitchener Camp, March 1939 to May 1940, The Second World War Recollections*, op. cit.
10. *Twilight Crossing*, a poem by Harry Rossney, published in *Grey Dawns*, op. cit. The poem is probably about a dawn crossing.
11. Quoted from Norman Bentwich, *They Found Refuge*, p. 106.

6

JEWS SELECTING JEWS

While there had been slow progress at Kitchener, in the concentration camps nothing had changed. Only the arrival of spring had made the regime a little less deadly. In the sunshine the days took on a routine of useless and back-breaking work and awful and completely inadequate food. Only beatings and shouting interrupted the monotony. As he wielded his mop and bucket in the huge shed that had become his home, Fred Pelican was relatively insulated from the brutality of the concentration camp regime but even so, like everyone else, he longed to get away. And he had begun to think there was no hope of release – ever.

One morning in April 1939 the camp tannoy crackled into life. Normally it played Nazi songs over and over again – the one Fred remembered when he came to write his memoirs was '*Heute gehört uns Deutschland und Morgen die ganze Welt*' – but this particular morning the loudspeaker played a different tune:

A bombshell fell: an announcement over the loudspeaker declared that those Jews in possession of emigration documents would be released. Those qualifying would have their names called and would immediately report for medical examination. We all were visibly shaken, some overcome by emotion, crying like babies.[1]

It was not surprising that the men were shocked. This was the very first sign that there was a way of getting out of the camp alive. Until that moment they had expected to stay there until brutality got the better of them and, like so many others, they died. But could this not be just some cruel Nazi joke? And even if it were true, what did this 'medical examination' mean? Would those still suffering from 'blisters, frostbite and other ailments' not be allowed to go? Most particularly they wondered which families had managed to get whose emigration papers together. Who would be the lucky ones?

At least it turned out not to be a joke. The next morning, around 10 a.m., a list was read over the loudspeaker of fifty to eighty names; and so it continued, every morning. 'One could daily observe the envy of those not called and the joy of those released, as well as the tragedy of those who had been called and were afflicted by ailments.'[2] For two weeks Fred waited to hear his name and for two weeks he heard nothing. He felt like 'someone forgotten, left to his fate'. Then, when at last he heard the call, he 'cried unashamedly'. He knew that for himself this meant immediate freedom. Having worked indoors all winter his body was free of frostbite so the medical held no terrors for him. But others, including his friend Henry, were knocked back at that stage and had to wait while their frostbite slowly healed in the warmer weather. The camp authorities were determined the world outside should have no inkling of the brutality of their regime and all the bodies that emerged from their camp should tell a story, not of cruelty, but of comfort – they even instructed Fred and his friends, as they left the camp, that, when asked, they should say they had been in Dachau on holiday.

Fred ticked all the boxes for release because he ticked all the boxes for entry to the Kitchener Camp. He was young (the age range for Kitchener was 17 to 45), he was in a concentration camp (men coming to Kitchener had to be able to demonstrate 'urgency' in their need to leave Germany), and he was fit and willing to turn his hand to any task, which made him particularly attractive both as an international migrant and as someone who could contribute to the refurbishment of Kitchener itself. He was also very lucky, in that he had a mother who had understood precisely what was needed and had worked frenetically, from the moment he was arrested, to get the papers together for him to leave Germany. As advised by the local Jewish Agency in Breslau, she had purchased a ticket for Fred to sail from Liverpool to Shanghai, in China, on 28 October 1939. Once she had done that, everything else had fallen into place. She could demonstrate that Fred, if admitted to a 'transit' camp in Britain, was indeed in transit and that he would leave the UK within a few months.

Admittedly it was a shock for Fred to discover, on his release from Dachau, that he was bound for China – '"Bloody Shanghai" of all places'[3] – but he comforted himself with the thought that there were thousands in the same position; he had, for example, a cousin who was shortly leaving for Lima in Peru. The outcome for Fred was the end of a long process that combined international bargaining with personal circumstance. His personal journey had begun in Britain, when the Home Office had given permission for a 'transit camp', it had faltered on the way when so many countries, including the USA, imposed quotas on the number of refugees coming from Greater Germany, and it had tripped but not fallen when his struggling mother had found the money to purchase a ticket for him to Shanghai, an international port that did not ask for visas but which did demand hefty 'landing fees'. In the background of his journey were many men, most of whom were drawn from their country's and their community's elites, and who worked in government departments and Jewish organisations both in Germany and in Britain. And of course, beyond these gentlemen, were the thugs of the Gestapo and the SS. It was a gendered process combining women in the family and men in the polity, and the end result was the rescue of many thousands of youngish men to safer shores. But Fred had also been lucky – there were after all only up to about 3,500 places at the Kitchener Camp, and there were about 30,000 men in the concentration camps, and probably up to another 300,000 men still in Greater Germany who were at very severe risk. Who chose the men who came to Kitchener and how were they selected?

In London, Norman Bentwich and Robert Waley Cohen were clear that the answer to the 'who' question was, initially at least, simple. The Fund in London should play no part in the selection process. Instead, the men should be chosen by the two relevant Jewish agencies in Berlin and in Vienna. The answer to the 'how' question was less clear cut. There were three selection criteria that were agreed by everyone, in London and in Berlin and Vienna. These were the men's age, the urgency of their removal from Greater Germany, and their prospects of ultimate re-emigration once they were in Britain. But it was very difficult to decide which of the criteria was the most important, and two of them were open to interpretation. 'Age' was clearly relatively simple: it was easy to administer and easily understood. The minimum age was to be 17 (in order to dovetail with the *Kindertransport* where the maximum age was 16) and the maximum age 45. 'Urgency' was much more difficult to define because the position of all Jewish men in Greater Germany at that time was so precarious – if they were not already in a concentration camp then they could legitimately claim that they were at immediate risk of being sent to one. Distinguishing different levels of 'urgency' became a time consuming and ultimately rather futile method of organising priority for rescue to the Kitchener Camp. Instead the third criterion of 'prospects of ultimate emigration' came to be used as a powerful tool. The men had to be able to demonstrate that they would leave the Kitchener Camp and Britain within a certain period of time. The accepted method of proving this came to be a 'high' number in the quota system operated by the USA, permission to emigrate to Palestine, or a dated ticket for a ship sailing, preferably from a British port, to some other part of the world.

Of the two Jewish agencies in Berlin and Vienna, the *Reichsvertretung der Juden in Deutschland* (otherwise known as the 'RV') in Berlin was the more mature. It was first established under the Nazi regime in 1933 when it was felt by both German Jewry and by the Nazi authorities that a national organisation of Jews was necessary within an overtly anti-Semitic policy context. As the Third Reich increasingly excluded Jews from public life, so the RV developed alternatives – Jewish schools, Jewish training centres and farms, Jewish health centres, support for destitute Jews. In effect, the RV became a mini welfare state, complete with a taxation policy, whereby when richer Jews emigrated they paid additional sums in 'taxes' to the RV, which were then used to assist the emigration of the less wealthy.[4]

As far as the Nazis were concerned the primary purpose of the RV was to organise the emigration of Jews from Germany. This the RV did effectively and in an orderly fashion – purchasing foreign currency at an extortionate and exploitative cost, insisted upon by the Reich, assisting emigrants in the paperwork which they needed, liaising with organisations, including the London Fund and the 'Joint' in New York, which could help with finding opportunities for emigration and with funding emigrants, putting pressure on national governments to accept more Jewish refugees. The relationship between the officers of the Third Reich and the officers of the RV was basically one of very uneasy and awkward colleagues, but colleagues nevertheless. They were, as one historian has put it, enemies with a common interest[5] – the Nazis engaged in a process of brutal ethnic cleansing, the Jews engaged in making emigration as easy and painless as possible, against a background of acute pain and loss.

The RV was led by two men: Rabbi Leo Baeck and Dr Otto Hirsch. Both were frequent visitors to London throughout the 1930s and one or other of them was almost always at the meetings of the London Fund's Executive particularly in the months between *Kristallnacht* and the outbreak of war less than a year later.[6] Indeed it was Otto Hirsch who had accompanied Sir Robert and Norman Bentwich to the Home Office meeting in early January 1939 where the details of the transit camp at Richborough had been finalised. They both were integrated Jews who found, after 1933, that the idea that they were no longer Germans quite astonishing, because being patriotic Germans had, until that moment, been a fundamental part of their identity.[7] Bentwich, who shared many of their interests and values, would have found them very congenial and personally trustworthy. However, these German Jewish leaders were in a very uncomfortable place. They were basically protected by the Nazis who found them very useful in their enterprise of making Germany 'Jew free'. For example, immediately after *Kristallnacht* the Gestapo had arrested Otto Hirsch, who was taken to Sachsenhausen concentration camp – but someone higher up the Nazi chain of command had realised that he was too useful to them and he was almost immediately released. Leo Baeck seems to have been left unscathed at that time.

Everyone, including the London Fund, was well aware of the fact that the Jewish agencies in both Berlin and Vienna were in certain respects doing the Nazis' dirty work. But they perceived both agencies as the place where order was imposed on potential chaos. For Bentwich, 'order' was a supreme value. At the back of his mind was the fear that if hundreds of thousands of German Jews tried to cross borders illegally, or took to the high seas, there would be a global upsurge, not in human sympathy, but in anti-Semitism.

In February 1939 Bentwich took himself to Germany proper to see for himself what was going on in Berlin. He was particularly concerned that, post-*Kristallnacht*, the Berliners would have moved completely under the thumb of the Nazis. This, it had become clear, was precisely the situation in Vienna (of which more later). His report on his visit to Berlin was, a bit like the curate's egg, reassuring – but only in parts.[8] He found his Berliner colleagues were, indeed, under a lot of pressure: 'They have been told that what is required is the evacuation within four to five years not only of the younger men who are able to work, but of the whole half a million Jews remaining in Greater Germany. The authorities require an emigration of 100,000 a year.' However, he found that the officers of the RV did not feel especially under threat. Admittedly, additional pressure was being brought to bear on individual Jews to get out of Germany by forcing them to relinquish all their fixed assets, but the men of the RV were continuing to work in their usual unruffled way:

> The organisation of German Jewry is still in great measure unbroken despite the events of last November. The Hilfsverein[9] has resumed its work in all its centres. The Reichsvertretung goes about its activities methodically and quietly; but demoralisation might set in if the Vienna methods were unchecked. It expects to be able to meet the whole of its internal budget for this year, because it has obtained from the authorities the permission to raise fresh taxes on the Jews who still have some means, and also to realise Jewish endowments in Germany for its purposes. They require help then from outside only so as to have foreign exchange as landing money for emigrants going overseas.[10]

Bentwich returned to London reassured that, despite *Kristallnacht*, the RV in Berlin had maintained its integrity. The Kitchener Camp would take a little of the pressure off and the RV was going to set about selection for the camp in an orderly, calm, and methodical way.

The difficulty was that, if anything, they were *too* orderly. The RV put in place a selection procedure for Kitchener that was slow, bureaucratic and elaborate. 'Ponderously Germanic' would not be too far-fetched. As to the application form itself, as a British visitor to the RV was to say later that year, '*das ist ja ein ganzes Buch!*' (this is a whole book!).[11] Not only did candidates have to detail their past, including their entire educational and employment history, they also had to tell the RV about their future plans, who they knew in the countries to which they might eventually emigrate, and they even had to tell them about their hobbies. In addition, they had to attach a one-page CV, testimonials about their career, photocopies of degrees and diplomas, and medical certificates.[12] And, of course, lots of passport-size photos. All this was submitted in the first instance to their local *Hilfsverein*, where the local committee made their comments. Then the heavy envelopes were sent to the RV in Berlin, but slowly. Eventually Richard Joachim, the appointed director of the 'Camp Department' of the RV, read every single one 'because he felt that the degree of urgency could only be assessed after having obtained a full picture of the whole situation'.[13] Once he had read them, made his comments, and put them in order of priority, they went to one of two weekly committees who made their own remarks, and finally made a decision.

Given the context, this bureaucratised system seemed extraordinary. Very quickly Norman began to indicate his frustration with the RV. As early as March 1939, he wrote to Dr Paul Eppstein, who was in overall charge of emigration at the RV, pointing out the Fund had given the RV a quota of 2,000 for Kitchener. The Austrians had only been given 1,000 places and had already, six weeks after the camp had started up, sent lists of men that totalled more than that. Norman hoped a sense of how much better the Austrians were doing would spur the Germans on. He expected that 'there may be about 500 from Germany by Passover'.[14]

German refugees did start to come in dribs and drabs, but not enough: two months later, in May, Norman drafted a letter that Robert Waley Cohen was supposed to sign, telling Otto Hirsch that they were sending their colleague, Julian Layton, to take a fresh look at the RV procedures and see what could be done to improve them. It was on that visit that Layton exclaimed that the German application form was the size of a book. In the same letter the RV were told that if they did not move more quickly, the Fund in London would simply increase the Austrian quota.[15] As time went on, Norman became tetchier and tetchier, writing sharp little letters when he personally encountered a difficulty – for example, when he had been told that dentists qualified to practise in Britain were on their way and then found, on one of his weekend visits to the Kitchener Camp, that months later they still hadn't arrived.[16]

Not much changed. The summer of 1939 rushed by and the Berliners still took their time. In many ways this was understandable – they knew through their own personal experience how desperate the circumstances of the applicants were and how their decisions could easily be a matter of life and death. Werner Rosenstock, who was the secretary of the Kitchener Camp committees at the RV and who was one of the very few of these officials who actually left Germany before war broke out, wrote, years later, of the difficulties they had in choosing who could be rescued. Unlike Norman, he thought they had worked quickly, but in very hard times:

The ultimate decision rested with two selection committees which met twice a week in the Kantstrasse headquarters of the 'Reichsvertretung'. The view from the window symbolised the situation: on the left the burnt-out shell of the Fasanenstrasse Synagogue, constantly reminding us of the pogroms and their victims in the concentration camps, and on the right the railway, with the trainloads of troops, impressing on us that there was no time to lose.

Under the circumstances, acceptance or rejection of an applicant was a matter of life and death. A proper grading of each case would only have been possible if all the applications had been scrutinised first. Speed, however, was the paramount factor and absolute justice was impossible. Outside intervention had to be eliminated and applicants or their relatives were therefore, in theory, not permitted to call on headquarters in order to plead their cases. It was, however, humanly impossible to ignore the presence in the corridors of visitors who, by their shorn heads, were recognisable as released K.Z. prisoners. When their cases were dealt with by the committee, the official who interviewed them had to forget the impression they had left, lest he be carried away by his emotions, to the detriment of others who relied on their written applications.

There were other cases where the Gestapo intervened and tried to press for the prisoner's acceptance. Should one yield to this pressure, thus inviting further pressure, or should one leave the prisoner to the mercy of his torturers? More often than not, this was not an easy decision.[17]

It was only in August 1939, when war was imminent, that the Germans recognised they had to move very fast indeed. Norman was mollified. On 11 August he wrote to Jonas May:

I have had a letter this morning from Dr Eppstein of the RV, about their transports from Germany. He tells me that he wired you about sending this week 116 men, because it was too late to reduce the number to 100. He is most anxious now that their remaining 600 or so men should come over with the shortest delay. They have got going at last. I have told him that 100 is not an absolute number, and that he will endeavour to facilitate the arrival of the balance of their men in every way. I feel with the Chinaman who remarked that 'the sky is black with the chickens coming home to roost', but I have sympathy with the Germans, because I believe they have made their selection with the greatest scrupulousness, and they, of course, have kept absolutely within the limit of 2000 which were given them.[18]

At the last possible moment, on 28 August 1939 an entire contingent of older boys along with their teachers – there were about 100 of them – from a Jewish

Technical School in Berlin were sent by the RV to Kitchener. The RV had finally fulfilled their quota.

The Jewish agency in Vienna was known as the *Israelitische Kultusgemeinde* (IK) and was a rather different organisation from its sister organisation in Berlin. A very similar organisation to the RV had been in existence in Vienna since the end of the nineteenth century but after the annexation of Austria by the Third Reich in March 1938, Adolf Eichmann, who was eventually to be tried and executed as a war criminal, had overseen its closure, and seen to it that the leaders were imprisoned. Two months later he was instrumental in setting up a new organisation with a very similar name, but one which was led only by Jews of whom he had personally approved. The head of the new IK was Josef Loewenherz who had been released from prison once he had produced a plan, on Eichmann's orders, for the mass emigration of Austrian Jewry.[19] This new organisation was not only completely under the thumb of the Nazi hierarchy, it was actually located in the same building as the headquarters of the Central Office of Jewish Emigration which Eichmann ran – ironically in the confiscated Rothschild Palace. Within that building Eichmann set up, in August 1938, what he later described as a 'conveyor belt': instead of Jews who wanted to emigrate having to hurry from building to building to pay the punitive emigration taxes, relinquish their property and collect their visas and permissions, all the necessary offices were relocated to the Rothschild Palace. As Eichmann said in his evidence to the Israeli police shortly before his Jerusalem trial for war crimes, 'The initial application and all the rest of the required papers are put in at one end, and the passport falls off the other.'[20]

Much of this process was actually staffed by Jews from the IK, and every week Eichmann insisted on reports from them on how the enforced migrations were going. A visitor to the Rothschild Palace was taken round by a proud and strutting Eichmann and witnessed one of these meetings. He described seeing Jews 'seated on several chairs where they had clearly been waiting for me for hours on end' and that 'Eichmann rapidly pointed out each by name, told me with equal rapidity which area they would report on; they then immediately droned through their information like trained animals. The expression of a justifiable mortal fear could be read in each face.'[21]

When Norman had visited Berlin in February 1939 to see what was happening at the RV after *Kristallnacht*, his worry had been that the 'Vienna methods' of ethnic cleansing would be used in Berlin. In his report on his visit to Berlin he had described the Austrian situation with horror:

Since the Anschluss the Austrian Jews have been dominated by the Gestapo, who, by ruthless pressure, have led thousands to flee in panic without any destination in which they can settle. Thousands have illegally crossed frontiers, and some thousands have fled to Shanghai and other lands to which admission was easy, without regard to any chance of absorption. Constant demands are made by the Gestapo to increase the number of emigrants and to liquidate the whole Jewish community of Vienna in a few months [...] In the last weeks there have been indications of a policy of the German authorities to make the Reichsvertretung imitate the methods of Vienna. The head of the Jewish department of the police, a Herr Heidrich, is a notorious enemy of the Jews; and officer Eichmann, who has been one of the principal Gestapo agents in Vienna, is to be brought to Berlin.[22]

None of this is surprising – the impact of the *Anschluss* on Austrian Jewry was far worse than the drip-drip of the persecution of the Jews in the *Altreich* which had, by then, been going on for six years in old Germany. But what is surprising is that an Englishman from the Fund was, for quite a lot of the time, in the Rothschild Palace. The Englishman was Julian Layton, a successful stockbroker of German Jewish parentage who had been born in London in 1904 some years after his parents moved from Frankfurt. The family had begun to acquire a British identity and between 1904 and 1924 each member of the family changed their name from Loewenstein to Layton. Debonair and charming, Layton was fluent in German, English and French and was already rich enough, at age 35, to spend a great deal of time working voluntarily on refugee issues. A free spirit – he never married – he had become a rather grand 'gofer' for the London Fund. His main task, from 1934 onwards, was to help Continental Jewish communities – first in Germany and later in Austria – select Jews for rescue, particularly for migration to British colonies and dominions. His second task was to be a peripatetic firefighter – whenever the London Fund thought there was some difficult issue in Greater Germany that needed sorting out with diplomacy, they sent for Layton. And Vienna, being deeply problematic, meant that Layton spent a great deal of time there in the eighteen months between the *Anschluss* and the outbreak of war.

It is not clear if Layton was ever directly involved in the humiliating weekly meetings held on a regular basis between Eichmann and IK officers, or if Eichmann handled him more gently and on his own. They certainly met quite frequently.[23] It is unlikely that Eichmann ever lost his temper in Layton's presence, let alone slapped him – as he did on occasion with IK leaders. He regarded Layton as an asset and at times protected him: for example, knowing he was in Vienna in November 1938, Eichmann had personally phoned him the afternoon before *Kristallnacht* and told him to stay away from the Jewish quarter.[24] Eichmann could be ingratiating in Jewish company, sometimes claiming he was a Zionist, a Hebrew speaker, and that he had been born in Palestine. None of this was true – but it is the case that he made alliances with Zionists and encouraged illegal entry by Jews into Palestine simply because he saw this as one of the countries to which

Austrian Jews could be forced to move. So Eichmann was probably coldly polite with Layton at all times.

The British Jews who came across Eichmann did not have the wool pulled over their eyes. They were, as Bentwich's comments on Eichmann indicate, well aware of his hatred of them – as Jews – even as he politely cultivated them. They were aware that it was Eichmann who was driving the relentless pressure to make Austria 'Jew free' in the shortest possible time.

In the early days in the life of the Kitchener Camp this pressure seemed to effect adversely the type of man who was arriving there from Austria – although it is impossible to tell what was meant by the term 'unsatisfactory', which they applied to the Austrian men. Consequently the Fund decided to send a small investigatory delegation to Vienna to find out what was happening and, if necessary, undertake the selection themselves. Maurice Baron – a director of the cigarette firm Carreras, which had donated large quantities of cigarettes to the camp, an Italian Jew named Gentilli, and Julian Layton, duly arrived at the IK on 19 February and stayed for ten days until early March 1939. Their report, entitled 'Selection of Refugees for the Richborough Camp', has a certain cryptic quality and is very short.[25] The point seems to have been that the Austrian men who were arriving at the Kitchener Camp at this early stage in its life were, in the words of the report, 'unsatisfactory'. The men who had so far arrived at Kitchener were well resourced, particularly in terms of family and friends who had already got away from Greater Germany and were able to maintain them. This was in contrast to the men who had *not* been given permission to go to the Kitchener Camp, who 'were in fact better fitted for emigration than those who had facilities provided them'.[26] The report recommended that the Fund release monies to the IK so that those 'who have neither funds nor relatives' could get away. Reading between the lines of the report, one can only assume that those men who had been selected for Kitchener so far had been able to lubricate their progress through the selection procedure by offering money, either to individuals or to the IK itself. This was not what the London Fund wanted: they had hoped that the Kitchener Camp would provide for those who did *not* have networks of support already resident outside Germany.

The report also recommended that 'it would be of great advantage that two British representatives, *one of whom should be a non-Jew* [my italics], should reside in Vienna as investigating liaison officers between the British Consular offices, the *Kultusgemeinde*, and the various refugee organisations in London.' This, they thought, 'would lessen the influence of the Gestapo over the Kultusgemeinde'. This indicates that they understood that Eichmann's anti-Semitism was always going to drive his passion to rid Austria of all its Jews. He was not just a man of cold logistics obeying orders – which was, of course, his now notoriously controversial defence in his 1961 trial for war crimes; they knew he was also a man of deep bigotry, and that no Jew could ever hope to influence him.

The cumbersome committee process of the RV in Berlin was not replicated in Vienna; Eichmann would not have tolerated it. And although it is certain that Julian Layton returned to Vienna and continued to help with the IK's selection process,[27] there is no evidence that a non-Jew was ever appointed as his colleague. We do know that an officer of the IK, Dr Benjamin Murmelstein, had day-to-day responsibility for selection to Kitchener. Decades later a British historian, Louise London, interviewed Julian Layton concerning this period, and reports that he 'felt a strong personal commitment to assisting men who did not have means but who would be suitable for re-emigration'.[28] However we do not know how far, if at all, Layton was able to put this commitment into practical effect.

The officials of the RV in Berlin and the IK in Vienna were in a completely paradoxical and basically impossible position. They could please no one. Subject to daily humiliation in the office, and persecution and confiscation of their property in their homes and neighbourhoods, they nevertheless continued to exercise considerable power over their fellow Jews. Inevitably this power and their ability to say 'no' led to deep suspicion that their motives were not always the purest. Each time they rejected a man for rescue or refused financial aid for a family there was a potential for deep criticism of them – even hatred.

If letters of complaint were sent to London very few of them survive. There is one, however, that indicates the level of anger that could be generated and the rumours that were current about who obtained favourable treatment – particularly in Vienna. The letter is a rant, but its content confirms, to some extent, the view the small delegation from London to the IK had taken that it seemed to be the case that officers of the IK, for whatever reason, looked favourably on the better resourced. Most of the letter is of the 'green ink' variety and cannot be taken as the truth, but it is quoted here at length because it conveys the convolutions that the potential emigrants had to go through to put together the monies they needed to emigrate and the utter humiliation of having to depend on charity:

My case, one amongst many, is this: with the aid of a Dutch benefactor I obtained two visas for Bolivia which had been bought in Paris. $350 were deposited for me to be used as landing money. The Hicem in Paris[29] bought two steamer tickets and two transit tickets; all I asked the Kultusgemeinde for are the tickets to Paris. Herr Dr. Driemer who, in the meantime, has emigrated, promised me that I would get them from them. The director of the department which grants money for travelling etc. is a certain Dr Marx who acts entirely to his own personal tastes and grants money only if and when he pleases. On receipt of the steamer tickets I had to run from one office to another and at length saw Herr Oberlehrer Muller in room 7 of the Kultusgemeinde who said to me 'As far as we are concerned you will have to walk to Paris. We will not give you the money for the fare' [...] [Dr Marx] is not interested in the fact that it is essential for me to emigrate and told me to come back in the evening at seven o'clock. In the meantime he was going into the matter of tax payments since 1930. I arrived at 7 o'clock, Dr Marx saw me at 8 and informed me that the money could not be given to me. When I asked him how he proposed that I should go to Paris he replied, 'You have been earning money haven't you?' 'Yes, until a year ago.' 'You should have saved something for your emigration.' 'What shall I do now?' 'You will have to find that out for yourself, this is the end of the conversation for me.'

There are thousands of people in Vienna who could have left a long time ago, if only the Kultusgemeinde were prepared to assist the poor. Real help is only given to those who come from Poland, who were born there, who still wear Peijes[30] and who have the necessary connections [...] Cases are known to me where children of rich parents were sent away with the first transports while children who are half starved and where parents are in concentration camps or in No-man's-Land are still here [...] if someone has good connections, plenty of furniture that has been sent in advance, they are given first or second class steamer tickets. Poor Jews can walk to Paris, according to Herr Muller and Herr Dr Marx.[31]

This man did eventually get away; having threatened suicide 'a Christian gave me money for the fare' and his fiancée, who had converted to Christianity, received some money from a Dutch fund and the Society of Friends.

He was one of the lucky ones. The men from the Jewish elite who stayed behind, who remained at their desks as they stripped out their communities, who assumed that their close contact with and utility to the Nazi authorities would serve as an insurance policy, were the seriously unlucky. Their illusion of safety was eventually shattered and almost all of them perished. As they walked towards the firing line or the torture chamber, or, with others, into the gas chamber it is unlikely they were comforted by the thought that through their efforts they had saved so many. But they had. And some of those they had helped to rescue had made their way, as a result of their decisions, to the Kitchener Camp.

Notes

1. Fred Pelican, op. cit., p. 24.
2. Pelican, ibid.
3. Pelican, ibid., p. 29.
4. For more detail about the financial arrangements, see Yehuda Bauer, *Jews for Sale?, Nazi-Jewish Negotiations, 1933–45*, Yale University Press, New Haven and London, 1994.
5. Ibid.
6. Both Baeck and Hirsch stayed in Germany although they could easily have left. Leo Baeck survived the war; Otto Hirsch did not.
7. As late as 1935, the Reichsvertretung was objecting to the fact that Jews could not join the Wehrmacht (regular German armed forces). 'Protest of the Reichsvertretung Against the Refusal to Include Jews In the Wehrmacht', March 23 1935, Jewish Virtual Library. The proclamation is signed by Leo Baeck.
8. Norman Bentwich, *'Note on Visit to Germany 17–19/2/39'*, BWP, File P174/25a.
9. The 'Hilfsverein' was the organisation concerned with international emigration with the exception of emigration to Palestine, which was handled by a separate agency. There were local Hilfsverein offices in all German towns and cities with Jewish communities.
10. Bentwich, *'Note on Visit to Germany 17–19/2/39'*, op. cit.
11. Werner Rosenstock, unpublished memo on 'The Selection of Applicants', kindly supplied by Dr Walter Marmorek and now in the author's ownership.
12. Application forms, found scattered in the archives of the Central British Fund.
13. Rosenstock, op. cit.
14. Letter from Norman Bentwich to Dr Paul Eppstein of the RV, 21 March 1939, BWP, File 174/17b.
15. Draft of a letter to be signed by Robert Waley Cohen, addressed to Otto Hirsch, 23 May 1939, BWP, File 174/17b.
16. Letter from Norman Bentwich to Dr Paul Eppstein, 23 June 1939, BWP, File 174/17a.
17. W. Rosenstock, 'Days of Emergency', *AJR Information*, November 1958, London: Association of Jewish Refugees.
18. Letter from Norman Bentwich to Jonas May, Director of the Kitchener Camp, 11 August 1939, BWP, File 174/15c.
19. David Cesarani, *Eichmann, His Life and Crimes*, London: William Heinemann, 2004, pp. 64–65

20. Cesarani, ibid., p. 67.

21. Cited in Cesarani, ibid., p. 69. This was the evidence of a Nazi colleague of Eichmann's, Bernhard Losener, in a post-war memoir.

22. Bentwich, '*Note on Visit to Germany 17–19/2/39*', op. cit.

23. Interview with Julian Layton, recorded 10 March 1979, Sound Archives of the IWM, Accession no 004382/03.

24. Interview with Julian Layton, ibid.

25. Report by Mr Layton, Mr Gentilli and Mr Baron on the Selection of Refugees for the Richborough Camp, Archives of the Joint Distribution Committee, Jerusalem. The interview with Julian Layton, op. cit., reveals that 'Mr Baron' was Maurice Baron.

26. Report, ibid.

27. Letter from Norman Bentwich to Otto Hirsch at the RV, 20 June 1939: 'It was reported at the meeting of the Richborough Camp Committee, by Mr Layton, who was recently in Vienna and Berlin to help in the selection of candidates for admission to the Camp …', Bentwich Papers, File P174/13b.

28. Louise London, *Whitehall and the Jews 1933–1948, British Immigration Policy and the Holocaust*, Cambridge, Cambridge University Press, 2000, p. 116.

29. This was the equivalent of the London Fund, based in Paris.

30. A Yiddish or Hebrew word meaning the long sidelocks worn by Hasidic Jews.

31. CBF Archives, reference number unclear, but probably 53/187.

7

MOVING TOWARDS A NEW LIFE

And so the lucky ones came to England. They were ordinary men – they weren't famous or well connected or especially intellectual. They were the German equivalent of butchers and bakers and candlestickmakers: mechanics, carpenters, watchmakers, clerks, patissiers, musicians from lesser orchestras, school teachers. They had been good upstanding Germans, many of whom had fought in the First World War, until their countries of origin rejected them and their fellow countrymen took to cruelly abusing them. They had said goodbye to their loved ones and had little idea if they would ever see them again, yet they, as individuals, were travelling away from terror towards freedom and safety. They oscillated between ecstasy and despair; their deepest wish was that this was the beginning – that once they were settled in England they would find the ways and means to get the people they had left behind away to safety too. Forty years later Fred Dunstan described that mixture of feelings to an interviewer from the Imperial War Museum:

> My father was in prison, he couldn't come to the station, my mother and sisters saw me off. But I wasn't a child – I mean I was 22 years old – and of course at least one knew one was travelling into safety so to speak. So it was very mixed. One had to say 'goodbye' to the past so to speak, but a feeling of being – er – I mean able to be free again and no more under this pressure which the Nazis and the SS caused, and to be a Jew in Austria or Germany. I […] was full of joy, that at last the moment had come.[1]

Their lives in Greater Germany had been chaotic and arbitrary but over it all had lain the heavy hand of Third Reich bureaucracy: in order to escape they were laden with documents and permissions. Before they left, they had had to apply to the Reich for a document to certify they had paid off all outstanding taxes and loans, and a similar document from their local tax authority. They had had to pay their local Jewish community taxes and outstanding loans and collect a statement from them saying they had done so; they needed a permit from their bank for foreign currency, which would pay for the transport of their luggage. Men still in paid work had to have an additional certificate stating that their 'Work Book' had been closed and there was no objection to their emigration from the Reich. Once they had amassed all these documents, always in triplicate and always accompanied by certificated passport photos, they had then been able to approach their local police station for an emigration permit. The police also had to provide a certificate stating that the man had no criminal record.[2] It was a huge task and for the Germans in Berlin, as opposed to the Austrians in Vienna, who were fast-tracked on the Eichmann-led 'conveyor belt'; it had taken many days of queuing and pleading to get the correct documents together.

The Berlin *Reichsvertretung* had responded in kind and developed its own elaborate procedures and, in its usual thorough way, had provided the men with a long document of advice and instructions.[3] From this the men knew that they would be travelling by train in a 'closed group' with an RV appointed leader who would take charge of their voluminous papers. Their route, via Aachen, through Belgian to Ostend, and thence a ferry to the English port of Dover, was spelled out for them. This document was intended to be reassuring but many of the men were anxious that even after all this effort their journey would come to nothing: they had heard rumours of the Jewish carriages being shunted into sidings at the German–Belgium border and left there for days, or of men being taken off the trains by the German border guards and then finding they were still trapped in Germany.[4] But if they thought that they would never actually get away, they underestimated the desire of the German Reich to get them out of the country. When they arrived at the border they were harassed and yelled at, their luggage searched and their property stolen – but that was the worst of it. They *were* allowed back on the trains. As they rolled slowly into Belgium they were sorely tempted to shout and cheer, but were under strict instructions not to draw attention to themselves: 'any bad behaviour (e.g. loud behaviour or leaving the train) could lead to great difficulties, not just for that group but all future groups'.[5] Despite the injunction some could not resist:

> And then when we arrived at Aachen, which was towards the late afternoon, we all had to leave. Because we were about 30 altogether coming together to England, we had to leave the train, with all our luggage and everything else. And the way they spoke to us, as one can imagine, wasn't very polite. Jew Raus! Alle Juden Raus! So we were then on the platform and they went through all the things, all our luggage, which most of us hadn't got much, and the train went.

So we had to wait for the next train, which we eventually got. And then we went across the border into Belgium. And we done something which wasn't very polite, but we were *safe*. We could see ourselves being safe. We were away from it![6]

They came with baggage – emotional and material. Close relatives had given them final messages and mothers and wives had filled their suitcases with mementos: family photographs, a little curl of a child's hair. They were going to have nothing in their new countries so they needed whatever they could possibly take with them. The RV had let slip in their instructions that they could, at their own cost, ship items ahead and that there was a large luggage store at Kitchener (as indeed there was). Even today there is someone in North London still using the pots and pans sent by his Kitchener father from Vienna.[7] But the message from the RV was basically that they should not send or bring too much – three 'medium' suitcases that could travel in the luggage van of their train, and a small piece of hand luggage they could keep with them. Whatever they brought with them had, of course, to be pre-checked and documented by German customs.

As well as the mementos and the items that they really wanted to bring with them, the RV had also issued a 'Kit List'. As a list it was somewhat daunting. Somehow or other they had to hit a happy medium – bring too little and they would be a nuisance or bring too much and they would be branded show-offs: 'most camp inmates will not have any money in Richborough and must therefore bring everything they need with them. Whoever does not do this will create great embarrassment, but on the other hand buying too much is also forbidden'.[8] There then followed a long list of all the pieces of kit that were compulsory. It summed up the life of the camp – its ethos, its discomforts, its leisures and its pleasures:

Everyone must take:
a) Work overalls
b) Work shoes – if possible rubber
c) Enough underwear
d) 2–3 blankets and 2 pillows (it is cold and damp in the camp)
e) 3 sheets and covers
f) Sports kit (gym trousers, shirt, plimsolls, running trousers and swimming trunks). (Without sports kit you will be at a great disadvantage)
g) Personal washing materials, especially hand towels
h) Sewing kit (everyone must darn and sew himself)
i) Shoe cleaning materials
j) Cutlery (spoon, fork and knife)
k) Writing materials, books for language instruction
l) Musical instruments where possible (guitars, violins etc.)

> Everything must be labelled with your full name, otherwise washing will not be returned to the owner. The Camp does not take responsibility for lost unlabelled items. So do not bring too much.[9]

They must have wondered quite what they were coming to: for those used to the well-developed tradition of German and of Jewish summer camps for young people it may well have sounded comfortingly familiar – except for the reference to the cold and the damp – but some might have detected a certain element of regimentation and uniformity. But it was also clear that this was a camp where life and living were secure and the request for musical instruments implied a certain soft humanity: this was certainly not going to be another Dachau.

The journey from Berlin or Vienna to the Continental coast of the English Channel took hardly a day, and yet for these many thousands of men this was *the* greatest journey of their lives. For some, particularly the Austrians, their arrival at a Continental Channel port was probably the first time they had seen the sea. The ferries that crossed the rolling English Channel were hardly luxurious and sometimes, in the early spring and into the summer, the seas were rough and the men were ill. There were so many reasons, both banal and profound, to be deeply relieved on reaching England's shores.

There were nervous moments still to come: in the English port of Dover they encountered their first brush with British officialdom. However, unlike their German counterparts, the British immigration officers turned out to be polite, careful, well informed. The arrival of men destined for the Kitchener Camp in the evening of most days meant that the scrutiny of their documents had become routine and there were hardly ever any problems.[10] There were slightly forbidding aspects to the phrase the officials stamped in every man's passport: 'Leave to land is hereby granted at DOVER on condition that the holder proceeds forthwith to Richborough Refugee Camp, registers at once with the police and remains at the camp until he emigrates.'[11] The customs officials were rather less formal but they, at first, were deeply suspicious of so *many* musical instruments. The customs officers devised a test: if the men could play their instruments then they were musicians, not smugglers. Phineas May in his diary of 27 March noted that 127 men from Vienna had arrived late that evening. An hour or two earlier they had performed 'an excellent concert to enrapt officials of the Customs House'.[12] By the time Phineas came to write about this event in the April edition of the *Kitchener Camp Review*, he had elaborated a charming scene:

> Many of them carried musical instruments [...] 'Unless you can play them,' said the Customs Officers, 'we are sorry but you will have to pay Duty on them.' Then instantly there began a concert, which would have warmed the cockles of even Sir Henry Wood's heart. Delighted, the Customs, Boat and Railway

Officials listened entranced to the 'Tales of the Vienna Woods' and the haunting, lyrical notes of the 'Blue Danube'. All work on the quayside ceased … but there was no Duty to be paid on those violins and piano accordions.[13]

A sentence later he wrote in the *Review*:

> Appreciation of the porters' assistance with their luggage was shown by the giving to them of cigarettes and biscuits. 'Baggage to the right of them, – Baggage to the left of them, – Baggage behind them … no porter grumbled.' At 10pm the 127 new arrivals at the Camp sat down to supper, served by the many willing hands of fellow refugees, whose welcome to their new comrades was overwhelming. Total in Camp noon 28/3/39 – 320. Expected in Camp by end of the week a further 150.[14]

Within the thick, mimeoed pages of the *Review* there was propaganda but there was also more than an element of truth: these men, for the first time in years, had encountered a state with a kindly face, and the physical and emotional space for a warm and cheerful welcome from their fellow refugees.

They often arrived in the late evening when it was too dark to see a great deal of the camp apart from the crowded hut to which they had been allocated and the large dining hall. It took the next few days to adjust to their surroundings and there were one or two surprises in store. As they explored the camp they found that their ideas of 'England' were not entirely satisfied by the Kitchener Camp – in certain respects it was rather like what they had left behind. Fred Dunstan recalled:

> Well I was born and brought up in Vienna, Austria, but the far bigger number of people at the Camp were Germans.[15] And the first thing that hit me personally was the accent which was of course like the SA and the SS. This is very difficult to describe. Although they were our own people, it took more than one week to shake off this feeling, this horrible feeling that we had.[16]

There were other aspects of the Kitchener Camp which also served as reminders of the world they had left. There was barbed wire, there was containment, and there was fierce discipline:

> One had to get used to the discipline of course, and the discipline was *very* strict. We were really behind barbed wire and that was in a way a bit of a shock. Once you are behind barbed wire you are of course not free. And it needed a permit, which one could obtain but not easily, to leave Camp.[17]

In many ways the retention of a barbed-wire fence and a single heavily guarded gate is, with hindsight, at best unthinking and at worst totally insensitive. Combined with a 10 p.m. curfew, the men's relative confinement served as a reminder that they were refugees with no rights of citizenship and that they remained in a precarious position in this new country. It was also a statement that the camp management had taken it upon themselves to police the demand of the British government, stamped into their passports, that every man 'remains at the camp until he emigrates'. But different men had different responses to these limitations on their freedom. Fred Dunstan, who had *not* spent time in a concentration camp before he arrived, found the barbed wire a shocking novelty. His namesake, Fred Pelican, who had been in Dachau, found the Kitchener Camp positively congenial and, as this Fred kept repeating to an Imperial War Museum interviewer, 'quite normal'.

If they had throughout their time in Germany, nursed a concept of 'freedom' that they thought existed beyond that country's borders, they were bound to be disappointed by Kitchener. They remained marginal men, with no civil rights and no right to work beyond the camp. Even though Britain had given them back their human rights, they were dependent on charity and for many this was a deeply uncomfortable place to be. However, the organisation of the Kitchener Camp left little time for reflection and anxiety. There was, certainly in the early days of the camp, a great deal of work to be done, just to get it into shape. If the camp managers had planned a place of occupational therapy they could hardly have done better and there are indications that the camp organisers did indeed have a very good idea of the recuperative nature of work. They had agreed, in April 1939, a statement on the kind of work that should be available:

> Every man in the Camp should have a full day's beneficial occupation. What
> is more, every man must *feel* that it is beneficial. Drudgery, or anything which
> might seem to the men to be valueless and time-wasting, would quickly have
> an adverse effect on the morale of the Camp and grave difficulties would follow.
> Work must be of such a character and so organised that each man feels that he
> is doing something of real value for the Camp, for his prospects of successful
> settlement, and for the support of himself and his fellows.[18]

The camp, particularly in its early days from February till June, was an absolute hive of activity: long working hours combined with manual labour were the order of the day. Fritz Mansbacher described the elaborate division of labour he discovered when he got there in early March:

> After breakfast we were divided into different work groups. Those who had
> worked in certain professions were grouped together in order to achieve the

greatest efficiency as well as provide leaders who could instruct others in the type of work needed. We all knew why we had come here and we were all very anxious that the work proceed as quickly as possible. The faster we worked, the quicker the huts would be ready and the sooner hundreds, and maybe thousands, of men could get out of concentration camps in Germany [...] We had groups of bricklayers, electricians, roof layers, carpenters, cleaners and so forth and one group hustled the other. The cleaners would start first [...] [they] were followed by the bricklayers ... [then] roofers installed reinforcing and roof supports prior to installing a new roof [...] the carpenters entered to install flooring ... and wooden walls in order to separate the huts into two areas [...] the electricians [...] were followed by the painters who brought in their spraying equipment. When all the inside was fixed and properly painted and the windows had been glazed, we would bring in the beds and tables and benches to make it livable [...] Plumbers were hard at work installing pipes for bathrooms, showers and sinks, while another group sawed and hammered wooden boards into cupboards into which future camp inmates could hang their clothes or store their socks and underwear. Work was going on all over the camp and no one complained about the work, working conditions or the long hours.[19]

On one point Fritz was wrong: there were complaints, first in February from the Orthodox Jews about having to work on Saturdays, and then, a month later, from the secular and Christian Jews that they had to work on Sundays. The Orthodox were told by Jonas that such hard work was essential and that it was a *mitzvah*.[20] This strategy and language worked. A month later when the secular Jews came to see him about Sundays he used more secular language: 'though they were fortunate enough to be in the Kitchener Camp, thousands of German Jews were waiting to come here and it would indeed be very selfish of them to wish for a free day when so much work was waiting to be done.' Phineas recorded that 'The "rebuke" was very well received and they are all willing to work like good boys on Sunday mornings.'[21]

The work was hard and unrelenting, particularly since, in the first few months, the weather was awful and men, tools, machinery and lorries often got stuck in the mud. But by June/July the huts were habitable and kitchens and washing facilities were fully functioning. There were, by that date, nearly 2,000 men in the camp with more refugees arriving on an almost daily basis. The sheer logistics of the day-to-day management of such large numbers plus their provisioning and feeding, their medical care and their entertainment became a major source of 'jobs' in the camp. In July 1939, there were 1,901 residents of Kitchener. Of these, 782 were involved in 'Organisation', 390 in the Kitchen, 552 in 'Workshops and Campshops', 177 in 'Agricultural Training'. The 'Organisation' group was a catch-all for jobs that were not included in the other three categories. For example, it included the camp police force: ten 'cycling guards', thirty-six 'night guards', forty-four 'day guards' and thirty-four 'gate guards'. There were almost a hundred cleaners, twelve men looking after the Woodstore and sixteen dealing with the Luggage Store. There were forty-five members of the orchestra – which compared rather well with the four 'Artists' who, in turn, were equal in number to the four 'Rat catchers'. Fifty-four office workers were supplemented by fourteen workers in the accounts department; forty-nine men worked in the medical department, although there were only four in the first-aid station. Eight men looked after the telephone box and eighteen men the post office.[22]

Harry Rossney was a signwriter at the camp and possibly included among the four 'Artists'; he also later on became a hut leader; Fritz Mansbacher was an assistant in the first-aid post, Fred Pelican was a night guard, Fred Dunstan worked in the bicycle store, and Philip Franks (another of the men later interviewed by the Imperial War Museum), who was a trained glazier, worked on refurbishing and maintaining the huts. All of them seemed happy with the jobs they did, Fred Dunstan particularly so:

> And in the end I got a marvellous job in the Camp! Because I and another friend were in charge of the Bicycle Shed and that was a real bonus, because there was shift work. That means you were 8–2, 2–8, the third day you had completely free as long as you had your English lesson. That means you were almost out of the normal Camp discipline. So that was really very enjoyable! … And in the meantime you could read a book or improve your knowledge of English, so that was a real stroke of luck. I mean that just happened that this job became available and I and a good friend of mine were sharing it.[23]

Work was the bedrock of the ethos of the camp and this was reflected in the Kitchener Camp song which Ivy May, wife of Jonas, had written:

> Any time you're Richboro' way,
> Any evening, any day,
> You'll find us all
> Working the English way Oi!
>
> Every man and every boy
> Helps to make the Camp a joy,
> You'll find us all
> Working the English way Oi!

Everyone bright and breezy
Everyone makes things easy,
Why don't you make your way here,
Work here, play here,

Any time you're Richboro' way,
Any evening, any day,
You'll find us all
Working the English way Oi![24]

There is no knowing whether Mrs May meant this song to be ironic; was she making some private joke about how the English do – or don't – work? But it certainly indicates what the camp management expected the men to do.

There was a German counterpoint. At one stage, in July, Poldi Kuh, who had brought with him his team of 100 young men from Niederschönhausen and was on the 'staff', produced an elaborate policy document entitled, 'Work and Training in the Kitchener Camp'. Poldi wanted the camp to have training courses, lasting six months, with graduation certificates for those who had completed their courses satisfactorily. The training was to be highly specialised, and was full of routine surveillance and assessment of the men's work performance. He even listed, under the heading 'Occupational Training', the domestic chores that all the men should be able to demonstrate competence in, including, for example: 'repairing button holes, lining sleeves, putting on batches [sic], darning stockings.'

The camp management seemed positively alarmed by this report and invited extensive comments, including from the Inspector of Technical Education for the London County Council. He was as kind as he could be, but within limits, describing the report as 'typically German', 'too ambitious' and 'too close attention to detail by far'.[25] What came of this argument is anyone's guess: all this debate about the nature of the training at the Kitchener Camp was going on in August 1939. It was extraordinary that nobody seemed to notice that war was about to break out and that radically changed circumstances might eventually determine that training would, in very short order, become entirely militarised.

At a late stage in the camp's development, and very shortly after war broke out, the Kitchener Camp Committee published a single issue magazine containing striking photos of activities in the camp. In a no doubt unintentional echo of the notorious phrase '*Arbeit macht frei*' a series of pictures of Kitchener Camp men appeared under the heading, 'They find Happiness in their new Work':

Every man in the Camp has a job. There are representatives of more than 30 different trades and professions, including doctors, architects, engineers, dentists, lawyers, electricians, clerks, bricklayers and business men. Between them they are rebuilding and maintaining the Camp and its services. Their day begins at 6.30. They take breakfast at 7, and work from 8 to 5.30, with a break for lunch at 12.30. After working hours they are free to leave the Camp at will, but must return at 10pm. for roll call. Only pay they receive is sixpence a week for pocket money. The refugees remain at the Camp until they are fitted for a trade. After that they become emigrants to the United States and British Empire centres.[26]

In the accompanying photos of men driving tractors, feeding ducks, harvesting hay, mending boots, sawing timber, almost everyone is smiling. There are one or two men wearing *lederhosen* as they mow lawns and hump hods of bricks. Some of this was no doubt exaggerated but this was certainly not the futile and often brutal 'work' of the concentration camp regimes. It was all work with a purpose, either to refurbish huts which would then house further refugees, or to build the self-sustainability of the camp, or to train men for their futures in some other country. Indeed, that was the point: these men were to have a future, however uncertain, and the skills they learnt at the Kitchener Camp were to equip them to be breadwinners wherever they finally found a permanent home.

Notes

1. Interview with Fred Dunstone or Dunstan, IWM Sound Archive, Accession number 13617.
2. 'Instructions for Emigrants to the English Transit Camp in Richborough, Kent', BWP, P174/17b. I am grateful to Joan Cromwell for helping with the translation of this document.
3. Ibid.
4. Interview with Fred Dunstan, op. cit.
5. 'Instructions for Emigrants to the English Transit Camp in Richborough, Kent', op. cit.
6. Interview with Philip Franks, IWM Sound Archive, Accession number 13618. Philip, who later settled in East Kent, was 19½ at the time.
7. Phone call from a gentleman whose name I could not hear who told me his father had been in Kitchener and had left him astonishing amounts of kitchen equipment, cutlery and linen, which his father had brought from the family home in Germany.
8. 'Instructions for Emigrants to the English Transit Camp in Richborough, Kent', op. cit.
9. Ibid.
10. Interview with Fred Pelican, IWM Sound Archive, Accession number 9222.
11. BWP, File P174/13a.

12. Phineas May diary, 27 March.
13. *Kitchener Camp Review*, April 1939. This article was written by Phineas May.
14. Ibid.
15. It was almost certainly not the case that Germans were in the majority, but it is interesting that Fred Dunstan thought they were – a reflection presumably of his fear of men with German accents.
16. Interview with Fred Dunstan, op. cit.
17. Ibid.
18. Comments by 'C.M.D.' on a policy document, 'Work and Training in the Kitchener Camp'. 'C.M.D.' was almost certainly Charles Davis, who was probably a member of the Kitchener Camp Committee and particularly concerned with arrangements for work at the camp. In his comments he quotes this statement as taken from the Committee minutes (which I have not found despite extensive searching both in British and Israeli archives). BWP, File P174/12d.
19. Mansbacher memoir, chapter on the Kitchener Camp, op. cit., pp. 3–5.
20. A Hebrew and religious term meaning a moral deed performed as a religious duty.
21. Phineas May diary, 24 March.
22. *Work and Training in the Kitchener Camp*, held in the Kitchener Camp box file, Sandwich Archive, the Guildhall, Sandwich. This document does not have an author's name but it was definitely written by Poldi Kuh.
23. Interview with Fred Dunstan or Dunstone, op. cit.
24. *Kitchener Camp Review*, No.2, April 1939, p. 9.
25. Comments by Mr J.H. Currie, Inspector of Technical Education, LCC, August 1939. BWP, File P174/12d.
26. *Some Victims of the Nazi Terror: the Reward of the Salvors*, published by the Kitchener Camp Committee, Odhams Press Ltd, 1939.

8

MINDS AND BODIES

In the century of war, of totalitarianism and of the Holocaust, as the twentieth century was destined to become, it was the disruption of family life that eventually became the most common experience of many millions of people. This was particularly true of Europeans. Camps of every description – gulags, death camps, prisoner-of-war camps, army camps, internment camps – were scattered across the Continent and beyond, and in each one, men and women were separated so life together, with their children, was rendered impossible. In that sense the Kitchener Camp, being for men only, was much more like these other camps than a twenty-first-century refugee camp, many of which contain whole families. Indeed, Fred Pelican, when asked about the Kitchener Camp, used an army camp as his point of reference and said that was what Kitchener was like.[1]

The masculinity of the Kitchener men had in fact been amplified. The original arrests after *Kristallnacht* of men but not of women reflected Nazi ideology concerning men's and women's separate spheres. Moreover, when it came to selection for rescue to Kitchener, many of the men had been chosen because they had traditionally male skills of craftsmanship and technology. These skills, in the camp itself were valued and used. However, the emotional and domestic core of these men had been profoundly disrupted; it was no longer persecution and torture that lay at the basis of their pain, but separation from the people they loved and who loved them. In addition, by separating from their families the men were acutely aware they could no longer see themselves, or act, as protectors of their families against the terrible depredations of the Nazi regime.

There were ways of staying 'in touch' with their families from within the Kitchener Camp. The camp had its own telephone exchange, with an English-speaking switchboard operator who quickly grew used to the names and the call numbers of the cities of Germany. And the men's weekly pocket money of 6*d* a week was supplemented by the issue, not only of cigarettes and chocolates, but also by two international stamps. Phineas was astonished by the length of the letters the men wrote. Writing in his diary as he sat in the new recreation hall in mid-February he said: 'As I write games of table tennis, chess, darts and Russian billiards are going on, while others read magazines or write the long, long letters that the German folk always write home.'[2]

But sending long letters and making expensive international phone calls, which many could not afford, were never going to be satisfactory forms of contact. Indeed these activities, in themselves, probably reminded the men of the distances between themselves and their loved ones and the huge difficulties that stood in the way if they were ever to hold them in their arms again. It is not surprising that for many of these men their time in Kitchener was an unhappy one and one that, over the years since the Second World War, they have preferred to forget. When Fred Pelican was interviewed in the 1980s and asked what morale was like in the camp his answer summed up the mixed feelings of so many, and also the anxieties that tended to prevail:

> Well – it depended on the age group. The elderly people – most of them were brooding. But by the same token they'd begun to realise that they've gained freedom – something which they didn't have for so many months. It depends on the individual but they were pleased to be here. They liked it. And by and large the morale in the camp – I won't say it was a high standard because a lot of them had to leave their dear ones behind: there were husbands who had to leave their wives behind or vice versa or children who had left their parents – like in my own case, I had to leave my mother and two brothers behind. So everybody had a feeling of anxiety just the same.[3]

Harry Rossney also refers to the difficulties of the Kitchener men: 'we were all affected by the events of our times, past and present. There was tension, strain, emotional pain, uncertainty and enforced separation'.[4] Everyone noticed this, including the people of Sandwich. A very kind couple, a Mr and Mrs Gray, invited Fritz Mansbacher to Sunday lunch. Maybe they knew that he longed for peace and quiet and something resembling family life. It is certainly what they provided and years later he recorded how special that afternoon's experience had been for him:

> After tea Mr Gray lit the fire and he and I settled into easy chairs in front of the fireplace. He had put out all the lights and only the light from the dancing flames in the fireplace lit up the room. Now Mr and Mrs Gray were sitting on either side of me while their dog had his head in my lap. How peaceful it was and how different from camp life. It was so enjoyable. In camp we had become numbers. There was no privacy, no place where we could be alone with our thoughts. In camp were were all in the same boat and there was little sympathy

for one another. Most of us had had to leave our parents, wives, children, our loved ones […] The peace, the warmth and the dancing flames made me realise how lucky I was to be where I was. I appreciated what they had done for me and I was grateful for their silent company. When I returned that evening to the camp and looked about me, I so much wished that I could change things and comfort many of the men in camp.[5]

Ivy Kum, an elderly lady in 2013 but a young girl in 1939, and a resident of Sandwich all her life, said to me completely unprompted when I asked her about the Kitchener Camp, 'They were very unhappy you know.'

It wasn't just the impact of separation that made the men sad and anxious. For so many of them, although not for all, there was the recent experience of detention in a concentration camp from which – somehow – they had to recover. The Kitchener Camp regime helped: during the day, particularly in the early months, the men were so busy that it was difficult to catch breath, let alone find the time to dwell on the horrors they had witnessed and the brutality they themselves had been subjected to. Despite the strangeness of being one among so many there were opportunities during the day to catch up with old friends from Berlin or Vienna, to find companionship and the opportunity to talk over shared problems. The nights were the bad times. Squeezed into crowded huts, sleep could catch men unawares. Their memories surfaced in their dreams, disturbing others and waking them. Fritz remembered that 'Many men had to overcome their maltreatment in Germany. Nightmares, sudden outbursts of crying or bewildered shouts for help were quite frequent. It was pitiful.'[6] Night terrors were so commonplace they became the subject of public jokes in the camp magazine:

> I like Stangl. He is taller than six feet, and has a sandy beard. When midnight approaches, Stangl lies in his bed and screams in a loud voice so that his fellows jump out of their beds believing that Doomsday has come. Awakened, Stangl insists upon his conscience being pure. (But I know quite well the reason of his sinister dreams; for four weeks he has owed me sixpence.)[7]

Stangl was one of those who was fine during the day – he was clearly a 'camp character' and he appeared, paradoxically and possibly significantly, in a Wee Willie Winkie hat, in a bunk bed and pulling a mock long face, on a float the Kitchener Camp sent to the Ramsgate Carnival.[8] But there were others for whom the days were as hallucinatory and terrifying as their sleeping dreams, and they sank into madness. Phineas recorded how one man appeared to invert the camp experience so that the Kitchener Camp water towers had become watch towers mounted by machine guns, which were protecting him:

A man who had suffered a good deal in the Concentration Camp have [*sic*] gone quite 'crackers' during the last few days – he put the grand piano on four chairs and covered it with some awful grease pretending to be a great Piano Polisher – a letter he has written home was opened in which he gave a description of the masterly way he had repaired (actually spoilt) the piano, how he had been promoted to a most important position in the Camp, and how to protect him machine guns had been placed at the top of the water towers – this afternoon they told him in view of his good work he was going to be taken out to tea with four of his comrades – who of course took him in a car to the local asylum – poor chap.[9]

Fritz Mansbacher worked briefly, probably for no more than a month, as an assistant in the first-aid station. He was only 17 at the time and saw men in very acute distress, which he had to handle. For example, he encountered someone who, in his delusion that his body was full of poison, was desperate that his arm be amputated:

He had already written to his wife not to come to England as he felt that his family had suffered enough and the sight of him without his arm would be too much for his wife to bear. My assurances that he was not sick, that his arm was not hurt, that there was no necessity for the arm to be amputated did not calm him. He begged and pleaded with me to get the job done as quickly as possible to get it over with.[10]

Eventually Fritz and his boss, a certain Dr Mink, pretended to drain the man's arm in the hope that that would calm him. It did, but only temporarily. Another man took to threatening all and sundry with a bread knife because he thought they were Nazis. Both these men were taken to the local asylum as were, to Fritz's knowledge, five other men during the brief period he was a first aid assistant. Phineas recorded, on 28 June, a death in the asylum; this was almost certainly a suicide and it could have been one of these men or equally someone else who had become deranged.

  These stories of madness, and the knowledge that so many men were unhappy in the Kitchener Camp, inevitably colour our present-day response to this rescue. The originators of the camp – Robert Waley Cohen, Norman Bentwich and their colleagues – had thought that it was desperately urgent to get the men out of the concentration camps, and their families, in particular their wives and children, would be rescued through some other route and over a longer period. For men there was urgency, for women and children there was time. Given time, the Fund assumed that many of the wives and mothers could come to Britain via the 'domestic service' route, which the Fund, with the Home Office's happy agreement, themselves ran. The work of the 'Domestic Bureau' at Woburn House was entirely concerned with finding refugee servants for British households who wanted them and it was successful in doing so, with about 20,000 German–Jewish women entering Britain in the late 1930s to work in British homes.[11]

This immigration of women as domestic servants and of unaccompanied children on the *Kindertransporte* meant that the Kitchener Camp Committee had reason to assume that, given time and resources, the families of the Kitchener men would eventually be reunited. They were, of course, optimists, particularly Waley Cohen and Bentwich, and it is possible that they really did think that either war was not imminent, or that, even if war were to break out soon, it would still be possible for German–Jewish women and children to cross European borders and move westwards to Britain.

It was the responsibility of the Kitchener Camp organisers, particularly the May brothers, to deal, on a daily basis, with the unhappy human consequences of this enforced hiatus between the arrival of the men and the arrival of the men's families. In certain respects Jonas and Phineas did remarkably well. Work and training were obviously the chief means of keeping the men's minds occupied, their bodies fit and, by the end of the day, fatigued enough to sleep moderately well. But there were other hours to fill: between the end of the working day and the 10 p.m. curfew, and the men's days 'off' once the camp was refurbished and they were working two days out of three. Phineas's diary and the *Kitchener Camp Review* are filled with reports of pastimes of every possible kind. They cover a huge range of activities: exercise classes run by Mr Banks morning and evening, football matches between Austria and Germany, daily compulsory English lessons with additional Spanish language teaching for those expecting to go to Latin America, theatrical performances and religious services. Table tennis and cycling, often with outside teams drawn from the neighbourhood, feature frequently in both diary and the *Review*. Sports days with the local grammar school, mock Parliaments for the refugees, inter hut drama competitions and, according to Norman Bentwich, university level courses, were all on offer. It was all amazingly *busy*. Phineas made certain it was so:

> Beautiful sunny weather helped to make this the happiest day yet spent in the Camp. Both Services[12] were good and in addition a Reading from the works by 'Heine' for those who did not attend, and a group in the open air studying the Talmud. And very excellent was the leader of it. Most successful physical training in the open was followed by a reading from the news in English and German by Prof. Bentwich. In the afternoon four of our men were playing for Sandwich Town against another small town team and for 2/- I was allowed to take as many Refugees as I liked. I had arranged to meet them at the gate and I was surprised at the large number who wanted to go. So lining them up

we marched in proper formation to the Stonar House Playing Fields singing English and German songs. In the evening we had a 'Do-as-you-please-contest' with prizes for all performers. It proved a great success and the room was packed. At 9.30 a further 130 Refugees arrived from Vienna.[13]

Perhaps the most extraordinary aspect of the organised leisure of the camp was the 400-seater cinema donated by Oscar Deutsch, a member of the Executive of the Fund and the owner of the Odeon Cinema chain ('**O**scar **D**eutsch **E**ntertains **O**ur **N**ation'). The original intention was that 'educational' films would be shown which would introduce the camp residents to life in Britain and in the colonies but very quickly the programme reverted to more standard fare of Donald Duck cartoons and romantic comedies. The films were so popular and so many of the men wanted to see them that a strict rota system, working on a hut by hut basis, was introduced, only to be overturned by the development of a brisk trade in cinema tickets. Next door to the cinema was a large concert hall complete with stage and heavy velvet curtains. Here, under the direction of the one time conductor of the Radio Stuttgart orchestra the camp orchestra gave regular concerts. Comedy sketches and variety acts performed by the men also frequently filled the hall; Phineas said they were hilarious and that the audiences loved them.

Fred Dunstan thought that, in certain respects, there was too much organisation of his time:

> Germans like discipline and for us [Fred was Austrian] it was almost too much discipline. There was a regular timetable, and I think one *had* to do two things: English lessons were compulsory, which didn't worry me because I had quite a good knowledge from school, and private lessons, a reasonable knowledge, and then one had to choose a subject, like carpentry, agricultural training, or whatever. And so time was divided and now and again – I wasn't a very great sportsman – but there was time for sport. And occasionally one could get a permit and of course have a chance to get to Ramsgate or Margate and see the sea, and enjoy an afternoon at the seaside.[14]

Fred was clearly one of those who found the disciplinarian ethos of the Kitchener Camp hard to take. But he had one memorable weekend (probably organised by Phineas) where he suddenly found a new sense of being both at ease and at the same time free:

> Well one had to have a permit, and of course money was limited. But one day, there was a call that all who were associated with the Boy Scouts movement either in Germany or Austria should come forward and it turned out that three or four, mainly my own personal friends, came. We were told that there was an

invitation to come to Biggleswade and to spend a weekend with some Rover Scouts from Cambridge. So we accepted very gladly; we still had our Scout uniform and we went to London, we were met there, and went by coach I think to Biggleswade. And had a lovely time! Of course it was the first time that we were really *free*, because after all as we arrived we were immediately behind barbed wire. This was the first time we were free and amongst real friends. So we really enjoyed that ever so much.[15]

It would be entirely wrong to give the impression that the Kitchener Camp was, at all times, a grim and dowdy place filled with unhappy and worried men. There is no doubt that there were also happy times, often arising out of Phineas' enthusiastic efforts to keep the men entertained, and there were good and plenty of reasons for laughter. Many men were fond of Phineas and appreciated his efforts to lighten their load. For his birthday on 9 May his 'office staff' greeted him with little presents and most particularly, a birthday song, which they must have had fun composing. Since it is a pastiche of the Kitchener Camp song, it is also possible they were poking gentle fun at that too:

> As we have in camp a stay
> On the day of Phineas May
> Everytime we say
> Phineas is OK. Oi!

> He is doing all his best,
> In recreation without rest
> Luck and health for him
> This is our request. Oi!

> Nobody of his staff is lazy,
> Only a little crazy,
> This the way to smile here,
> That's the style here.

> As we have in Camp to stay,
> On the day of Phineas May,
> Everytime we say
> Phineas is OK. Oi![16]

Phineas' diary is full of examples of where he himself had a good time along with some Kitchener men, which more often than not involved the Dovercourt boys. For example, on 23 April the boys came second in the 'Best Kept Hut contest' and were rewarded with, as Phineas put it, 'a Ride round the Country and Tea':

> There were two coaches, it was a delightful drive, the boys singing and very happy. We had an excellent tea at an inn called the 'Half Way House' and all was very jolly. The coach drivers and the people at the Inn (who refused to take a tip) doing all they could to make the boys happy. They were all delighted with the outing, as were the others [who had won the first prize of Tea at a Ramsgate Restaurant] who also had a wonderful time.[17]

There were also ample opportunities for friendships to develop. After all these men, who had in common their ethnicity and their persecution, were now thrown together in very special circumstances and were in each other's company at work, at play, at mealtimes and at night. For those that wanted it, companionship was easy and it is clear from the memoirs that exist that friendships did form in the Kitchener Camp.[18] Some of these friendships were lifelong: for example, Harry Rossney wrote a poem in 2008 recording the moment when one of his Kitchener friends phoned him to say that he was dying ('We shared a past. Broken childhood. Separation. Language. Culture. Faith and Nation.')[19]

Sadly, though, one disaster occurred in this regard. The Dovercourt boys, all of whom had originally arrived in Britain on a *Kindertransport*, were suddenly sent away from Kitchener in early June. The reason given was managerial – that their places were needed for men coming out of the concentration camps and that the Fund had found places for the boys at an agricultural training farm near Oxford. This was almost certainly an arrangement put together by Robert Waley Cohen and his brother Charles, the latter being in charge of agricultural training for the Fund.[20] But it is also clear that these boys, who had already left their own parents once when they boarded the trains in Berlin or Vienna, had begun to make surrogate child/parent relationships in the Kitchener Camp. Now they were being sent away – again. There was a certain logic to this decision but there was also a certain inhumanity. Phineas and everyone else in 'management' at the camp were furious:

12 JUNE 1939

> This is a very unhappy day for the Camp, for despite every effort by the Camp authorities the ex-Dovercourt boys will be leaving tomorrow to go on a farm in Oxfordshire. The boys have been extremely happy here and hate the idea of leaving and have threatened to refuse to go when the time comes. The Movement for the Care of Children who are responsible for these boys has treated them very badly. Prof Bentwich had done his utmost to prevent them

going and telephone calls all day have been made to London about them to try and keep them here.

What is worst of all is that my office boy Werner Kaufman has got to go and he could not restrain his tears, as we have be [*sic*] such very good friends and he has worked wonderfully hard. I shall miss him very much indeed.

I saw J specially in the afternoon to phone or telegraph London to put in a special plea for him, but J said Prof Bentwich said he had been so badly treated it was useless trying further.

We spent the last evening together but I fear we were both very heavy of heart, it is astonishing how attached one can become to somebody in so short a time.

There was also a farewell party to another excellent worker in the camp.

13 JUNE

Awoke early and took a box of chocolates to each of the Dovercourt boys. J gave them a farewell speech at Breakfast and I had a photograph taken with the two boys I have been most friendly with – Heinz and Werner.

The coach to take them away arrived at 10am and before they left the Mayor of Sandwich got in the coach and said a few words of farewell. There were wet wet eyes in the coach and tears were streaming down Werner's cheeks, yet he was trying to joke. There was no doubt they have been very happy here. I went with them as far as Canterbury, they are going to the Wallingford Farm Training Colony, Turners Court, Benton, Oxford. Somehow I feel we shall hear more about those excellent boys.

As I waited in Canterbury for a bus to take me back to the Camp, a magnificent car stopped and Mr Ernest Joseph said 'Jump in.' Was that not a bit of luck.[21]

These had been valued relationships for these very young men and yet again they were being forced to lose them.

The big – and generally unspoken – issue was sex and its conjoint, intimacy. There were some comings and goings with girls in the neighbourhood but it is highly likely that this was largely the realm of the younger and single men. For the older men, used to the intimate companionship of their wives, it must have been particularly galling to know that a very few of the refugees (Poldi Kuh for example) and most of the English 'staff', including Jonas May who had recently become a father for the second time, were able to live with their wives. Some of the men somehow managed to find places for their wives to live in Sandwich and for them, and for the others whose wives were working elsewhere as domestic servants, there were probably snatched opportunities for intimacy. But the camp leaders clearly saw sexual relationships as something they should regulate and in effect forbid. For example, in a letter marked 'Strictly Personal' Norman Bentwich wrote to Jonas May about a young man in the camp:

> The mother of the young woman in London with whom he is in love has ordered him not to visit her house while she has to be away. It would be wrong for him to get leave to London in these circumstances. And I think you and Dr Bondy should speak with him about his conduct, and point out how dishonourable it would be for him to take advantage of the mother's absence. We must endeavour to keep him in the camp.[22]

Jonas May replied instantly that 'no leave will be granted to the individual in question'.

Sometimes the level of frustration that must have prevailed in the camp percolated through to the public domain. For example, Phineas was very shocked to be told – by the Camp Police – that an older man had tried it on with the young wife of a young Kitchener resident when the older man was entrusted with her care on a trip to London. Nothing had happened but the camp authorities, in the form of Jonas, had been very angry:

> A day of incidents amongst them was a call at my office from the Camp Police with a member of my artists group. The fellow is an awfully nice young man of 23 who has been married only 8 months, and his 21 year old wife has a job as a domestic in Sandwich. Last week she had occasion to go to London, and as he could not go with her he entrusted her in the hands of a middle-aged and responsible member of the German staff who was a friend of his, and who was going to London at the same time. He said that his wife complained that he had suggested as he had not much money that he should share a room together and that she should be nice to him and kiss him. She left him at once and went to stay for the night at some friends, and returned next day to Sandwich and told her husband. I arranged to see J. with the Police and we told him – so J. arranged to interview the offending member of staff, who subsequently denied everything and said it was a complete misunderstanding as he was a respectable married man, and that he would see the young couple and explain everything.[23]

There was discipline and the occasional punishment, there was surveillance, there was total lack of privacy and there was a single gate and barbed wire. Nevertheless this camp did have permeable boundaries. It was *not* a prison and the camp authorities were, within rather strict limits, fairly liberal and happy to see the men moving beyond the camp into its hinterland and into the local towns of Sandwich, Ramsgate and Margate. The incentives for the men to do so were enormous: once out of the camp they could, if they wanted, be alone. They could get away from a prevailing mood of unhappiness and the pressure of the company of the masses of forlorn. If they could speak English well enough, they could seek out the company of men and women who had different worries, different comforts, different norms from the men they saw day in, day out within the camp. But the 'outside world' they had come from so recently had been a terrifying place, full of hatred and brutality. A camp full of Jews would have been a comfort for many. What would they find beyond the gate? Would it be a place all too similar from the one they had come from, full of hatred and fear? Or would there be something resembling a welcome and a warmth that had been, for so long, missing from their lives?

Notes

1. Fred Pelican, IWM Sound Archives, op. cit.
2. Phineas May diary, entry for 18 February 1939.
3. Interview with Fred Pelican, IWM Sound Archives, op. cit.
4. Harold H. Rossney, *Grey Dawns*, History Web Limited, www. britishlocalhistory.com, undated, p. 21.
5. Peter Mansbacher, memoir, op. cit.
6. Peter Mansbacher, memoir, op. cit.
7. *Kitchener Camp Review*, No. 4, June 1939, p. 18.
8. I am grateful to Adrienne Harris, the daughter of Phineas May, for pointing this out to me when we went through her father's photo album of the Kitchener Camp, now deposited in the Wiener Library. Stangl became a long standing friend of the May family after the war.
9. Phineas May diary, entry for 27 May 1939.
10. Peter Mansbacher memoir, chapter on the Kitchener Camp, op. cit., p. 14.
11. Tony Kushner, *The Holocaust and the Liberal Imagination*, Oxford, Blackwell, 1994, p. 57
12. By this time there were two Services held on the Sabbath – one Orthodox, one Liberal.
13. Phineas May diary, entry for 8 April.
14. Interview with Fred Dunstan, op. cit.
15. Ibid.
16. Phineas May diary, entry for 9 May 1939.

17. Phineas May diary, entry for 23 April.

18. See for example, Harold H. Rossney, *Grey Dawns*, op. cit. Walter Marmorek and Poldi Kuh were lifelong friends; Phineas May stayed in touch with Stangl and with Werner Kaufman. These are just the few I know about. There must have been many others.

19. Harold H. Rossney, 'Friday Night....19 September 2008', ibid., p. 59.

20. Letter from Norman Bentwich to Charles Waley Cohen concerning agricultural trainees, 25 April 1939, BWP, File P174/12a.

21. Phineas May diary, entries for 12 and 13 June.

22. BWP, File P174/15b, 28 March 1939.

23. Phineas May diary, 16 July.

Jonas May, Director of the Kitchener Camp, outside a hut. (Wiener Library)

Phineas May, on the left, leading a sing-song. (Wiener Library)

Jonas May showing the Archbishop of Canterbury round the camp, with Robert Waley Cohen in the background, October 1939. (Wiener Library)

Fritz Mansbacher's registration document for Sandwich. (Wiener Library)

Archibald Ziegler, *Portrait of Professor Norman Bentwich*, oil on canvas, 52.5 x 42 cm. (Ben Uri, The London Jewish Museum of Art: Presented by Sam Trilling, 1948)

An overview of the Kitchener Camp. (Wiener Library)

The camp gate. (Wiener Library)

Raising the camp flag for the first time, 1 March 1939. (Wiener Library)

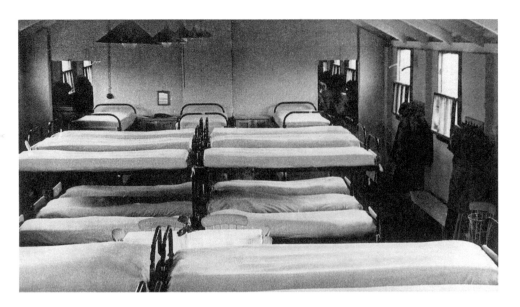

A hut, ready for new arrivals. (Wiener Library)

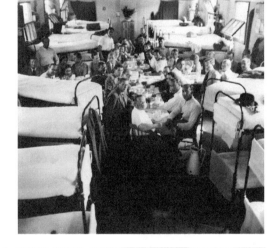

A party in a hut. (Wiener Library)

Trying to get some privacy. (Wiener Library)

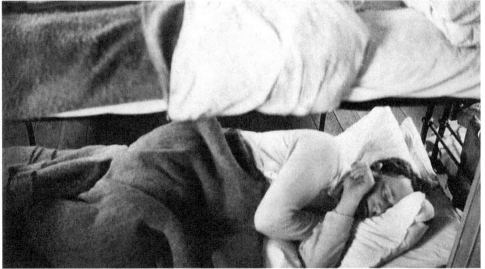

The camp library. (Wiener
Library)

Writing home. (Wiener
Library)

The Camp Post Office.
(Wiener Library)

The First
Aid Station.
(Wiener
Library)

Carpenters
at work.
(Wiener
Library)

Agricultural
training.
(Wiener
Library)

Theatricals – a man and a 'woman'. (Wiener Library)

Jolly kosher cooks. (Wiener Library)

English lessons in the open air, with Sandwich in the distance. (Wiener Library)

The camp float at the Ramsgate Carnival – 'Our Thanks to England'. (Wiener Library)

Hilda Kimber in her new dress, on her way to a Kitchener Camp concert. (By kind permission of Mrs Hilda Keen)

A Kitchener Camp concert. (Wiener Library)

3 September 1939: young men listening to the Declaration of War, by Hans Jackson. (Kind permission of Allen Sternstein)

Listening to German messages in the monitoring centre, by Hans Jackson. (Kind permission of Allen Sternstein)

Drilling the Pioneer Corps, by Hans Jackson. (Kind permission of Allen Sternstein)

Stella and her father on a Sunday outing. (Wiener Library)

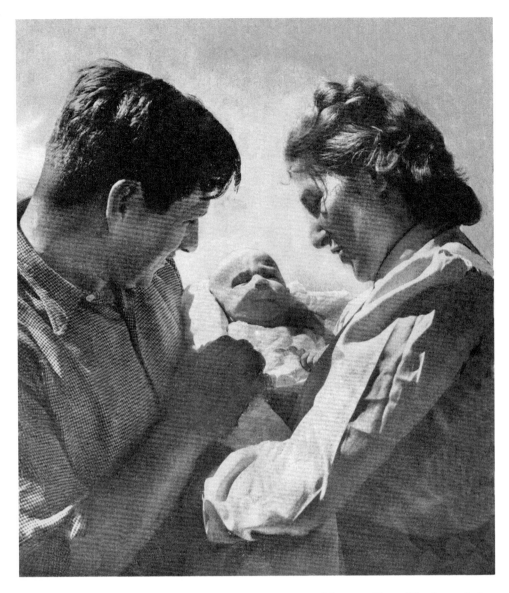

New life: the baby was named Winston. (*Some Victims of the Nazi Terror: The Reward of the Salvors*, Sandwich Guildhall Archive)

Mechanics at work.
(Wiener Library)

Front cover of a single
issue magazine published
by the Kitchener Camp
committee in October
1939. Fifty thousand
copies were printed,
possibly to raise funds
from American Jewry.
(Sandwich Guildhall
Archive)

SOME VICTIMS OF THE NAZI TERROR

B 13

362.87

The Reward of the Salvors

Inside the
magazine
'After work'.
(Sandwich
Guildhall
Archive)

Flower beds and lawns are already re-
placing the weed-grown wilderness round
the huts as a result of the work some of the
refugees have done during their leisure
hours. With many gardening is a hobby and
recreation. The writing room is always
crowded with men who keep constantly in
touch by letter with their tragically scattered
families.

'Work'.
(Sandwich
Guildhall
Archive))

They find Happiness in their new Work

Every man in the Camp has a job. There are representatives of
more than 30 different trades and professions, including doctors,
architects, engineers, dentists, lawyers, electricians, clerks,
bricklayers, and business men. Between them they are rebuilding and maintaining the Camp and its services.
Their day begins at 5.30. They take breakfast at 7, and work
from 6 to 5.30, with a break for lunch at 12.30. After working

hours they are free to leave the Camp at will, but must return
at 10 p.m. for roll-call.
Only pay they receive is sixpence a week for pocket money.
The refugees remain at the Camp until they are fitted for a trade.
After that they become emigrants to United States and British
Empire centres.

NEW FOUND FREEDOM

Facing the future with renewed confidence and hope the community at Richborough are rapidly absorbing the habits and customs of the people who have given them sanctuary. After the day's toil the men attend classes at which English is taught. A gramophone is used to help with the teaching of pronunciation. The camp director insists that everyone shall learn to speak the language that will soon become his own.

New ways and a new language. (Sandwich Guildhall Archive)

The original caption reads: 'Fine specimens of manhood are to be found everywhere in the camp. Brave fellows with spirits that no cruelty or adversity can break.' (Sandwich Guildhall Archive)

9

SANDWICH

One afternoon in late March 1939, one of the Dovercourt boys decided to walk into Sandwich for the first time. He had finished work at 5 p.m., and now the days were getting longer there was time before supper to take a stroll round the town in daylight. He didn't much like the Kitchener Camp – he thought it was a 'dump'[1] – and preferred his own company, so he was keen to find another place where he could feel more comfortable. He went through the camp gate, telling the day guards where he was going, and then turned immediately right, passing a large girls' school and another crumbling First World War army camp on his left and open fields to his right. As he walked straight ahead he could see, in the middle distance, buildings, a river, small boats moored against a long stone embankment. He came to a wrought-iron swing bridge that crossed the river, and at its far end he saw a striking and obviously much older building, with a high arch below and a dwelling above with a dramatically curved gable end. Bridge tolls were being collected from the few cars and horse drawn carts that were waiting patiently to pass through the archway. Once over the bridge and through the arch he was immediately within the town of Sandwich and he could see that the river, far from constituting a proper port, was just a quiet resting place for a few workaday boats and some leisure craft.

He had brought his sixpence pocket money with him and was hoping that, despite being slightly under the age to be allowed into an English pub, he might be able to sneak into one for a pint of beer. Immediately beyond the arch there were two pubs, one on either side of the street running off to his right. They were obviously many centuries old and looked attractive, but when he tried their doors he discovered to his surprise they were shut. So in the hope of finding somewhere he could have a drink that was open he wandered farther down the street to the right. He walked past some more half timbered centuries-old buildings and a few shops. It all looked charmingly old fashioned. But he had not gone far – a matter of 30 yards or so – when his eye caught a flash of red, white and black that was part of a display in a large shop window. He looked more closely. There was a flag that looked very like the Swastika. In addition there were a few dusty photographs, amongst them a large portrait photo of a man with regular features and a moustache and another of men dressed in black military style uniforms standing to attention for this same man, their right arms raised in the Fascist salute. He knew immediately what he was looking at. The Fascists he hated and whom he knew hated him were *here* in this quiet and ancient town, no more than a few minutes' walk from where he and his Jewish companions were living. His first and only thought was that the one safe place for him was back in the Kitchener Camp. His so-called 'freedom' had had very short shrift.

This Dovercourt boy never bothered with Sandwich again. But there were other Kitchener men who chose to ignore the Sandwich Fascist headquarters at 13 Strand Street and who began to make a habit of wandering into Sandwich when they had a spare moment. Sandwich then, as now, was a very pretty town, surrounded by the remains of a medieval town wall and its accompanying moat and full of charming domestic architecture, many of the houses dating back to the fourteenth and fifteenth centuries. The town, though small, was very well provided with independent shops selling everything from bicycles to ladies and gents fashions.[2] A cattle market every Thursday brought the local farmers into the town. As well as buying and selling their livestock, they bought and sold their produce on the market stalls and on that day the local people crowded into Sandwich by bus, car and cart to make their purchases. On market days the streets were crowded, at other times the pace slowed. The total population of Sandwich was recorded in the 1931 Census as 3,687.[3]

All this would have been immediately visible to the Kitchener men. But what they would not have been aware of is that Sandwich, though small, with a population not much bigger than the Kitchener Camp, had a rather unusual populace. It had become, since the turn of the twentieth century, a fashionable watering hole for the rich and powerful. There was no flamboyance about this at all; indeed, the rich and powerful were very effective in keeping their pleasures to themselves and making certain that only they had access to them. The great attraction of Sandwich for them was golf. Two golf courses lying between Sandwich and the long beach of Sandwich Bay had been established, one in the late nineteenth century – the Royal St George's – and the other in the early twentieth century – the Prince's. As their names indicated, both were closely associated with British royalty, with the Royal St George's patronised by Edward VII, and both golf courses patronised by his grandson, the Prince of Wales, who later abdicated in order to marry Mrs Simpson.

As a result of these royal associations, very rich people made their way to Sandwich and began to buy property there from 1900 onwards, in particular in a gated community located between the Royal St George's and the sea. This new housing development was known as the Sandwich Bay Estate. By the late 1930s an extraordinary roll call of 'important' people had houses there.[4] On Marine Parade alone, Viscount Waldorf Astor and his wife Nancy Astor (the first woman MP to take her seat in the House of Commons in Britain and, as a couple, probably second only to the royal family in their wealth) had a house next door to Lord St Just, whose father had been a governor of the Bank of England, and who had been Conservative MP for the City of London between 1922 and 1935. Between Lord St Just and his next titled neighbour stood the huge bulk of an exceptionally ugly and pretentious hotel, the Guilford, to which many visitors came including the Prince of Wales and George Bernard Shaw (in pursuit of Mrs Patrick Campbell who was staying there). Beyond the hotel was a house owned by Lady Alastair Innes Ker, who had married a grandson of the Duke of Roxburghe and a member of the Spencer-Churchill family. Her immediate neighbour was Sir Percy Daniels (an industrialist) and on his other side was A.E.L. Slazenger, the founder of the tennis equipment manufacturers. At the other end of the road, next door to the Astors, was the prominent Fascist, Captain Robert Gordon Canning, who owned and chaired the Fascist newspaper *Action*, and who had been a close friend of Oswald Mosley. Others who owned property on the estate included Lady Dorothy Macmillan, wife of Harold Macmillan, the future Conservative prime minister, and the Earl of Donoughmore, a one-time Conservative Under-Secretary of State for War and a prominent Irish Freemason. In Sandwich itself there were, on the golf course side of the town, a number of other personages including retired admirals, and Lord Airedale, an industrialist and Liberal politician. To all intents and purposes, this was Mayfair by Sea, with a considerable input from the Palace of Westminster.

None of this would matter in a story about the Kitchener Camp, if these people and their other titled neighbours had had no knowledge of the camp's existence or had chosen to have nothing to do with it. Such people were very unlikely to bump into Kitchener men in the shops and pubs of Sandwich, although it is certainly possible they passed each other by on the beach at Sandwich Bay. But the fact is that some of them, from the extreme right to the more centre right of 1930s British politics, chose to make a connection with the Kitchener Camp. The Fascist, Captain Gordon Canning, had his own take on the camp and of course never visited it. But some of the others definitely did so, including, to Phineas May's delight, Nancy Astor, who took out a subscription to the *Kitchener Camp Review* and almost certainly gave a contribution to the camp Welfare Fund.[5]

Nancy Astor was a complex woman with networks that crossed the whole spectrum of politics; for example, she frequently entertained Ribbentrop, the German ambassador and a committed Nazi, while one of her sons, David, became the editor of an important Liberal newspaper, *The Observer*, which the

Astor family owned. She was very actively pro-appeasement and also had some notoriously anti-Semitic friends, and both these facets of her character have led to her being described, occasionally, as a closet supporter of Hitler.[6] As far as her views on Jews were concerned, she was probably no worse and no better than most upper and middle class people in Britain at the time, thinking Jews were distasteful as a whole but happy to include Jews in her circle when they themselves were rich or distinguished enough.[7] Her visits to the Kitchener Camp were probably driven as much by curiosity and a sense of *noblesse oblige* as by any particular sympathy for Jews or any particular hostility to the policies of Nazi Germany. The men made a huge fuss of her when she visited and no doubt this was also part of her motivation:

> We took them [Nancy Astor and Ronald Tree MP] into the dining room and Lady Astor addressed a few words of encouragement to the men and received tumultuous applause. She walked out and they rose and bowed to her and one man to whom she spoke bowed and kissed her hand. It was all very pathetic.[8]

Nancy Astor clearly did not feel inclined to invite any of the refugees to her huge house and garden on the edge of the golf course overlooking the sea (it had fifteen bedrooms and she called it her 'seaside cottage'[9]). This lack is striking because others in the upper class Sandwich set did. Lord and Lady Airedale invited thirty-two men to tea in early May. That said, they made certain that they kept a certain distance:

> A coach arrived at 3.50 and drove to the house. There 'her Ladyship' with her Butler was waiting to receive us. The grounds of the house are beautifully laid out and I have never seen such a display of flowers so early in the year. The lawns were perfect and the house – recently painted white – almost a mansion made a lovely picture. She shook hands with everybody and chatted with them – and we had photographs taken with her. Then the Butler served Tea for the Men on the Lawn and she invited us to take Tea with her in the house ...[10]

Lady Airedale must have enjoyed this event because nine days later she invited another group to tea, and her next door neighbours, a Mr and Mrs Peto, did so too – they invited fifty to her thirty-two. Not all the smart set invitations were motivated by generosity and a hands off kindness: another 'sodding Earl', as Phineas described him, who had rented a house for the Sandwich 'season' asked the Kitchener Camp band to play at a cocktail party. The band was free of charge because they were not allowed paid employment, and they complained afterwards that the earl had treated them badly.[11] Presumably the expected refreshments in lieu of pay had not been provided.

The fact that powerful people with money and influence were aware of the Kitchener Camp, and, within limits, were well disposed to it and the men who lived there, may have influenced the wider political culture concerning British attitudes towards Jewish refugees from Greater Germany and attitudes to the Third Reich. There really is no way of telling: the impact could have gone either way, encouraging a complacency that Britain was 'doing her bit' to help the refugee problem and need do no more, or encouraging a sense that terrible events were taking place in Germany and that more had to be done. What is certain is that powerful people were well aware of what was going on in Nazi Germany, and that the Kitchener Camp was part of that network of knowledge. Moreover, the presence of important people who weren't Jews as occasional visitors within the camp and their offers of occasional kindliness beyond the camp would have had considerable significance for the Kitchener Camp men. These men had come from countries where, by 1939, interaction between Jews and members of national elites had been rendered impossible.

Sandwich was a complicated and layered place. While some of the rich and influential were hospitable enough to invite the men to visit their gardens, local officialdom and local organisations were much more generously disposed. Indeed it was at an organisational level that camp and town first began to meet in large numbers. The Mayor of Sandwich, Lieutenant Colonel Prescott–Westcar, obviously felt he should set an example of friendship and respect in relation to the camp and he seems to have made a point of always being on hand when men were leaving the camp permanently, presumably hoping the men would leave with a good impression of a town that had welcomed them. Even more striking was the appearance, almost as soon as the camp opened, of no less than eighty teachers drawn from the immediate neighbourhood who gave of their time voluntarily to help teach English to the men on a regular basis. In the month of June alone, the ladies of the Sandwich Congregational Church took to darning vast numbers of camp socks; fifty-two men were invited to the local RAF station at Manston airport;[12] Ramsgate Technical Institute organised a dance in aid of the camp Welfare Fund and invited all the hut leaders; the Betteshanger Colliery Social Club invited men to join them at a social[13] and they later sent Phineas one guinea for the camp Welfare Fund.[14]

The headmaster of the local grammar school invited the camp men to school sports days, made available the school's extensive sports grounds for the camp's own competitions and the camp orchestra was invited to give a concert at the school in July. In April the Sandwich String Orchestra invited Kitchener men to join them and lent them instruments; its conductor, a Mr Burwood, also came to the camp to conduct the camp orchestra. Phineas noted in his diary that the Sandwich String Orchestra, over the summer, acquired so many players from the camp that it had really become the camp orchestra in all but name.[15] The local football teams were delighted to have this large influx of potential football players on their doorstep and a number of Kitchener men were recruited to play for teams in Ramsgate, Margate and Sandwich. The camp table tennis players got on so well with their local rivals and there was such good equipment at the camp that Phineas felt obliged to make the point, when he discovered the local lads were using the tables at Kitchener as much as the camp men, that the Sandwich lads should play their table tennis elsewhere.[16]

There were some philanthropically minded individuals in the local community who felt that they had a special obligation to be helpful to the men at the camp. A local vicar took to driving down the Ramsgate road towards the camp in the early evening so that he could give lifts to men who were hurrying back for supper, or, later in the evening, so that they could get back to the camp by the 10 p.m. curfew. Fred Pelican found that, unbeknownst to him, he already had a friend in the area who had been instrumental in getting his cousin Irmgard out of Germany and into a job as a nurse at Margate General Hospital. To his astonishment a Mrs Joyce Piercy appeared at the camp one Saturday afternoon very soon after he had arrived and whisked him off to her 'smashing bungalow' in Broadstairs (about 8 miles from Sandwich) where they had afternoon tea and slightly stilted conversation. When he got back to the camp that evening he was in a kind of delirium of pleasure:

> Has all this really happened to me? I couldn't have dreamed it up. I, who a few months ago went through a process of dehumanisation, kicked about and spat upon, immune to dead bodies, had now experienced a reversal in a strange land among a strange people, a sort of kindness and humanity completely strange to me, and, above all, it came from a non-Jewish person.[17]

He and Mrs Piercy rapidly became 'Freddie' and 'Joyce' to each other, and 'her house was for me at all times an open door'.

There was another warming moment when some of the customs officials who had been regularly inspecting the luggage of the men as they arrived at Dover, and who had been regaled with musical interludes at the dockside, went to see Phineas to suggest a bike ride with the Dover Cycling Club.[18] This was no doubt prompted by their insider knowledge that many of the men had brought their bicycles over from Germany. A report on this bike ride appeared in the June issue of the *Kitchener Camp Review*. Entitled 'Up Hill and Down Dale' it is headed by a drawing of three men on sit-up-and-beg bikes puffing up and down hills. The man at the front, who is pointing the way, is wearing a flat cap and a checked jersey and is, presumably, a local, the man in the middle seems to be wearing *lederhosen* and the man at the back is quite definitely wearing a brimmed Tyrolean hat complete with a little feather plume:

When we returned to the Camp on Sunday, 14 May, at nightfall, in sleat [*sic*] and wind, after a ride of more than 37 miles, we were of one opinion only – that this ride had made a supremely happy day for all of us. The warmth and joy of this day lay in the simplicity and unconventionality of the English sportsmen to whom we owed this outing …

They had had lunch at a pub in Petham (this is a good stretch from Sandwich on a push bike) and afterwards played games 'like children' including sack races and cycling blindfold. Later they had tea in a British Legion hut where 'Happy English girls serve us with tea and cakes and keep on helping us in their hearty way'. Then they cycled back through Canterbury and 'were shown the ancient and beautiful Cathedral'. At the end of the ride one of their hosts made a short speech and told them how pleased he and his friends were to 'make a few hours more cheerful for men who have suffered much unhappiness'. 'This little speech of good fellowship brought us nearer to feelings that we thought were long dead within us.'

Even as he wrote about how much he and his colleagues had enjoyed their day out, the refugee writer of this article seems to have been struck by what he presented as the naïve charm of the English 'local yokel'. It is of course true that most of the Kitchener men came from the European capitals of Berlin and Vienna and that many Sandwich people had probably never even been to London; inevitably there was a disparity in their life experiences and possibly a sense of urban sophistication amongst the Kitchener men. But it was through such joint and organised activities that the refugees began to meet the people of the neighbourhood and develop closer, one to one, relationships with them. Fritz Mansbacher, for example, met the thoughtful and generous Mr and Mrs Gray, who had given Fritz such a memorable Sunday lunch, through the fact that Mr Gray was a builder and worked alongside Fritz refurbishing huts. The camp men were so often invited back to the homes of local builders that it was remarked upon in the *Kitchener Camp Review*.[19] It is clear that a great many residents of Sandwich welcomed the opportunity to get to know these polite and urbane foreigners rather better. It does not seem to have mattered to them that the identity of these men was so confusing or potentially so harmful to closer relationships. Whether they were 'Germans', so recently the 'enemy' in the First World War, or 'Jews', so frequently vilified and loathed in Europe as a whole, this was immaterial. They were 'refugees' and thus pulled at their heart strings. They were also young or youngish, cosmopolitan and intriguingly different. At the same time, they were of a similar social background to many Sandwich residents, who were also, like the Kitchener men, predominantly small shopkeepers and skilled artisans.

It wasn't just sport and working together at the camp that brought Sandwich and Kitchener together. Over many months the Sandwich shopkeepers and publicans grew accustomed to finding German-speaking Jews on their premises, spending money and chatting, and this despite the fact that most of the Kitchener men had very little cash. Their sixpence a week pocket money was only enough to buy a single pint of beer. But some men acquired money through other routes, possibly from relatives already in England with access to further resources, or by sneaking out of the camp to work illegally, usually for local farmers who needed extra labour at harvest time.[20]

This large influx of newcomers had, in effect, doubled the size of Sandwich, and the shopkeepers were naturally well disposed towards them since they brought extra custom. Sometimes this was considerable: for example, a vogue developed for jackets in the English style and some of the men had enough money to pay a Sandwich gents' outfitters to make them. But most purchases were rather more modest and there were little touches of kindness that indicated a straightforward generosity on the part of the shopkeepers. Fritz Mansbacher went to the local shoemaker to buy some shoe polish:

An elderly man shuffled into the store and asked what we wanted. I told him that I wanted some black shoe polish. He brought it and then asked almost in a whisper: 'have ye got a brush?' I did not, but told him cloth was just as good. Then he asked me if I was one of the boys from that new camp for refugees and how I liked being in England and if we were comfortable at the camp. We told him that we had been impressed with the kindness and hospitality of the British people and how much we appreciated it. Then with a 'god bless ye' and a 'good luck' from the shoemaker, we departed. When we returned to camp I noticed that the bag was unusually heavy for a little bit of shoe polish and when I opened the bag found not only the shoe polish, but also a polishing cloth as well as a brush inside![21]

As Fritz's use of 'archaic' language, spoken by the shoemaker he remembers, implies, the Kitchener Camp men were to some extent aware that they were metropolitans and cosmopolitans meeting small townspeople whose world, so far, had been much smaller than theirs. Sometimes the difference between them had to be handled with a certain diplomacy, and in the case of the Kimber family who ran a bakery in the middle of Sandwich, this seems to have been done rather well. Mr Kimber was the baker and Mrs Kimber ran the shop, known as the Golden Crust Bakery. The family lived upstairs, with Hilda, aged 12, and her older sister, Peggy, occupying one of the two bedrooms, with Mr and Mrs Kimber in the other. Hilda was 'the clever one' and attended the girls' grammar school in Dover where she was learning German, and this proved very useful when two Kitchener Camp men, anxious to maintain their Jewish dietary rules and not eat pork, first appeared in the bakery:

Two young men who couldn't speak much English wanted to know what was in some pies that were on sale. I just managed to say 'Fleisch' and my mother mooed like a cow! That was the first we knew about the Jewish refugees fleeing from Germany who had been given refuge in the old huts on the Ramsgate Road.[22]

Behind the main shop the Kimbers ran a tiny tea room with four tables and some chairs. Word must have got round because, in ones and twos, the 'quiet, polite' Kitchener Camp men began to congregate there. But, Hilda remembers, 'they didn't want a pot of tea: they wanted coffee. So we made them coffee – Camp Coffee it was called, from a bottle.' This 'coffee' was truly revolting, consisting mainly of chicory, and not surprisingly the Kitchener men found it a big disappointment:

'Mrs Kimber' said Dr Laski, when he had introduced himself 'You should make *proper* coffee – the way we do in Austria. You must buy some ground coffee and put it in a linen bag and infuse it.'

Mrs Kimber was happy to oblige: 'She would try anything to help trade.' She bought an urn, some proper coffee, and a cotton bag. It was a great success:

And word must have got around the Kitchener Camp because numbers increased and the tables at the back of the shop were crowded. Once or twice I trailed home from school at Dover, getting home about half-past five, only to have to stand in the kitchen because the table in the living room was full of men drinking coffee and talking mostly in English but occasionally slipping in a foreign word.[23]

Thus two very different worlds met and came together. A Viennese coffee house had been successfully replicated at the Golden Crust Bakery, Sandwich.

The bakery became a social hub for the Kitchener men. The Kimbers had recently bought a gramophone and Hilda heard her first classical music that summer, courtesy of Frans Mandl who had brought some of his precious records with him from Vienna and, despite Mrs Kimber's objections, played them in the little tea room. Hilda's horizons began to shift a little, and they shifted even more when Mrs Rosenberg, 'a fine boned lady [...] suddenly appeared in the shop lugging a suitcase'. Mr Rosenberg, 'a quiet shy man', had obviously told his wife to make her way, on arrival in England, to Sandwich and the Golden Crust:

What to do with her? Mum took her upstairs, via the shop stairs, to our new sitting room with its settee and two armchairs and sent me up there to 'keep her company' while, I suppose, word was got through to Mr Rosenberg. I was a shy, gauche 12–13 year-old, totally struck dumb by this lady, with (to me) strong make-up on, sitting with her on the settee with her suitcase next to her. I suppose she took pity on me and opened her case to show me, on the top layer, a tray divided into small compartments in which were rolled-up stockings. I had never seen anything like that before: we had no suitcases, we had never been on holiday.[24]

Hilda was entranced. And then the Kimbers did something that many people did in Sandwich that summer. They took in Mrs Rosenberg as a tenant, and moved out of their bedroom so that Mr and Mrs Rosenberg could have some privacy together. Hilda does not remember if they paid rent (Mrs Rosenberg only stayed a week), but others did. Ivy Kum remembers that her mother squeezed some refugee wives into the parlour of their little cottage in order to make some pin money.

These relationships, between shopkeepers and customers and between landladies and tenants, were essentially commercial but they brought people into close proximity who would, under normal circumstances, never have encountered each other. For some, these new relationships formed the basis for continuing friendship, for others an opportunity to offer discrete acts of kindness. The Kimbers made long-term friends of the men they met, and if and when their relatives arrived, made them welcome; well disposed shopkeepers made gestures of generosity. There were other Sandwich residents who no doubt maintained a strictly commercial distance, and yet others who wanted nothing to do with the Kitchener Camp at all.[25] But in the main the people of Sandwich were intrigued, even fascinated, by these polite young men with their musical interests, their odd looking clothes, their attempts at English and their sad circumstances. And once a few of their wives began to appear in the town, there must also have been, as Hilda's memoir demonstrates, a perception that there was a certain exoticism about them, with their bright make-up, their silk stockings and their urban ways.

The London Fund had been worried about the response the camp would receive in Sandwich, and, given the presence of Fascists, and the anti-Semitism that ran so close to the surface across all social classes in Britain, they were right to be anxious. But what they had underestimated was the desire of the local populace for novelty and change in dreary, depressed inter-war Britain. The arrival of strangers who were different, but not too different, was a source of interest to many rather than alarm.

A real test of the town's collective response came when, instead of the camp going to the town, the town was given the opportunity to come to the camp. It was Phineas who realised that the Kitchener Camp entertainments, which had originally been put on to amuse the camp men and only the camp men, were good enough to present to a wider audience. But when, one Sunday afternoon in early May, he came to organise the first public show he was worried that the new concert hall, which held one thousand, would be loomingly empty: 'As we had only invited people by word of mouth and in no other way, we had no idea how many would attend.'[26] On the Sunday morning the orchestra, which had been feeble at the dress rehearsal, was given a pep talk by Jonas and immediately held a good rehearsal, and 'the Hall was made to look spick and span for the afternoon'. After lunch the camp gates were pushed wide open. There were nerve racking moments when at first the people of Sandwich came 'very slowly', then the pace picked up and 'eventually their [sic] must have been between 600 to 700 people'.[27] The local newspaper published a rave review (quite possibly written by Phineas):

> The acts were excellently given by a violinist, jazz singers, a whistler, dancers and singers, a saxophonist, gymnasts, accordionists, a lightning sketcher in charcoal [Phineas] and a magician. The show ended [...] by the orchestra playing Strauss' 'The Blue Danube'.[28]

It had been a huge success, not just in terms of the show itself but also because the people of Sandwich had voluntarily given £10.8s.8d towards the camp Welfare Fund.

This was the first of a number of shows to which the public were invited. They were very popular: Phineas noted that there was an audience of 800 for the entertainment in June and 1,000 in August, remarkable numbers given the total population of Sandwich was under 4,000. Hilda went to the June show with her sister Peggy and there is a charming photo of Hilda Kimber standing in a field in high summer wearing a very pretty dress which she had made especially for the occasion.[29] At the concert there was still a sense of strangers meeting, but meeting in happy circumstances:

> When the pianist (a woman) started to play, the music disturbed some swallows which were nesting in the rafters [...] some of the refugees felt they should do something about this and arrived with long brooms to sweep the nest and the swallows away. But the audience made it clear that the swallows should be left alone, with cries of 'Oh no! Let them be!' and the like and we had music accompanied by swallows. We felt very English – a kind-to-dumb-animals feeling![30]

At the end of the concert, according to the daughter of another Sandwich shopkeeper, they were all given tea and 'delicious small cakes'. 'It was all very formal, but sociable.'[31]

There were other musical opportunities which endeared the Kitchener Camp to Sandwich that summer, not least the jazz band, which played up and down the Kentish coast at festivals and fêtes. The band was not only excellent, ('the band has quite a professional touch by the inclusion of a "mike" and a crooner')[32] and smart (they wore a uniform of grey flannels and red jerseys) it was also free – because the Kitchener men were not allowed to take up paid employment. This meant it was in very high demand from local charities for their fundraising events, and the only people who were upset about this were, understandably, the local musicians who wrote to the local paper to object: 'while we English are willing to offer hospitality to these unfortunate fellow men, it is expecting rather much if they are permitted to take engagements, whether remunerative or otherwise, in competition with existing bands …'[33]

It was commerce and entertainment that provided the social 'glue' that brought Sandwich and Kitchener together that summer. There was good will and curiosity on both sides, but there was also a great deal of behind the scenes public relations on the part of the camp management. Opening the camp up to masses of visitors from the neighbourhood had clearly been part of a very effective strategy. Maintaining a good press was also part of that strategy. Either Phineas or Jonas met with a local journalist on a weekly basis and consequently over those few months in 1939 a short report on the activities at the Kitchener Camp appeared every week in the *East Kent Mercury*. Almost always on page 5 and headed 'Kitchener Camp' in bold, it appeared alongside similar reports of the Women's Institute, the girl guides, the sea scouts and the local churches. The Kitchener Camp had been normalised and become part of the Sandwich topography. If there was to be an effective Fascist counterblast, the Fascists would have to pull a number of rather vicious levers.

Notes

1. Interview with Mr Andrew Kodin, author's notes.
2. *Deal, Walmer, Kingsdown and Sandwich Directory for 1937*, Pain and Sons, Deal, 1937.
3. Ibid.
4. Ibid.
5. Phineas May diary, entry for 20 May.
6. See for example, Christopher Sykes, *Nancy: The Life of Lady Astor*, Collins, London, 1972; John Grigg, *Nancy Astor: Portrait of a Pioneer*, London, Sidgwick and Jackson, 1980. Both these authors make reference to Nancy Astor's possible Nazi sympathies and, in the case of Sykes, refer to her anti-Semitism. Neither author thinks she was a Nazi, although Sykes writes at length of her friendship with Hilaire Belloc, who was a notorious Jew hater.

It is interesting to note that her latest biographer, Adrian Fort, makes no reference to her attitude to Jews at all: Adrian Fort, *Nancy: The Story of Lady Astor*, Jonathan Cape and St Martin's Press, 2012.

7. Her niece, the actress and comedienne Joyce Grenfell, whose mother was Nancy Astor's sister, wrote to her mother about Myra Hess, the world-class pianist, who had become her friend: 'I wish you knew her: she's one of the most attractive people in the world. Gentle, humourous, gay, quiet, intelligent, kind and above all this world's greatest woman pianist. Jewish of course, but, for once, not Jewish looking. I always feel that when she plays she does so in a sort of 'this-is-what-my-race-is-really-like' spirit. And does the job perfectly.' Letter written in December 1939, quoted in Joyce Grenfell, *Darling Ma, Letters to her Mother 1932–1944*, edited by James Roose-Evans, Hodder and Stoughton, London, 1988.

8. Phineas May diary, entry for 19 April.

9. Adrian Fort, op. cit., pp. 122–123.

10. Phineas May diary, entry for 9 May.

11. Ibid., entry for 29 July.

12. *Kitchener Camp Review*, No. 4, June 1939: 'in a speech of thanks one of our members said that it was astonishing for them to be turned out of one country and then to be invited as guests to the Airport of another', p. 3.

13. Ibid., p. 3.

14. Phineas May diary, entry for 25 May.

15. Ibid., entry for 8 June.

16. Ibid., entry for 26 April: 'I have decided to put the ping pong tables out of bounds for the visitors as the Sandwich people now use our place as a very nice club and are depriving the Refugees of the opportunity to use the tables intended for them.'

17. Fred Pelican, op. cit. pp. 36–37.

18. Phineas May diary, entry for 3 May.

19. *Kitchener Camp Review*, No. 4, June 1939, p. 3.

20. Information from an American descendant who told me her father used to creep out in the long evenings in the summer to help local farmers for pay.

21. Peter Mansbacher memoir, chapter on Kitchener Camp, op. cit., p. 17.

22. Hilda Keen: 'A Sandwich Resident remembers the Kitchener Camp', *Association of Jewish Refugees Journal*, January 2010, pp. 4–5.

23. Ibid.

24. Ibid.

25. One person in Sandwich, whose father was a local Sandwich haulage contractor at the time, told me that her father was an avowed anti-semite and refused to have anything to do with the Kitchener Camp, even though he knew he was losing trade by doing so.

26. Phineas May diary, entry for 7 May.

27. Ibid.

28. *East Kent Mercury*, 13 May 1939, p. 5.

29. Reproduced in Hilda Keen, op. cit. (See picture section, page 9.)

30. Ibid.

31. Enid Miles, extract from her unpublished memoir, entitled 'Chapter 4: World's Stores'. I am grateful to her son Patrick Miles for sending it to me in a personal communication.

32. *East Kent Mercury*, 10 June 1939, p. 5.

33. *East Kent Mercury*, 17 June 1939, p. 5.

10

FASCISTS OFFENSIVE

Within a few months a strange transformation was taking place. Not only did the erstwhile military barracks change into a veritable camp city with all amenities, but also the old picturesque town of Sandwich awoke from her centuries-long sleep. Suddenly, thousands of men thronged her narrow lanes, talking in loud voices, dressed outlandishly, who did not understand English, or worse, mutilated it by their pronunciation.[1]

Thus wrote Herbert Freeden, a one-time Kitchener man, recalling, twenty years later in 1959, the impact in 1939 of the Kitchener Camp on Sandwich. It is an extraordinary statement by a German–Jewish refugee because it seems to be written from an anti-Semitic and xenophobic point of view. Like all such statements, it is not true. It was never the case that 'thousands of men thronged her narrow lanes'; there were careful limits kept on the numbers of men allowed out of the camp at any one time, and not a single one of the Sandwich residents has ever mentioned the overwhelming of Sandwich in this way. Secondly, Freeden uses the classic accusation of Jews in large numbers – that by talking in 'loud voices' and dressing 'outlandishly' they draw attention to themselves and their 'otherness'. Hilda Keen (née Kimber) noticed quite the reverse: the Kitchener men were 'quiet' and 'polite',[2] and, according to the son of another Sandwich resident, 'they [his mother and her female Sandwich friends] also welcomed the *intelligence*, the liveliness, civility and *wit* of the refugees they mixed with'.[3] They were 'other' but in a wholly attractive way.

If one reads further into Herbert Freeden's 1959 article one comes to realise that, as he wrote, he was trying to think himself into what he assumed to be the minds of the Sandwich residents of the time. He was imagining how 'the conservative, small-town, insular element of the English people, their customs and prejudices …'[4] would have determined their response to the Kitchener Camp. He was seeking to establish, given the contrast between the traditional tightly knit community of small town Sandwich on the one hand and a large influx of Jews from Continental Europe on the other, that this was fertile ground, in 1939, for an explosion of xenophobia and anti-Semitism.

It is quite possible, even probable, that the Sandwich Fascists were delighted when the Kitchener Camp refugees began to arrive in large numbers. They must have hoped, even expected, that the local response would be hostile and thus provide a fruitful basis for further recruitment to their cause. The leaders of the Sandwich Fascists were not insignificant – both Lady Grace Pearson, who was the prospective candidate for the British Union of Fascists for the parliamentary constituency of Canterbury, and Captain Robert Gordon Canning feature in various histories of Fascism of the period.[5] Moreover, both these individuals were very well off and willing to spend their money promoting British Fascism. In addition Lady Grace was a recent president of the Sandwich Chamber of Commerce, a part of the Sandwich establishment, and clearly commanded the respect of the business people of the town. Thus the pair of them were well resourced and well positioned to take advantage of any grass-roots xenophobia that might arise out of the presence of so many foreign-born Jews on the edge of Sandwich.

Lady Pearson and Captain Gordon Canning certainly knew each other. Not only did they live in the same place, they also came from the same social class and would have mixed in the upper echelons of Sandwich society including the upper class 'golfing crowd'. They had also shared a mutual friend, Oswald Mosley, the leader of the British Fascists, who was rumoured to be Lady Pearson's occasional lover; Gordon Canning is said to have been Mosley's best man when he married Diana Mitford in Hitler's presence in Berlin in 1936. However, Lady Pearson only gets one very brief mention in Gordon Canning's MI5 file; (there is no way of checking if Gordon Canning featured in Lady Pearson's MI5 files because they no longer exist.[6]) By 1939, in the year of the Kitchener Camp, Gordon Canning and Mosley had badly fallen out (they had quarrelled over money) and Gordon Canning had resigned from the BUF so it is possible that he and Lady Pearson no longer had a great deal to do with each other. Sandwich cocktail parties were, in 1939, the one place they were certain to meet. It is a matter of informed speculation as to whether the various Fascist flurries against the Kitchener Camp were organised by them together or separately.[7]

The first sign of an orchestrated anti-Kitchener campaign occurred in late March, 1939. Phineas went into Sandwich on Sunday 19 March and that evening wrote in his diary:

In Sandwich today. I am informed that the Fascists have put up notices: 'A GERMAN IS WORTH TWO ENGLISHMEN' – a very subtly worded notice.[8]

This was not just a 'subtly' worded notice – it was also, if it was meant to denigrate the Kitchener Camp men, a completely nonsensical statement, since it suggested that one German was 'worth' twice as much as one Englishman. The statement was almost certainly intended to mean the exact reverse.

However, it is also possible that Phineas had misheard or got the wrong end of the stick. He himself had not seen any of these notices – he says he was 'informed' of their existence. Others, who had seen a single notice, or claimed to have seen one, reported rather differently and had a different interpretation of its origins. Somewhat surprisingly this relatively insignificant incident – at least on a national scale – came to the attention of the Whips Office in the House of Commons possibly because one of Sandwich's important personages had reported it there. Three days after Phineas had heard of the notices, the secretary of the Board of Deputies of British Jews wrote to Sir Robert Waley Cohen to tell him the National Liberal MP for St Ives[9] had been to see Neville Laski, at that time the president of the Board, to inform him that 'on the walls of the Richborough Camp there had been observed the words chalked up 'One Jew is worth two Englishmen.' The MP understood what the statement was actually saying about relative 'worth' and was convinced that a refugee from the camp had written this statement: 'the suggestion was that there should be continual inspection at the camp to find out who is responsible in order that appropriate action might be taken'.[10] But the Board of Deputies recognised a familiar Fascist *modus operandi*. The remainder of the letter from the Board reminded Sir Robert of a recent incident:

You may perhaps remember that last November a young Fascist called Flockhart was summoned for fixing to a telegraph pole a stickiback with the inscription 'Any Jew is worth two Englishmen.' He was fined 40/-. There would therefore seem to be little doubt as to the source of the chalk inscriptions.[11]

However unclear the 'notice' was, something was obviously afoot, it was Fascist in origin and it had come to parliamentary attention.

The odd phrasing of the 'notice' and its nasty intent probably passed the people of Sandwich by. But it was the Kitchener men who were all too aware of local Fascist activity and who adjusted their behaviour to take account of it:

The only other thing we had – we had problems with the Blackshirts. There were some Blackshirts in Sandwich and Deal and around who used to come past the Camp with their flag to maybe intimidate us – to upset us. And they even held meetings in Sandwich so our Camp Director didn't allow us on that day to go into Sandwich – because we knew there would have been a brawl. Because we couldn't stand that. And as there is a very small Toll Bridge between the Camp and Sandwich, so it was easy for us not to go in.[12]

Intimidation of the Kitchener men was clearly one part of the Fascist strategy. Since Lady Pearson ran the local Blackshirts it was probably her decision to encourage her local branch to put up the 'notice' or notices, and to march along the Ramsgate road in order to show the Kitchener men the colour of their Fascist banners. She certainly did not pursue a national strategy – there was hardly any mention of the Kitchener Camp in the national newspaper of the BUF, *The Blackshirt*, and this was quite possibly because she did not want to upset her colleagues in the Sandwich Chamber of Commerce for whom the arrival of the camp had been an unalloyed blessing.

The other part of the Fascist strategy was to foster and promote local anti-Semitism amongst the people of Sandwich and this was probably the task for which Gordon Canning took responsibility. In May a correspondence, of a generally anti-Semitic nature, began in the letters column of the local press. The first letter, appearing in the *East Kent Mercury* on 20 May, blamed the Jews for their own persecution: 'The persecution of the Jewish people down through history has, in my opinion, been mainly due to the unnatural and pernicious persistence of the Jews to remain a race apart.'[13] The following week another letter appeared, also from a Londoner, attacking the suggestion of the first letter that intermarriage between Jew and Gentile should be encouraged:

> According to the Jew Israel Cohen, in 'Jewish Life in Modern Times' various authorities state that 'the frequency of mental diseases among Jews is from four to five times higher than among non-Jews' [...] inter-breeding between human races which differ so greatly as do the native of Britain (Nordic or Mediterranean race) and the Jew (Armenoid and Alpine race) would be a dangerous experiment. It is known that certain unions of races markedly different from each other cause a mental retardation in the offspring of such unions, as also a marked tendency to certain spasmodic diseases such as 'St Vitus' dance, stammering and asthma [...] If Mr Jones' remedy were adopted, the downward path of Britain would follow the example (the warning example) of Spain and Portugal which died from that remedy.[14]

Racism wrapped up in pseudo-science, and a quotation from 'Israel Cohen', an author known to have been invented by anti-semites, demonstrate the Fascist origins of this letter from a person calling himself 'Henry Hedges'. The two letters, each appearing a week apart under the heading 'The Jewish Problem', apparently arguing against each other but both profoundly anti-Semitic, seem to be part of a set up 'debate'. It was designed to frighten the Sandwich populace away from the Kitchener Camp and recruit them to Fascism via anti-Semitism.

Somebody, almost certainly Robert Gordon Canning and his cronies, had decided that the powerful driver of local anti-Semitism would be sex, in particular fear of the outcome of sexual relations between Jews and Gentiles. This must have been a considered move: it was early summer, the sap was rising and some of these polite young men were making headway with some of the local girls. (Hilda's older sister Peggy became 'unofficially engaged' that summer to a young man from the camp, Ivy was stepping out with Oscar.) If the Fascists could persuade the people of Sandwich that the Kitchener Camp housed degenerates who were disease carriers to future generations, and whose genes constituted a peril of such power that they threatened annihilation of the nation itself, they could create an atmosphere of disgust, alarm and hatred.

At about the same time that these letters were appearing, Gordon Canning also wrote to the local paper. His letter got into the public domain, not because it actually reached the pages of the *East Kent Mercury* – it did not – but because it was published in his personal fiefdom: the weekly Fascist newspaper, *Action*. Gordon Canning funded *Action* and chaired its board. The letter appeared under the bold banner heading 'REFUGEES', as follows:

The following letter was sent to the 'Deal and Sandwich Mercury'. The Editor, however, refused to publish it.

Dear Sir,

By the number of stories concerning the camp of aliens established by the courtesy of Dorman Long near Sandwich, some no doubt unsubstantiated, others fully substantiated, the life of Sandwich citizens has been particularly disrupted by the intrusion of this Central European mass into its quiet and orderly existence.

It would have been thought that refugees receiving the hospitality of Great Britain would have done their utmost to live an unobtrusive and unprovocative existence. This appears to be far from the fact, so that the good name of this ancient town, its repute as a beauty spot of England, is becoming endangered by the presence of this foreign excrescence which visiting motorists will presumably take for citizens of Sandwich.

Only recently a young girl assaulted by two of these aliens was put on probation for two years, while the culprits were exonerated. Sex-starved they may be, but it is not for British womanhood to appease their appetites.

Finally, I would like to ask the Mayor of Sandwich whether his duty is not first to the welfare of Sandwich, to the needs of the unemployed, and to the safeguarding of its citizens. Is it necessary, then, for the Mayor to promote social intercourse between these aliens and Sandwich citizens which may endanger, not only the amenities, but the morals of this ancient and renowned town?

Is not the duty of the Mayor first to Sandwich and to England?

Yours faithfully,
R.GORDON CANNING[15]

It was a disgraceful letter, wholly untrue, and racist in tone and language. Perhaps the editor of the *East Kent Mercury*, who had been lulled into publishing the previous anti-Semitic 'debate' by pseudo scientific language and an apparently moderate tone, finally realised what was going on, or – more likely – he checked and discovered that there was absolutely no evidence of a young woman being assaulted and of men from Kitchener being 'exonerated'.

The publication of this letter in *Action* was hardly going to impact on the people of Sandwich; even nationally the newspaper had a very small circulation. It could have been left to lie. However one of the policies of the Board of Deputies of British Jews was to pursue all statements in the public domain that were defamatory to Jews. Anything and everything, from graffiti to press statements, were followed up. The letter in *Action* was no exception and the president of the Board, Neville Laski, asked for counsel's opinion. The lawyer took it upon himself to check with the Clerk to the Justices at Sandwich as to the truth of the allegation and discovered that it was sheer invention and anyway did not make sense: 'he [the Clerk to the Justices] has not heard of any such case of assault as is contained in that letter, but even if that case be true, it was the girl who was convicted and the men who were discharged'.[16] The counsel advised that 'a strong and timely prosecution [...] might act as a brake to what cannot be regarded otherwise than as an attempt to import [...] the racial doctrines and practices of Germany'. Neville Laski sent the opinion to Robert Waley Cohen, suggesting that, if he agreed, they should pass the papers to the Director of Public Prosecutions.[17] Nothing further seems to have happened – either Sir Robert or the Director of Public Prosecutions thought it was not worth pursuing.

Once the editor of the *East Kent Mercury* had stopped the oxygen of publicity for the local Fascists and other anti-Semites there was little they could do that would have much impact on Sandwich – apart from their usual activities of occasional marching and regularly selling *Action* and *The Blackshirt* in the Market Square on market days. However, there was one more effort, which, like the Gordon Canning letter, involved sexual slurs and sheer invention. It came much later, after war had broken out, and began in November 1939. This time the Fascists used a sympathetic monthly journal to spread another set of lies. A right-wing magazine, called *Truth,* published an article claiming that the Kitchener

Camp refugees had printed 'in thousands' a 'scurrilous postcard', which they were circulating 'to the people in the neighbourhood, including the troops'.[18] The postcard contained some kind of image, probably a cartoon. The Board of Deputies were immediately on to the case (they must have had someone constantly monitoring the Fascist and right-wing press) and they deputed Norman Bentwich to write to the editor of *Truth*. Norman's letter, which the journal published in full, said that a thorough enquiry had been made at the camp and there was no possibility that this postcard had been printed, let alone circulated in the neighbourhood. He also pointed out that previous 'notices' purporting to have been chalked up by the refugees turned out to have Fascist origins. 'The police in Sandwich were able to put a stop to that nuisance, and it is proposed to put this matter, also, in the hands of the police.'[19]

The editor of *Truth* was determined to counter this veiled threat with his own threat to prosecute. Beneath the Bentwich letter he added an editorial note:

> The postcard was not scurrilous; it was filthily pornographic. On that account I should be interested to have details of the inquiry that was carried out. Necessarily the circulation of the postcard was surreptitious; to circulate it openly would entail immediate prosecution.[20]

The editor may have thought he was having the last word, but he had underestimated both the determination of Norman Bentwich and the Board of Deputies to pursue this matter and their ability to take it to the highest possible level of government. A month later Norman was able to reply, in the letters page of *Truth*, that no less than the Home Secretary himself had taken a view:

> We have now received a letter from the Home Secretary himself, in which he states 'I have made enquiries of the Chief Constable of Kent, who is unable to substantiate that the postcard originated from the training camp; the Kent police are satisfied that this card is not, and has not been, in circulation in the neighbourhood of the camp. Moreover, this card is identical, except [for] one or two insignificant alterations, with a card which was found in a Sailors' Home at Chatham, in the cubicle of a man who was arrested on a charge of sodomy in the spring of 1937, and later sentenced to three years penal servitude at the Central Criminal Court. At the time of his arrest he stated that he purchased the postcard at a public house in Stepney.[21]

The whole affair had taken on a really awful dimension. Once again, Norman's letter to *Truth* was published in its entirety and yet again the editor of *Truth* appended a note:

I gladly give publicity to Mr Bentwich's letter. I would have been grateful for fuller details of the inquiries of the Chief Constable of Kent, so that I and my readers might judge of their worth. If murderers can outwit the police, circulators of postcards would not find it difficult to do the same.

This postcard is not the sort that would emanate from a Gentile brain, even with the design of injuring the Jews. I am not suggesting for one moment that Gentiles are incapable of equally revolting pornography; I am merely saying that it would not be done *in that particular way*. ED.,TRUTH.[22]

The editor obviously considered he had had the last, and – to him – satisfactory word. Enclosing a copy of his disgusting journal, the editor wrote to Norman Bentwich on 4 January 1940:

I have made my statement about the postcard; you have made yours. So the matter is at an end. If the Home Office is incapable of stemming – as I have said in TRUTH often enough – the influx of illegal refugees into this country, it cannot expect its 'inquiries' to be taken over-seriously. And you are, of course, at liberty to repeat that statement.[23]

Many people would have been tempted to throw this letter and its accompanying journal into the rubbish; Norman, a careful, orderly man with a commitment to the proper truth filed them away, and left them for future researchers to uncover them.

These four efforts of the Fascists – the intimidatory marches, the 'notices', the letters to the press, and the episode in *Truth* – were all of them very high on the scale of sheer nastiness. It is possible that the Fascists' inclination to lies and inventions, which they must have known could be very easily discovered as complete falsehoods, was an indication of their inability to get a purchase on Sandwich sentiment. That is the one comforting thought in the midst of the poison unearthed here. They did have their nuisance value, particularly in the light of the determination of the Board of Deputies to follow-up every piece of defamation. But the impact on local attitudes to Jews in general, and to the men in the Kitchener Camp in particular, seems to have been very low. At the meeting of the British Board of Deputies Defence Committee in November 1939, someone, under the heading of 'Reports from the Provinces', submitted the short report: '*East Kent*: no evidence of any increase in anti-Semitism. Neutral area.'[24] The people of Sandwich had, it seemed, chosen to take a much more enlightened approach to the camp. They were not going to be provoked into anti-Semitism and xenophobia by the odd lying letter in their local newspaper or the parading of the Sandwich BUF banner in their narrow streets. This was not Germany – and that, after all, was the point.

Notes

1. Herbert Freeden, 'Sandwich Revisited', *AJR Information*, Vol. XIV, No. 3, March 1959. Herbert Freeden was née Friedenthal and had been a Kitchener Camp man.
2. Hilda Keen, op. cit.
3. Personal communication from Patrick Miles, 21 September 2009.
4. Freeden, op. cit.
5. On Lady Pearson, see for example, Robert Benewick, *Political Violence and Public Order: a study of British Fascism*, Allen Lane, The Penguin Press, 1969, pp. 126–127; Martin Pugh, '*Hurrah for the Blackshirts!': Fascists and Fascism in Britain between the Wars*, Jonathan Cape, 2005; Julie Gottlieb, *Feminine Fascism: Women in Britain's Fascist Movement, 1923–1945*, I.B. Tauris & Co., 2000. Robert Gordon Canning has had less attention although, through his close association with Mosley until they quarrelled in 1939, he was more powerful within British Fascism than Lady Pearson. He occasionally appears in Martin Pugh's book.
6. This is somewhat surprising because it is highly likely she was under surveillance of some kind, but if there were files they have long since disappeared from the National Archives, possibly because her influential brother, Henry Page Croft MP, made certain that they vanished. When, after the fall of France in May 1940, Lady Pearson was interned, her brother, by making a tremendous fuss, managed to get her out of Holloway prison after only nine days.
7. They definitely met after war broke out, when they were part of a widespread Fascist campaign to make peace with Germany immediately. See Martin Pugh, op. cit., pp. 297–298, who mentions their meeting at private fortnightly meetings designed to bring prominent Fascists together in order to develop a peace strategy.
8. Phineas May diary, entry for 19 March.
9. The MP was Nevil Alexander Beechman. There is absolutely nothing in his Wikipedia entry to indicate a particular interest in German, Jewish, Fascist or anti-Fascist matters. It is a mystery as to why he got involved. Perhaps he was a golfer.
10. Letter from Mr A.G. Brotman to Sir Robert Waley Cohen, dated 21 March 1939. Board of Deputies of British Jews archive, ACC/3121/E/01/106.
11. Ibid.
12. Interview with Philip Franks, IWM Sound Archive, Accession number 13618.
13. *East Kent Mercury*, Correspondence, 20 May 1939, page 5.
14. *East Kent Mercury*, Correspondence, 27 May 1939, page 5.

15. *Action*, No. 173, 17 June 1939, p. 19.
16. British Board of Deputies Archive, file ACC3121/E3/247.
17. Ibid. Letter from Neville Laski to Robert Waley Cohen, dated 11 July 1939.
18. Letter from Norman Bentwich to Neville Laski, dated 1 December 1939, BWP, File P174/21c.
19. Letter from Norman Bentwich to the Editor, *Truth*, 15 November 1939, BWP, ibid.
20. Quoted in Bentwich to Laski, 1 December 1939, op. cit.
21. Letter from Norman Bentwich to the editor of *Truth*, headed 'Richborough Postcard', dated 1 January 1940, BWP, File P174/21c.
22. This edition of *Truth* is held in the BWP, File P174/21c.
23. Letter from the Editor of *Truth* to Norman Bentwich, 4 January 1940, BWP, File 174/21c.
24. British Board of Deputies Defence Committee, minutes for the meeting of 8 November 1939, 1658/1/1/1, Folder 2.

11

RACE AGAINST TIME

The months of that spring and summer of 1939 had sped by. International events of very great importance had crowded together and the prospect of another devastating European war had grown ever closer. In March, the Germans occupied the city of Prague and its hinterland regions of Bohemia and Moravia; it was clear that the Munich agreement and the policy of appeasement were both now dead in the water. Two weeks later Hitler turned his attention to Poland and denounced Germany's 1934 non-aggression pact with that country; in response the British and French governments guaranteed Poland's independence. This meant that if the Nazis invaded Poland, war would begin. In anticipation, Britain moved further towards war readiness, introducing conscription in April 1939, preparing for total blackouts at night, drawing up plans for mass evacuation from the cities, distributing gas masks against weapons of mass destruction, and preparing shelters to protect the British people from incendiary bombs. Coastal defences, particularly those on the beaches facing Continental Europe, were strengthened.

The Kitchener Camp, tiny compared to the overall British population but of very high density, was not ignored in these preparations. Phineas, who was himself a qualified Air Raid Protection (ARP) officer showed a Sandwich ARP officer round the camp on the day it opened on 1 February, and, again in March, probably in response to the invasion of Bohemia and Moravia, he was invited to a meeting with what he called a Sandwich 'Burgomaster' to discuss arrangements to protect the camp in the event of fire bombing.[1] The men in the camp would not themselves have been aware of these arrangements, but what they did notice, and which Phineas mentioned in his diary, was the invasion of Bohemia and Moravia: 'a day of depression all round owing to the news regarding Slovakia and rumours which were not allayed with the 6 p.m. news that all German frontiers had been closed'.[2] The fact that the German frontiers had been closed would have been of particular concern to the men since so many of them were hoping that their families who were still in Greater Germany would be able to join them in England.

On 29 April, the day after Hitler had rejected Roosevelt's peace proposals and denounced the German–Polish non-aggression pact, Phineas again noted that 'everybody was in bad spirits – perhaps the gloomy international situation helped towards that end'.[3] On 8 July there was a blackout rehearsal across the whole of Kent. The men were marshalled into their huts, all the camp lights were put out at 10 p.m., and the Sandwich air raid sirens were sounded.[4] August was really alarming. At the beginning of the month the Royal Engineers arrived to practise bridge building across the Stonar lake, just over the road from the camp.[5] And the main international event was the announcement, on 23 August, of the Nazi–Soviet non-aggression pact, which indicated the imminent carve up of Poland by the two great totalitarian entities of the Third Reich and the Soviet Union. Even before that alliance, which shocked the world, the tension at the Kitchener Camp had reached an hysterical pitch. On 14 August, Phineas recorded that he had been told that 'there was considerable excitement during the night, as one of the men […] went round a number of the huts ringing a bell and saying the Concert Hall was on fire and that war had commenced. The men got up and rushed to the Concert Hall, some feinting [sic] when they were informed that it was a Hoax [sic].'[6] Just over two weeks later the real war began.

During those few months living on the edge of Sandwich all the Kitchener men knew that war was, at most, months away, possibly as little as a few days. They had seen the remilitarisation of Germany for themselves and were well aware of what it entailed.[7] For a few of the men, time spent in Britain waiting for war was not that important: their arrival at Kitchener was the final link in a chain of family migration and they had been able to join wives and siblings, even children, who had already found another route to England.[8] But most of the men knew that they were the first link: once in England the hope was that they would find a means to get their wives, their children, their siblings and (most difficult of all) their parents away from Nazi Germany. It was a very heavy responsibility, and, given the restrictions on visas both to Britain and to the rest of the world, a formidable one. Worst of all, it was a task that would take both money and *time*. They had neither.

They would have known that the urgency was growing day by day, not just because of the imminence of war and how that would impact on the ability of their loved ones to cross international borders, but also because the circumstances of those they had left behind were getting worse on a daily basis. Norman Bentwich went to Vienna in early August 1939 (his intention was to persuade Eichmann to take the pressure off – never a remotely feasible objective) and his report of what he found there is absolutely chilling. As he put it, 'The aim which has been remorselessly pursued is to make life literally unendurable, and so force the people out – anyhow.'[9] He observed how rapidly the Viennese Jewish community had declined in one year – from 165,000 to 67,000 – and he could not help remarking that while most of the reduction was due to emigration, the death rate had quadrupled and, such was the prevailing despair, 'of the death rate one eighth part is due to suicide'. The circumstances of the remaining community were desolate. Stripped of their assets, removed from their homes and their jobs, forced to change their names to 'Israel' if they were men and 'Sarah' if they were women, they were dependent on struggling Jewish charity:

> The poverty and destitution of the remnant of a great community are heartrending. Well over half of the 67,000 are fed daily through communal soup-kitchens, most of them collecting for their family their one square meal of the day from the kitchens. They have no meat; and a large number are glaringly undernourished. Some thousands more of the old, infirm and children, are maintained by the community in such charitable buildings as remain to it – all of them sadly bare and gaunt. The hapless people cannot even enjoy God's air; it is an offence for them to enter a public park or garden, or to sit on a bench in the Ring. One small park near the Jewish quarter was reserved for them, but it is not safe to enter it.

There was only one hope and it was to get a domestic service post in England:

> The one hope for all, young and older, is emigration; and the main interest is preparation for emigration. During the year nearly 40,000 have passed through classes of training and re-training, which embrace a thousand different branches of manual or domestic work. There is a class [...] for bar-mixers and several for butlers, which are attended by lawyers, doctors and industrialists. The possibility of domestic service in England has been a Godsend. Thousands of children and adults are learning English somehow, for there is scarcely a family which has not a relation in Great Britain or the United States.[10]

Small wonder the men were desperate to get their families away.

The Kitchener Camp management were keen to provide the means whereby the men could begin to organise the process. They had made certain the camp had its own telephone exchange and post office and each man received two stamps a week which he could use for international mail; it took a little while but eventually they established an advice centre run by the refugees themselves. But that was the limit of what they provided. The people connected to the camp who were in touch with the Jewish agencies in Berlin and Vienna on an official basis were of very little help. Indeed Norman Bentwich made certain that early on the men at the camp got the message that he could do nothing. In March he wrote to Dr Bondy, a staff member at the camp:

> I do not think that we ought to be troubled with these applications from wives. The Domestic Bureau is endeavouring to place a certain number of the wives in domestic service; and, as you know, applications have been made for two or three of the wives of the heads of the staff to come to the Camp, that is all that can be done at present. It is a little disquieting that so much of our time is taken up with these personal applications from persons of the Camp about their families. I understand their anxiety, but we did make it quite clear that the men would have to come without their wives, and till there is a *Beratungsstelle*[11] in the Camp they must be patient.[12]

Norman was a man of order and it seemed to him that the men had made a contract to come to Kitchener on their own: all this fuss about wives was not in accordance with what had been agreed. But he did love working quietly behind the scenes and something in this instance must have pricked his considerable capacity for kindness – perhaps it was a conversation with his wife Helen. Two days later he wrote two letters, the first to Lord Duncannon who worked at the High Commission for Refugees. He wanted him, in that capacity, to ask the German government to 'leave [the wives] unmolested' while they waited until they could 'join their husbands in emigration to their ultimate destination'.[13] He wrote a similar letter to Dr Eppstein at the *Reichsvertretung* in Berlin, which he obviously hoped would help in handling desperate women folk at his end:

> We are, however, making every effort to arrange the emigration of the husbands; and when that is done it will be arranged that their wives are to accompany them. It is hoped, then, that the wives will be allowed to remain in Germany until the emigration of the couples can take place.[14]

He must have known in his bones that the Nazis were well beyond reasoned requests and that time was the last thing they were willing to grant, but at least his conscience was salved.

He wasn't always kind, even in the light of the most eloquent of pleas, even, and perhaps particularly, when they came from his own colleagues. When a Mrs Schwab from the Welfare Department of the London-based German Jewish Aid committee got in touch about 'a number of cases where the poor men are over here in Richborough after concentration camp in Germany and their wifes [*sic*] are still in Germany, in two cases expecting babies very shortly'[15] he was brusque in negative response:

Their case has been brought fully and several times to the attention of the Domestic Bureau, which is doing all it can. It is a pity, though, of course, it is inevitable that the men will worry everybody about the same case.[16]

When Mrs Schwab came back by return, saying not only that 'our Domestic Department have informed me quite officially that they cannot do anything for the wives of the men in the Camp when they are pregnant', but also that 'we have been told by the Vienna *Kultusgemeinde* that there are no hospitals over there who will take the women'.[17] he brought the correspondence to a close. There is no reply in the file. He knew there was nothing to be done.

The situation was grim. The odds were so loaded against these men and women, divided by international frontiers and by the well-meaning efforts of good and philanthropic British Jews determined to rescue the men arrested after *Kristallnacht* and get them out of the concentration camps. Essentially the Kitchener men were on their own: it was a question of their energy, their commitment, and straightforward hustling. And the most important ingredient for success really seems to have been luck. Phineas, for example, in his capacity as camp welfare officer, was often at the receiving end of men who were at their wits' end. Sometimes, though rarely, he was able to do something:

Early in the day one Refugee who had done some special work for me begged me to give him a private interview. I did so. He burst into tears and showed me a picture of his mother, a widow, whom he wants to come over here and does not know how to help her. I promised to try and get her a domestic position – I told him it was very difficult but would do my utmost – he completely broke down and kissed my hand. I do hope I can help the chap, he is such a nice fellow and a very hard worker [...] During the afternoon a Mrs Williams called to see me and said she had had my name given her by a tradesman in the town and did I know of any Refugee who had a female relative who would be suitable to do domestic work in her house. What an amazing coincidence. I went into full details with my Refugee friend of the morning and the other Depts in the camp concerned and if there is no hitch he will be able to bring his Mother over within a week or two.[18]

Two days later he was able to add to this man's joy:

The Lady [*sic*] who had come to see me about having a Refugee as a Domestic phoned me up and said a friend of hers close by would also like somebody and so you can imagine the happiness of the man here when I told him I had found a place for his Financee [*sic*] where she could be a close companion to his Mother.[19]

It was personal contact, and particularly contacts in the Sandwich neighbourhood, that worked to the men's favour. Stella's story indicates the sheer serendipity surrounding these encounters. Her father, Schulim Schatzberg, was a Viennese dentist who had been arrested after *Kristallnacht* and who was released from Dachau on condition he went to Kitchener. From the day he arrived in Sandwich he worked to get his wife and little girl – Stella was 10 years old at the time – away from Vienna. His wife was fortunate – she managed to get a domestic service position in London – but the problem was that she couldn't get Stella on to a *Kindertransport*. Without Stella, Mrs Schatzberg would not leave. Stella's father was apparently 'very charming' and it was this that worked its magic on one of the many local teachers who had volunteered to teach English to the Kitchener men. It could have been 'Auntie Mab', 'Auntie Bessie', or 'Auntie Dorothy' (seventy years later Stella isn't sure which one of these ladies was the volunteer teacher) who responded generously to Mr Schatzberg's desperation and offered to look after Stella in the house the three ladies shared near Sandwich. They were already looking after another little German girl, the daughter of a Kitchener man, and Stella would be company for her. So, with their support, Stella and her mother obtained their entry visas and arrived in England on 28 August 1939, five days before war was declared. After one night in a bed and breakfast for a joyful reunion, the Schatzberg family separated, her mother to a domestic post in London, her father back to Kitchener and Stella to 'The Gables, Minster'.

For Stella it was a memorably happy time. There was a garden, a dog, a cat, the other little girl, and her three 'really lovely' aunties. It was all very different from the Viennese flat she had come from. She went to Minster Primary School where she thrived and every alternate Sunday her father would pedal the couple of miles from the Kitchener Camp and see her for afternoon tea at 'The Gables'. It was for Stella, looking back, a time of sunshine and happiness: her English 'aunties' 'were just wonderful people' and 'they were so kind. It didn't damage me at all.' She stayed with them for nine months, a time she thinks of as among the most important of her life.[20]

Quite how many wives and children were reunited with their menfolk is impossible to tell. Norman Bentwich, in the three books he wrote after the war about his pre-war work, was always careful to use the word 'most' or 'many'.[21] He thought that the main route to England for the wives was through local contacts in and around Sandwich. It was, he said, the refugees' popularity in Sandwich that made it 'possible to bring over some hundreds of wives of the men in the camp to be domestic servants in Kentish homes'.[22] He was speaking from experience – he and Helen had employed a refugee wife as their housekeeper for their second home in Sandwich.[23] Every now and then a hard figure emerges from the documents, although, it has to be said, always in round numbers and always different. Robert Waley Cohen confidently pronounced, in early August 1939, that 'of the 650 married men in the Camp, between 350 and 400 will now have their wives in England, because they have obtained domestic permits and are being placed in service'.[24] In January 1940, a Dr Plaut, the Kitchener man in charge of the camp's Social Welfare Department, produced a rather larger figure: 'Among the Campmen there have been about 900 married men. We succeeded in bringing over about 600 wives, almost all of them for domestic service were granted.'[25] These figures were obviously guess work but some hundreds can legitimately be added to the number of lives that were actually saved by the Kitchener rescue as a whole. Both Waley Cohen and Plaut thought that about two-thirds of the married men had managed to get their wives away, but at the same time some hundreds had not succeeded.

The other group of people who were desperate to get to England and the Kitchener Camp were, of course, other men. Unlike the wives, Bentwich clearly regarded the promotion of the rescue of particular men as a legitimate call on his time. Much of the bulging paperwork in the Bentwich archives consists of hundreds of letters, written by Norman to the Jewish agencies in Berlin and Vienna, asking them to take a look at a named 'Herr x' or a 'Doctor y'. As a committed bureaucrat, with a love of order, precedence and equity, he sometimes made it clear that he really did not enjoy promoting individuals, writing occasional apologetic little notes to his counterparts in Berlin and Vienna.[26] The London Fund had always been formally clear that selection should be left entirely to the RV and the IK; nevertheless, he kept the letters coming.

It is not easy for a reader of his many letters to understand why he took up some cases and not others. That is with one exception: his treatment of supporters whom he saw as influential 'outsiders' was consistently more obliging than his treatment of his immediate colleagues from the Fund. For example, the Labour MP Josiah Wedgwood, who was not a Jew but was a staunch supporter of Zionism and the cause of German refugees, wrote to him a number of times about particular cases and Norman always made an extra effort to oblige him.[27] This is in quite sharp contrast to his response to his closer colleagues. For example writing to Robert Waley Cohen, with copies to all the other members of the Kitchener Camp committee, in May 1939 he said:

> I would point out that it is not really sound for us on the Camp Committee here to be putting up every day cases for the special consideration of the RV or the KG. Our principle is that the selection of the persons is to be made by the responsible Jewish bodies in Berlin and Vienna according to their judgement of
> a) the urgency of the case
> b) the prospect of emigration
>   It is impossible for us to judge of these things on letters which are sent by friends and relations, and so forth. I have in my correspondence every

morning, I should think a dozen letters of the kind, from you, Ernest Joseph, and all the other members of the Committee, asking me to recommend this person and that person. I have been doing it in most cases, but I know it is wrong, and we are giving ourselves and the Committee in Berlin a lot of unnecessary trouble. The right answer to most applications of the kind is that the person must apply himself to the organisation in Berlin or Vienna, and we can do nothing. Only in a very exceptional case should we intervene.[28]

Norman was a kind man, and he did not do as he said. His sense of orderliness and equity collided with his sympathy and sympathy tended to win: he continued to send his little nudging letters to the agencies in Berlin and Vienna. Their response is not known (until someone links the names with a systematic search of the various databases of the Holocaust). But what can be said is that more often than not, when I have followed up a particular name, that person appears on the lists of those murdered in the Holocaust. To take just one example, a man who was initially recommended by Josiah Wedgwood, and whom Bentwich kept on promoting, perished in Auschwitz in 1942.[29]

Even if Norman knew that little notice was taken of his recommendations in Berlin and Vienna, he and his colleagues on the Kitchener Camp Committee were under enormous pressure. The letters they received from desperate men in Greater Germany and sometimes beyond were so touching, so full of moving personal detail, so human, that they could not but respond. Amongst the many that Norman himself received, here is one example:

Vienna, 9th of February 1939

Dear Sir,
Although unknown to you, yet I venture to solicit a great favour of you. The full confidence I have in your kindness and humanity and not presumption of my part emboldens me to take this liberty.
I have present myself at the Israel.Kultusgemeinde in Vienna for the camp in Kent and was registered with Number 1412. To-day I was informed that the Kultusgemeinde has not given my act to you, because I have left some years ago the jewish religion and am now without confession.

I am in a awful situation now. Because there is in Vienna only the Israel. Kultusgemeinde who could help and as they will not, I am in a dreadful state of distress. Allow me therefore to beg your kind offices for me and to tell you the reason wherefore I have to beg you to make it possible for me to come to England.

I was born on the 1st May 1904 in Vienna and was always living there.

After having finished my studies I was educator in a children-home during two years and afterward I became an official at the 'Magistrate of Vienna' where I worked 12 years in the service of my native town. In March 1938 I was dismissed because I am a jew. In the last year I have learnt the cultivation of bees and got a testimonial as apiarist.

On the 10th of November 1938 I was put in prison and remained there during two months. When I was dismissed I was obliged to leave this country till the 15th of March. As the day of my departure is approaching and I have no possibility to start I don't know what I am to do because I shall be punished if I should not leave the country in time. This means prison and perhaps perishing.

Moreover I am in another great danger. On the 26th of February I have got a letter from the Reichsstatthalter in Vienna that they will not pay further my pension. So I have nothing for my livelihood. And I am afraid to be put in prison again because of the news this letter contains.

Though I am not a member of the jewish religion, my whole family (mother and brothers) are good jews and I myself am a jew too. I should only stay in the camp for short a time because I shall receive the visum for the immigration in USA – I hope – in a nearer future.

Please dear Sir, don't be angry that I have ventured to trouble you are my only hope and if you would not help, I should be at the end of my life.

Please help me in my great despair.

My gratitude for you can only be equalled by the profound respect with which I have the honour to be your most obedient servant,
O… K…
Vienna, [address given in original][30]

There are many similarly eloquent letters to Norman, some from men who had already left Germany and gone eastwards to, for example, Hungary and Romania, others from men already in the Kitchener Camp, pleading the case for brothers, fathers, mothers and wives. As one reads them, one's eye is drawn to the date in the letter's heading – how close is this particular date to war? How long did they have before the frontiers closed?

There is one example of a correspondence which stretched over the months of that spring and summer of 1939. Meyer Stephany was the secretary of the Central British Fund in London and for some reason, when it came to two young men who were distant relatives of his wife, he did not contact Norman Bentwich about them but chose to run the correspondence without his help. Perhaps Mr Stephany had a sense that Norman's efforts were often minimal and all too easily discounted and thought that his own direct contact with Berlin would serve better and that, unlike Norman, he would simply insist and thus succeed.

He first wrote to Dr Eppstein of the RV, on 3 April 1939 about two brothers called Alfred and Kurt Jacobi from Göttingen.[31] They were, he said, 'very distant relatives of my wife' and that 'I know that when I tell you that I personally am interested, you will do what you can to help.' Dr Eppstein replied by return. He knew about the brothers but unfortunately their quota numbers for entry to the USA were too high and this meant they failed an important criterion: they would not leave the Kitchener Camp within six months.

This reply was not good enough for Stephany, who on 24 April, wrote to the Director of the RV, Dr Otto Hirsch, whom he knew well and personally, asking him to intervene. The Germans played strictly by the rules and they didn't do what Stephany wanted: instead they wrote to a distant relative of the Jacobi brothers who was living in London and asked her to provide 'the necessary guarantee of £100, obtain a trainee post and maintain them'. Nearly a month went by before, on 19 May 1939, Stephany wrote again – this time to his original correspondent Dr Eppstein – telling him that the distant aunt could not help and 'I should be obliged if something could be done to facilitate their emigration from Germany as soon as ever possible'. Eppstein replied that he had asked the brothers' local branch of the *Hilfsverein* to see if they could do anything.

At this point the Jakobi brothers evidently decided to take matters into their own hands: they took a train to the German–Dutch border with a view to coming to England under their own steam. This was a strategy that others had pursued with some success but it did not serve them well. Dr Eppstein, at the RV, reacted with fury. On 6 June he wrote to Stephany:

In the meantime I have had the deplorable news that, without waiting to see if there was any other possibility of emigration besides the Camp for them, they tried to cross the frontier near Emmerich into Holland and were arrested [...] we might add that the two young men have taken this step against our express warnings.

Evidently Stephany already knew this – his letter dated 5 June crossed with Dr Eppstein's. He pleaded 'that some exception may be made in their case to bring them to the camp?' There was no reply.

Three weeks later, on 30 June, Stephany heard directly from the brothers that they had been released and were back home. Apparently they were now being told by the RV that 'everything must be left to the British Committee'. Surprised by this, Stephany once more wrote to Dr Eppstein. Yet again the case went to the RV committee, and yet again they were turned down for Kitchener 'because they cannot re-emigrate within the specified time'.

At this point Stephany tried, again quite explicitly, to get Eppstein to bend the rules: 'If there is any possibility which you can think of, I shall be much obliged if you will use your influence on their behalf.' There was no reply. Five days before war broke out, on 28 August, the *Hilfsverein* in Hannover wrote to the London Fund stating that the prospects of re-emigration of the young men 'within two years appears to be certain' and asking for information from the London Fund as to how much money they could make available to maintain the young men either in England or another country. On 31 August 1939 Stephany replied, saying 'we are doing our utmost to assist' but repeating that the boys' aunt was unable to help financially. Three days later, on 3 September 1939, the Second World War began.

Then there was silence. Nothing was heard of the Jacobi brothers again until 1981.

Notes

1. Phineas May diary, entries for 1 February and 24 March.
2. Phineas May diary, 15 March.
3. Phineas May diary, 29 April.
4. Phineas May diary, 8 July.
5. Phineas May diary, 1 August.
6. Phineas May diary, 14 August.
7. For example, Fred Pelican, in an interview held at the IWM Sound Archive, said: 'I was aware that they were building up an enormous army because every town you went to you would see masses of soldiers, people in uniform, everybody was in uniform.' IWM Sound Archive, Accession number 9222, Reel 6.
8. For example, an American correspondent's father, who had come to Kitchener, joined his wife and sister who were already working as domestic servants in London. Some other men also already had children in England who had come on a *Kindertransport*.
9. Norman Bentwich, *Report on a Visit to Vienna*, dated 17 August 1939, CBF Archives.
10. Ibid.
11. Advice Bureau.

12. Norman Bentwich to Dr Bondy, a staff member at the camp, 27 March 1939, BWP, File P174/12c.

13. Norman Bentwich to Lord Duncannon, 29 March 1939, BWP, File P174/12d.

14. Norman Bentwich to Dr Eppstein of the Berlin *Reichsvertretung*, 26 March 1939, BWP, File P174/17b.

15. Letter from Mrs Schwab, originally addressed to Meyer Stephany, Secretary of the Central British Fund, and passed by him to Norman Bentwich, 1 June 1939, BWP, File P174/13b.

16. Reply from Norman Bentwich to Mrs Schwab, 5 June 1939, BWP, File P174/13b.

17. Mrs Schwab to Norman Bentwich, 7 June 1939, Ibid.

18. Phineas May diary, 10 May.

19. Phineas May diary, 12 May.

20. Meeting with Stella Curzon, 2006, author's notes. I am grateful to Ruth Bleasdale for introducing me to Stella.

21. Norman Bentwich, *I Understand the Risks*, London:Victor Gollancz, 1950; Norman Bentwich, *They Found Refuge*, The Cresset Press, 1956; Norman Bentwich, *My 77 Years*, The Jewish Publication Society of America, 1961.

22. *I Understand the Risks*, ibid., p. 29.

23. Letter from Norman Bentwich to Lord Samuel (Uncle Herbert), dated 22 July 1940:'we had a refugee woman as housekeeper in our cottage at Sandwich. Her husband was in the Kitchener Camp, an excellent watch maker', BWP, File P174/70.

24. 'Report on the Kitchener Camp', signed by Robert Waley Cohen, dated 2 August 1939, CBF Archives, report to the Council for German Jewry.

25. Letter from Dr Plaut, Head of Social Welfare Department, Kitchener Camp, to Major H.J. Ratcliffe OBE, C.H.Q. Coy, 5 January 1940, BWP, File P174/21a. One striking aspect of both these sets of numbers is how few of the Kitchener men were married – apparently considerably less than 25 per cent overall. There is some evidence that married men may indeed have been in a relatively small minority, in which case this was possibly a reflection of selection procedures in Berlin and Vienna which informally favoured single men, or a reflection of self-selection whereby married men decided to stay with their wives and children in Greater Germany, however awful their circumstances.

26. 'I feel I ought to send you a personal note of apology for the many individual cases with which I worry you about admission to the Kitchener Camp. I am reluctant to send you some of these recommendations and applications for members of our Camp committee, and others, because, on principle, I object to this method of protectia. But some of our Committee

will have the cases which are brought to their attention referred to you. I shall however always do my best to uphold your decisions.' Norman Bentwich to Dr Eppstein of the Berlin *Reichsvertretung*, 17 July 1939, BWP, File P174/17a.

27. See for example a number of letters from Norman Bentwich and Chaim Raphael to Dr Murmelstein of the *Israelitische Kultusgemeinde* in Vienna, pressing the case of an individual whose sister had been in touch with Josiah Wedgwood. Wedgwood's name is always mentioned in the letters from London to Vienna, BWP, File P174/14c.

28. Norman Bentwich to Robert Waley Cohen, 26 April 1939, BWP, File P174/18c.

29. 'Kurt Libochowitz was born in Wien, Austria in 1906 to Hermine née Spitzer. He was married to Sophie. During the war he was in Wien, Austria. Kurt was murdered/perished in 1942 in Auschwitz, Poland. This information is based on a List of Jews murdered in Auschwitz found in Auschwitz Death Registers, The State Museum Auschwitz-Birkenau page 43246/1942.' Central Database of Shoah Victims' Names, Jerusalem.

20. BWP, File P174/14b. There is no record of this person on the Shoah victims' database so perhaps he got away. A pencilled note at the top of the letter suggests his case was sent to the Quakers who handled the applications from 'non Aryans' – i.e. converted Jews.

31. All the following correspondence concerning the Jacobi brothers is taken from the CBF Archive, filed on microfiche under 'Reichsvertretung', held at the Wiener Library, London.

12

WAR

Throughout August 1939 Phineas's diary entries became increasingly terse. Normally a man who saw positive aspects to all events, the tone was apprehensive and on 23 August even more so. That was the date Hitler announced that Germany had made a pact with the Soviet Union, and it was clear that the invasion of Poland was imminent. As Phineas reported, the Kitchener men reacted with concern: 'Chief topic of course everywhere is chance of war, and all Radio and Newssheets [sic] are surrounded by men with anxious faces and you can feel the tension though the spirit is still cheerful.' On 26 August Phineas wrote of 'a general air of depression though considering the men were amazingly calm. The hospitals are very full.' His very last diary entry, on 30 August, recorded that the BBC, which had been hoping to come down to Kitchener to do a live broadcast of one of the camp orchestra's concerts, had postponed their visit 'until things are more settled'.[1]

Phineas probably stopped writing his Kitchener Camp diary because he had lost heart. War was going to be a very different experience from the excitement of helping to run a large-scale rescue project and it seems he had no wish to record this new experience for posterity. The cancellation of the BBC concert, which would have been a superb accolade of all his work at Kitchener, must have been a bitter blow and would have brought home to him how much the world had changed since his Kitchener adventure had begun those few months earlier in February. Moreover, the main *raison d'être* of this so called 'transit' camp now hardly existed. With war the international borders with Germany would close and it was very unlikely there would be any more refugees arriving (he had anyway noted on 24 August that a new transport of 100 arrived that day and that it meant 'our object achieved'. There were now about 3,500 men in the camp). He would have known that the nature of the camp was going to change radically.

Indeed the camp did change, and almost immediately. Very suddenly, from 5 September onwards, there were women in the camp – about 200 of them, and all wives of the camp men. This extraordinary turnaround, and one so many of the men had been continuously asking for, was the consequence, not of a sudden change of heart on the part of the camp management, but of a change in circumstance brought about by the onset of war. The day after war was declared the evacuation of school children from the nation's cities had begun. The county of Kent was, at that time, a destination for evacuees, and about 200 wives, many of whom had been living in and around Sandwich, had suddenly found themselves evicted by their landladies and employers who needed their rooms for a different set of strangers.

The men were delighted – some of the wives were even able to bring their children into the camp and whole families were reunited in the one place. But the camp management and the local police were utterly dismayed. On 14 September a Mr Oates from the Aliens Section of the Home Office wrote to Norman Bentwich to tell him that a concerned Chief Constable of Kent had been in touch and that 'The Police seem to think that this mixture of the sexes at the Camp may lead to complications.'[2] Norman promptly replied in reassuring mode:

> At the present moment most careful measures are being taken at the camp to keep the women separate from the men. They are together with the few children lodged in a separate compound which is divided from the camp by a wire fence, and the camp police see that they do not pass into the men's camp and vice versa, except at certain visiting hours. We believe that the position is well controlled.[3]

Looking back seventy or more years, the division of married couples by a fence seems absurd. Couples had to learn to live with it though, and Robert Fraser, writing from Western Australia, has written how his parents broke the Yom Kippur fast sitting on either side of the fence, cooking on a primus stove and handing each other food through its gaps. Husbands and wives could meet on undivided ground, but only for one hour a day.[4]

Norman, in his letter to the Home Office, was at pains to indicate the arrival of the wives as strictly temporary: 'The camp committee, together with the Domestic Bureau are making every effort to remove the women to hostels and other places until such time as they can find fresh employment. We are anxious that it shall be terminated as soon as possible by the removal of all women and children.' Threatened with removal to a hostel, a month later Robert Fraser's mother found herself in the very fortunate position of being invited to live in a grand house near Sandwich by a lady she met on a train. Her experience was similar to that of many others in Sandwich in the previous months: she was helped to transit from one culture to another by kindly and generous people. Her son has written:

> It seems that as winter 1939 approached, it was decided to move the women out of KC, possibly to hostel accommodation in London. Mrs Farquhar and Mrs Davis immediately offered my Mother a room in their house, as they could see what a dilemma she faced, and on 3 October she moved into the Grange […] She was given a room of her own, overlooking the lawn and was allowed to help in the household routine. She got on well with both the ladies. The staff comprised Hazel the parlour maid, Harry Carrier, the gardener and the cook, Mrs Bailey. As Christmas approached, my Mother helped to prepare the rooms for family visitors and experienced the preparations for a traditional Christmas in an English upper-class household. The delicious smell of mince pies filled the house and a little Christmas tree was placed in the hall and my parents were invited to take Christmas lunch in the kitchen with the servants – they had Christmas crackers and a glass of port […] they never forgot the kindness and generosity of these ladies who offered their assistance when it was sorely needed, as the Bible told them to. It was in their home that my Mother really started to learn English; in their drawing room, she learned the expressions of the English middle-class, and in their kitchen and garden she picked up the everyday vernacular. On the occasions that her Husband visited the Grange, one of the ladies would often surreptitiously drop a half-crown coin into his pocket – something like several pounds in today's money.[5]

It was, at the start of war, a very English idyll; it seems likely that the rest of the Kitchener wives were also eventually rehoused away from the camp, but not necessarily in such gracious surroundings.

The reunion of a few families within the camp, however temporary, was a boost to the morale of those families involved. Paradoxically perhaps, the immediate onset of war also brought other reasons for an improved atmosphere at Kitchener. Many of the men had been very disappointed, on their arrival at Kitchener, to find that they were not allowed to take up paid employment outside the camp – quite apart from getting away from the camp itself, paid work might have given them the income that would help them get their relatives out of Greater Germany. But from early September, the embargo on paid work began to be relaxed and some men were able to get work helping local farmers get in the harvest. In addition the advent of war meant that the coast of East Kent, so close to Continental Europe, was particularly vulnerable to invasion and many men from Kitchener were immediately engaged in building coastal defences. Their main task seems to have been the filling of sandbags, particularly in Dover.

These early war efforts gave the men a real sense of purpose and renewal. At last they could engage in a fightback against an enemy they knew only too well. There was a further boost to morale when the head of the Church of England, the then Archbishop of Canterbury, Dr Cosmo Lang, paid a visit to the camp at the beginning of October. All the grandees of the London Fund were there to greet the elderly figure, who was dressed in nineteenth-century garb including a black top hat and gaiters. Robert Waley Cohen introduced him to the packed audience as 'the first citizen of the country after HM the King'. Dr Lang gave a speech that the men loved – amongst many sympathetic comments he said that 'I am very proud to be an Englishman [...] and that my country has had the honour of being able to give you a place of refuge and of hope.' He stressed how they could join with the British in the fight against tyranny: 'I am sure you can make common cause with us. You have all the suffering and all the cruelty which has driven you from your own country to encourage you to come to our aid if for no other wish than to rid your country and the world of a tyranny which has too long been allowed to lie upon it.' At the end of his speech the audience had gone wild. As the local reporter put it, the applause at the end of his speech was deafening: 'Hats, hands and handkerchiefs were waved in the air, and it was many minutes before anything approaching silence could be secured.'[6]

The archbishop's message was clear (and he had probably been primed to say this by Sir Robert): the men should find a way of contributing to the war effort and find 'a place where you can prove to be good citizens'. All of the men would have welcomed such encouragement of activity beyond the camp, and for the war effort. However at that particular moment they could not do much more than help with the harvest and fill sandbags on Dover beach. Before they could take their anger to the enemy in a more direct manner, there was one further step to be taken. If these men were to be of greater use in war time, they had to be checked out; it was essential to ensure that they would contribute to the British war effort rather than that of the Germans.

Thus, in late September 1939, six senior lawyers proceeded to Sandwich to investigate the men's loyalty and decide, under the Aliens Act of 1919, whether they were 'friendly' or 'enemy aliens'. The lawyers were provided with special offices at the camp to undertake the interviews and they seemed very well informed about the *structure* of each of these men's previous lives. Fred Pelican wrote: 'I was most surprised, because they seemed to know more about me than I could have remembered, especially odd dates and odd times.'[7] In fact the men's files were lent to the tribunals by the camp management. But what these bare details did not speak of was the *quality* of their lives under the Third Reich. The Kitchener men understood that their loyalty to Britain was being investigated, and, as a consequence many of them told these lawyers, in graphic detail, the terrible ordeals to which they had been subject in their countries of origin. Day after day the men queued up to unburden themselves, many for the first time, to these representatives of the British state. They talked of torture, beatings, arbitrary death, starvation, untreated disease in the concentration camps; of the confiscation of their property, loss of employment, 'aryanisation' of their businesses. It was as if a dam had burst – these Germans and Austrians could not, would not, *ever again*, feel loyalty to Greater Germany.

The tribunal chairmen were horrified at what they heard. Moreover they recognised that the information, coming as it did at the start of a war with Germany, had a wider importance: it indicated the nature of the enemy. As a consequence, they took the decision to put their evidence on record in a letter to *The Times* newspaper. Taking up the whole of that newspaper's Letters page on 1 November 1939, a sub-editor gave their letter the large black headline: 'THE DARK AGE. GERMAN WITNESSES IN ENGLAND. A LETTER FROM THE TRIBUNALS.' Indeed, it was 'the Dark Age'. The letter outlined, in astonishing and horrible detail, the precise treatment so many of the Kitchener men had endured at the hands of the Nazis. (The full text of this letter is in the Appendix.) The details of torture, thus presented to a British public (and beyond, into the outer reaches of the British empire) must have proved a really shocking accompaniment to breakfast or the daily commute on the morning of 1 November. Perhaps even more striking, just at the moment right wing commentary was beginning to press for a negotiated peace with Germany, *The Times*, which had historically been a newspaper that supported the policy of appeasement, ran an editorial that day which used the details of the letter to liken Nazi Germany with 'a manifestation of anti-Christ' and to use that metaphor to justify war:

> To seek by all means to exorcize it, to try to restore civilized standards to the individual nation as to the international life of Europe, is in the fullest sense of the word a crusade, and one which is worthy of the united efforts of France, Great Britain, and all the nations of the British Commonwealth who have set out to defeat Nazism. This war has been described by an American publicist as a civil war to bring Germany back into Western civilization; and the definition is apt.[8]

It is possible that some of the Kitchener men were aware of the publicity their ordeals had received, and that in itself might have given them some satisfaction. But far more important to them was the fact that all but two of the approximately 3,500 men who had been interviewed by the tribunals were found to be 'friendly aliens' (and later of the two 'enemy aliens', one was found to be perfectly safe). The phrase 'A victim of Nazi oppression' was duly stamped in their passports, and as one of the refugees wrote in the *Kitchener Camp Review*, 'this country will not regret having treated us as the human beings and sons of God we are – brethren to any people of the same mind ...'[9]

The Kitchener men were now, officially, 'friendly' and despite still being 'aliens', they were also a *resource*. A large group of men, with craft skills, the German language, a culture of co-operation inculcated by months of living together in an ex-military camp located close to Continental Europe, could be very useful in wartime Britain. Someone sensible in the War Office clearly realised this; within weeks, Gerald Rufus Isaacs, the 2nd Marquess of Reading, son of a Viceroy of India and himself a Jew, arrived at Kitchener to start the process of enlisting these one-time Germans and Austrians into the British Army.

What Lord Reading had to say to the Kitchener Camp men when he arrived is not on record, but we know his impact was considerable. The men flocked to register their interest in enlisting (Norman later claimed 2,000 had done so[10]). The single men and other men who knew their families were safely away from Germany were delighted that they were invited to wear a British Army uniform and participate in a project – winning the war – extremely close to their hearts. In addition, once they were finally enlisted they would earn the same 14*s* a week that every British Army private earned – true *richesse* compared to the 6*d* a week pocket money they had had to rely on so far. Moreover, before the formal enlistment process began, a group of younger men were asked to man a special listening post that had been established at the camp and record the radio messages of German ships in the English Channel and the North Sea. This was thrilling – quite suddenly they were spies – and it was of vital importance at a stage in the war when most of the action was still at sea rather than on land.[11]

However, just as there was a wave of enthusiasm for joining the war effort so there was also a strong undertow of reluctance. The married men whose wives were still in Germany were deeply anxious that the Nazis would discover that they were fighting for the British and take revenge on their families. This may have been paranoia, but it also reflected the men's understanding, based on experience, of the extraordinarily long arm of the Third Reich. Even in the case of men who had left the Jewish religion and eschewed their local Jewish community, the Gestapo had nevertheless been able to find them and persecute them. Moreover, they had been told when they left the concentration camps, as the letter to *The Times* indicates, 'We have our spies everywhere'[12] and they clearly assumed, however much the Tribunals had indicated otherwise, that there were Nazi agents amongst the Kitchener men.

The pain of separation, which had been bad enough before the war, now became unbearable. The day after war broke out married men began to write to Norman begging for help to get their wives and children into Britain. At first he replied with kindness and sympathy but also indicating that there was nothing he could do: 'At the present all communication between this country and Germany, whether direct or indirect is cut off. You must all be patient for a time, and trust in God.'[13] The use of the word 'patient' must have persuaded the men that, given time, they would eventually get their families out. To that end, Dr Plaut, in charge of the Social Welfare Department at the camp, began the onerous and depressing task of drawing up a list of all the children that the men had left behind. It was very long – there were 582 children in total – each one listed by their full name, their date of birth and their full address in Greater Germany and often with extra details of, for example, a potential guarantor in Britain. This was sent to Norman on 4 October. There is nothing in his papers to indicate what he did with it other than filing it away. Perhaps he thought there would come a time when he could send it to the Home Office but that the time was not yet ripe.[14]

When enlistment became a possibility the married men began to wonder if there might be a *quid pro quo*: if they joined up, then maybe the government would let their families enter the country? A typical letter, sent to Norman in November, said:

> I have been summoned to join the Pioneer-Corps, which is to be formed in this camp, and I am faced with the necessity wether [*sic*] I am to join or not. My wife is still in Germany and she is likely to be exposed to great oppressions, if the German authorities, anyhow, should learn I am joining the English army. First of all, I, therefore, have to care for my wife and to rescue her from Nazi oppression. Of course, I will play my part in this struggle for justice and freedom and do my duty to England. I, however, beg to ask you urgently to let me know whether my wife would be allowed to come to England in case of my joining the army.[15]

Norman did not reply directly to this letter, but he did ask Jonas May, who continued for the moment to be camp director, to see the man and explain the situation: 'It is no good writing back to him, but would you see him and make the position clear. It is impossible, as you know, to bring out the wives.'[16]

It is not surprising that Norman passed the buck back to Jonas. He was becoming increasingly irritated by the despair of these men, about which he could do nothing. He had written to Jonas two weeks earlier to complain about the number of men coming to see him personally in his London office:

> I have had to-day nearly half a score of men from the Camp who came to see me about the question of getting their wives and children out of Germany or neutral countries, or about their emigration and that of their wives who are still in Germany. It is not that I am tired of helping, I am tired of telling people that I cannot help, and it is a waste of their money and my time that they come here without the previous consultation with the Camp staff.[17]

Norman did still have a smidgeon of hope that wives who had managed to get to 'neutral' countries such as Holland, Belgium, the Baltic states, might get permission to come to Britain and he continued to maintain that hope into early 1940. But he too was not averse to using the issue as a lever, in this case to get the men to enlist in the Pioneer Corps. He told an officer at the High Commission to Refugees to advise a Kitchener man that: 'So far from prejudicing [his wife's] chances by joining up before she is in England, he would certainly increase those chances, and he may be sure that the officers of the PO will do everything possible to enable men in the Corps to bring over their women.' He also knew that he was flying a kite, ending his letter with 'I appreciate that it may not be possible to get the concession at once.'[18] Eventually he gave up, writing in May 1940 to a sympathetic anti-Fascist Conservative MP who was pursuing a case:

> It is true that, in a number of cases of men who had been in our Refugee Camp at Richborough and joined the Corps, I made application to the Home Office for a permit for their wives in neutral countries to come to England. In recent months the Home Office has not been willing to grant any permits. You may have more weight, particularly if the woman was in the neutral country before the outbreak of the war.[19]

Norman was a kind man and had been an influential man but now that war had started the Home Office had become completely deaf to his entreaties.

The men in the camp grew increasingly disillusioned and intractable; their initial enthusiasm to enlist began to evaporate. They presumably felt that a government that refused to allow their families into the country, even when they were living in so-called 'neutral' countries, did not warrant their commitment to war service. However, the timing of their increasing reluctance to move into employment by the British Army came at a particularly awkward moment: the London Fund which had been supporting them had, by the end of 1939, run out of money. Despite the British government offering some funding on a pound for pound basis to support indigent refugees (this was the first time the British government had offered money to directly fund refugee rescue and support), the Fund was facing a deficit of £126,000 by early January 1940.[20] This was the equivalent of £3.6 million at 2005 prices.[21] It was only an advance of £25,000 (£718,000 at today's prices), on a loan basis, from the Executive Chair, Anthony de Rothschild, that was to keep them going for the last two weeks of December 1939.[22]

The Kitchener Camp was in itself a large call on their diminishing funds. A three-month estimate at the 28 December meeting of the Executive put the total expenditure on the camp at £36,000 (just over £1 million at today's prices) of which the British government would pay half. The only way out of this looming deficit was if the refugees were to enlist. The men would thence become the responsibility of the British Army, which would not only pay them a wage, but would also maintain them. There was a compelling logic to the Executive's position, but the problem was that for the logic to work, these anxious and traumatised men had to volunteer. A leaflet was produced urging refugees to volunteer for the Auxiliary Military Pioneer Corps. Entitled 'The Salvation of the World Lies with the Victory of Democracy: What YOU can do to help' the leaflet promoted the idea of debt repayment:

> And now, the opportunity has arrived for all Refugees to repay the debt they owe to England, and the way they can do it is by standing shoulder to shoulder with their English brothers, whether Jewish or Christian, to take up the work whatever it may be and to share the responsibility and the burden which has been thrust upon this country…
> THERE IS NO CONSCRIPTION
> ALL JOIN UP AS VOLUNTEERS
> We have no doubt as to what your decision will be, on the contrary, we know.
> YOU WILL DO YOUR DUTY![23]

The leaflet may have had some impact, but it seems more likely that it fell on deaf ears. There were men at the camp who felt they had reasons *not* to be grateful: too little had been done to help their families, the Kitchener Camp was confining and uncomfortable, they were bored and deeply unhappy. Six of the men, claiming to represent all the men who had not so far enlisted because they were close to getting their visas for the USA, wrote to Norman on 5 December pleading with him to arrange for their 'shiptickets' to the United States to be paid for. Their poignant letter demonstrates how they felt themselves psychologically unfit for national service, and desperate for 'a bit of private life' that would not be available to them if they were to become soldiers:

> One could not say anything against the idea of Refugees joining [up]. If they were normal men if they had passed years of normal life like every free citizen, then I expect they would be only too glad to do their duty but these men will not join the Auxiliary Corps nor any other military force because they are psychically [*sic*] unable to do so. These are men who suffered very very much in Germany, they passed the hell of Germany, they are broken men who endured years of physical and psychical [*sic*] terror and persecutions, who were tortured in German Concentration Camps for months and years, whose homes are torn up, whose families are dispersed all over the world, they have nothing in their heart but one ardent desire. Once again to live like a normal man, to have a

home, to be united with their families, once again to live their bit of private life, free from camping like gipsies and all these things. Of course this Camp saved them from danger and persecution, brought them out of hell, but evidently it did not, better could not consider these feelings and the men are and remain downhearted people with broken hearts and deranged minds. After several months of life in Camp they feel it torment to be forced to be together with so many others, seldom they can find a possibility to be alone with their thoughts and even during the night when they should recover in sleep they turn sleepless from one side to the other full of thoughs [sic], grievances and troubles about their beloved whom they left in the hell of Germany, full of heavy troubles about their future, and all the night whether they like it or not they are forced to hear the sounds produced by their colleagues who sleep with just the same uneasiness as they do.

From these psichological [sic] facts you will certainly understand that they although thankful for all what kind people have done for them cannot overcome the overwhelming desire for a bit of private life. Sooner or later they will go mad if the Camplife does not end or there is no hope that it does. Psychologicaly [sic] they are not fit to be soldiers because to-day they cannot be considered as normal men. And all those who were able to overcome all difficulties have joined already. It would be the best thing to help them as soon as possible, to send them away if they have proceeded so far, to enable them to build up a new life before it is too late, before the passing time makes them unable for that they become useless members of the human Community and a public charge forever …[24]

The case for funding the 'shiptickets' for the approximately 200 men with visas for the United States, at £40 a head, was rejected at the executive meeting of the London Fund on 14 December[25] (although they did later try to persuade the American Consulate to extend the period of their visas[26]). The London Fund felt the men were being obstinate, ungrateful and unwilling to translate themselves from refugee to soldier. As a consequence, the language of the Executive of the Fund began to slip into critique – for example, the refugees were minuted as 'recalcitrant' at a meeting on 21 December.[27] Both sides in the argument had right on their side: the men had always expected to leave Britain eventually – indeed that had been a condition of their entry into the UK in the first place – and now it seemed that, because no one would pay their fares, they were unable to do so. The only other opportunity open to them was to become British soldiers, which for many and arguable reasons they felt they could not do. The London Fund was desperate to get them off their 'books' but unable to find the money to pay for them to emigrate.

Explosions of frustration began to erupt, sometimes reaching into the public domain. A Mrs Sugden from Broadstairs had offered to house and support a

Kitchener Camp man on a permanent basis, but this was theoretically contingent on permission from the Home Office (but actually from the camp management). She had submitted her forms, outlining her income and her willingness, in the first week in November 1939 and then heard nothing. Six weeks later, and very close to Christmas, she wrote to Norman on 13 December asking if he could expedite matters. In the course of her letter, she said she was 'anxious that Mr Levin should leave this cold and comfortless camp and spend Xmas in comfort after having spent the last *three* Xmas's in concentration camp.' She also enclosed 'a paper that was handed to the refugees today. You can see that conditions are not too satisfactory there and the committee will be glad to release Mr Levin.'

For all this trouble, Mrs Sugden received an absolutely blistering reply, not, it has to be said from Norman himself, but from his assistant Chaim Raphael:

> I am returning the copy of the message from Sir Robert Waley Cohen which I think Mr Levin should keep with him.[28] The purpose in issuing this message was to remind men of the humanitarian reasons which prompted the organization to establish the Camp and of the very great financial difficulties that we are now faced with. I must add, and this is purely a personal comment, that when I hear complaints, either directly or indirectly from the men about what you call 'this cold and comfortless Camp', I feel that the men are not making the same effort to understand our present difficulties as this Committee made to understand theirs.[29]

These Kitchener men and the various grandees of Anglo–Jewry who looked after them had seriously fallen out with each other. Finance was always going to be the London Fund's Achilles' heel; war with Germany was always going to be a problem for the Kitchener men and for some it had become the catalyst for profound despair.

Notes

1. Phineas May diary, entries for 23–30 August, passim.
2. Mr H.L. Oates, Aliens Section, Home Office, to Norman Bentwich, 14 September 1939, BWP, File P174/13b.
3. Norman Bentwich to Mr H.L. Oates, 18 September 1939, BWP, ibid.
4. Robert Fraser, personal communication via email. His mother arrived at Kitchener on 5 September 1939.
5. Email from Robert Fraser to the author.
6. *Kitchener Camp Review*, No. 8, October 1939. The text of the article is copied entirely from the report in the *East Kent Times*.

7.   Fred Pelican, op. cit., p. 42.
8.   'The Nazi Blot on Europe', editorial in *The Times*, 1 November 1939.
9.   '"You are a Friend …"The Tribunals', by Dr A.W.W., *Kitchener Camp Review*, No. 9, November 1939.
10. 'The position is that some 2000 men of the Camp volunteered for the Pioneer Corps when the first appeal was made …', Norman Bentwich to Mr G.G. Kullman of the High Commissioner for Refugees office, 1 February 1940, BWP, File P174/20b.
11. Interview with Hans Jackson, author's notes. Hans Jackson was an accomplished artist and years later he produced many pictures of his war experiences, including his life and work in the Kitchener Camp.
12. See Appendix.
13. Norman Bentwich to Mr Felsner of the Kitchener Camp, 6 September 1939, BWP, File P174/13a.
14. Dr Plaut, with enclosures, to Norman Bentwich, 4 October 1939, BWP, P174/15a.
15. Kurt Fischer, Kitchener Camp, to Norman Bentwich, 27 November 1939, BWP, File P174/13a.
16. Norman Bentwich to Jonas May, 28 November 1939, BWP, File P174/15c.
17. Norman Bentwich to Jonas May, 13 November 1939, BWP, File P174/15c.
18. Norman Bentwich to Mr G.G. Kullman, High Commission for Refugees, 1 February 1940, BWP, File P174/20b.
19. Norman Bentwich to Commander O. Locker-Lampson MP, 16 May 1940, BWP, File P174/20b.
20. Minutes of the meeting of the Executive of the Central Council for Jewish Refugees, 14 December 1939, CBF Archives, 2/425–428.
21. The National Archives currency converter.
22. Ibid. 'The Chairman said he felt we should have to make arrangements to tide over the next fourteen days until we got the Government proposals in shape and that he and his brother would be prepared to make an advance of £25,000 to carry on …'
23. CBF Archives, 1/13.
24. Letter from six Kitchener Camp men, possibly addressed to Robert Waley Cohen with a copy to Norman Bentwich, 5 December 1939, BWP, File P174/12d.
25. Minutes of the meeting of the Executive of the Central Council for Jewish Refugees, 14 December 1939, CBF Archives, 2/428.
26. Minutes of the meeting of the Executive of the Central Council for Jewish Refugees, 28 December 1939, CBF Archives, 2/436.

27. 'Mrs Sieff also referred to the difficulties which were being encountered by the Agricultural Committee in dealing with recalcitrant refugees', Minutes of the meeting of the Executive of the Central Council for Jewish Refugees, 21 December 1939, CBF Archives, 2/430.
28. This was presumably a note, written by Robert Waley Cohen, and distributed to all the men at the Kitchener Camp who had not so far enlisted. It seems to have outlined the financial difficulties facing the London Fund. I have not found this note in the archives. That does not mean it is not there.
29. Chaim Raphael (for Professor Norman Bentwich) to Mrs H.M. Sugden of Broadstairs, 19 December 1939, BWP, P174/14c.

13

SAME DIFFERENCE: MILITARY SERVICE, INTERNMENT AND CLOSURE

In November and December 1939 general morale at the camp plummeted. Many of those who had initially taken up the offer of military service with enthusiasm grew increasingly anxious about that commitment and fed up with having to fill sandbags all day.[1] Moreover, many of them felt trapped. The possibility of further emigration to other parts of the world had been largely halted by the outbreak of war and, even if there had been ships that would take them, the London Fund seemed unable to fund their fares.

They were not only trapped in Britain. They also seemed to be trapped at Kitchener. Some of the men clearly assumed that once they had been found by the tribunals to be 'friendly' that they could leave the camp permanently and, given that by November 1939 it must have seemed that the whole country was on the move, this was not an unreasonable assumption. But the Kitchener Camp Committee was determined that the men should not leave the camp. At the end of October, Robert Waley Cohen wrote to Jonas May that:

> I feel that we should not give leave too lavishly now. The 150 people whom you sent up on leave created quite a little ripple at Bloomsbury House. Some of them applied for maintenance grants which were of course refused and others were heard to be boasting that they had now left the Camp and were never going back to it [...] I should be grateful if you would let me know how many have had leave since the Tribunals started work and how many returned at their due date.[2]

Quite why the committee was so determined to keep the men at Kitchener is not clear. Perhaps it was the age-old worry about the image of Jewry, particularly indigent Jewry who might become a 'public charge', and the possibility of provoking anti-Semitism as a consequence. The London Fund certainly wanted to avoid dependence on public funds, insisting that individuals who wanted to help men who wished to leave Kitchener permanently sign a so-called 'Form of Guarantee' which, in block capitals, contained the sweeping words: '[I] hereby unconditionally guarantee to hold myself responsible for his maintenance and upkeep during such time as he may be allowed to reside in this country.'[3] But the curious thing is that at this particular juncture it is likely that the men would actually have been able to support themselves. The national embargo on all refugees taking up paid work had been dropped in November 1939[4] and, given the introduction of national call-up to the armed services at the beginning of September 1939, jobs were increasingly available. Fear of anti-Semitism arising out of the men 'taking British' jobs from British workers had a decreasing basis in reality. A commentator at the time suggested that from November 1939 onwards, 2,000–3,000 refugees a month were obtaining paid employment.[5] There does not seem to have been a logic to the Waley Cohen position, apart from his wish that somehow or other the presence of all the Kitchener men in a camp that was about to turn into a military camp would aid their recruitment into the British Army: 'It will enable us to slide gradually from the civil to the military basis with the utmost convenience and goodwill.'[6] There was a sense in which the grandees of Anglo–Jewry saw themselves so much as part of the British Establishment that they were incapable of distinguishing between themselves and government. Moreover they, and particularly Robert Waley Cohen who so loved to be the boss, wanted to remain in control of their rescue operation and not let the men disperse to a place beyond their reach.

These months of containment and idleness immediately preceding Christmas 1939 were deeply miserable at Kitchener; they possibly had a profound impact on how Kitchener has, in more recent years, come to be confused with an internment camp. However, in January 1940 the culture of the camp changed profoundly when, under the overall command of Lord Reading, most of the camp was transformed into a Pioneer Corps Training Centre and thus became, at least partly, a British Army camp. Although there had been a falling away in the numbers of men who had been willing to enlist when first approached, nevertheless over 1,500 of the Kitchener men immediately confirmed their commitment to join up. Some failed the medical, but those deemed fit enough were rapidly recruited and most of the camp moved on to a military footing.

For those many hundreds who had enlisted, days that had previously been occupied with sandbag filling and thoughts of family still in Greater Germany now became occupied by different routines: square bashing and kit polishing. The camp began to reverberate to the sound of sergeant majors shouting orders and the tramp of marching feet. The men changed into the khaki uniforms of the British Army, although the camp tailors were kept busy altering the uniforms that were provided – the caps were too small![7]

There was a very serious purpose to all this activity and change, and it was a relief to have something 'real' to do. Six Pioneer Corps companies of 300 men apiece were established at Kitchener between January and May 1940. All the officers were British, veterans of the First World War, and many of them older than the general run of officers in the current British Army. They were astonished to find themselves commanding Germans. Lord Reading reported that 'the environment was strange and might well have proved uncongenial [...] the officers adapted themselves with energy and goodwill to the novel atmosphere and developed a genuine pride in, and affection for, their men'.[8] No doubt this goodwill was helped by their discovery of such a curious collection of British patriots. One of the first officers to arrive at Kitchener, a Lieutenant Gordon-Smith, remembered going round the huts on his first night and, to his delight, hearing the men 'singing in their, then, broken English':

> There vill always be an England,
> And England shall be free;
> If England means as much to you
> As England means to me.[9]

Perhaps Phineas, who, along with Jonas, had also joined the Pioneer Corps had been leading yet another sing-song when Lieutenant Gordon-Smith passed by.

Most of these new and rather strange British soldiers were already at Kitchener as a result of their rescue directly to the camp, but there were other 'aliens' who had been living elsewhere in Britain, and who, on enlistment, were sent by the army to be trained there. Not all these newcomers were Jews or refugees. Some of them, like Nicolai Polakovs, who was a famous Bertram Mills Circus performer known as 'Coco the Clown', were simply foreigners living in Britain who had responded to the call to war.[10] On arrival at Kitchener Coco seems to have had something of a run in with Phineas, who, despite – to Coco's chagrin – claiming that he had never heard of him, put him in overall charge of the camp theatre from day one. In vain Coco protested: 'Sir, I have been a circus proprietor, a clown, a conjurer. I was even buried alive for twelve minutes [...] [I] have joined the Army not to look after the theatre but to be a soldier.' But Phineas prevailed, Coco agreed to run the theatre (he was after all under orders to do so), and within a very short time, after a number of hugely successful shows (according to Coco), he was promoted to lance corporal by a grateful commanding officer: 'I walked out of the office with the feeling I wasn't just a lance-corporal but a general, and I was very proud of myself. Soon afterwards I was promoted to full corporal.'[11]

One strange aspect of Coco's memoirs (he published two, one in 1941[12] and the other in 1950) is that nowhere does he mention that almost all his fellow soldiers at the Kitchener Camp were German–Jewish refugees. He must have noticed: apart from anything else, they all had foreign-sounding names, and the huge majority had names that were instantly recognisable as German or of German–Jewish origins. The army certainly noticed and took action. If the Kitchener men were going to be part of the British Army it would be in their interest, if captured, not to be recognised as one-time German nationals; with the support of their officers, most of them anglicised their surnames as soon as they joined up. Helmut Rosettenstein became Harry Rossney, Fred Pelikan changed to Fred Pelican, descendants of a Sandwich family who became friendly with one Kitchener Camp man have told me that he changed his name to 'King' after 'King and Country'.[13] In the list of 'aliases' of Pioneer Corps men at the end of a book on the Pioneer Corps by Peter Leighton-Langer (himself a German refugee and one-time Pioneer Corps soldier) many of the new names reflected the meaning of the old ones – a Gruenbaum became Greenwood for example – and sometimes there was a certain social meaning embedded in the change – a Baron Heinrich Berger Waldenegg became the equally upper class sounding 'Henry Oswald Burgleigh'.[14]

Slowly but surely these Kitchener men were sloughing off their old identities and taking on a new one. Fred Pelican remembered how proud he felt:

> I was very proud of myself, very excited and ready to submit to whatever was required of me. I reflected upon the transformation that had taken place in a comparatively short time. Here was I, a fully-clad soldier in the British Army, while six months ago my young life had been in jeopardy in a German concentration camp – a remarkable transformation![15]

However there was still some hesitation on the part of the authorities; in their minds, the difference between these men and the ordinary British soldier could not be so easily expunged by a change of name and khaki uniform. For example, the authorities were sensitive to the fact that, by dint of their biographies, these men were in a rather special position. Every new recruit had to sign a statement declaring that:

I hereby certify that I understand the risks, which have been fully explained to me, to which I, and my relatives, may be exposed by my employment in the British Army outside the United Kingdom. Notwithstanding this I certify that I am willing to be employed in any theatre of war.[16]

To sign this statement would have been hard, because it was an acknowledgement of the risk their enlistment and the possibility of their capture by Germans entailed for the families they had left behind. That so many did sign was an indication of their very great willingness to take revenge on the Third Reich. However, paradoxically, it was a defining feature of the Pioneer Corps that the men were not equipped with arms of any kind. Ultimately the authorities did not completely trust these men to kill Germans. Instead, the role of the Pioneer Corps was to support a fighting force, not to participate in it, and to that end, they built defences, dug trenches, assisted with transport – all the dogsbody jobs necessary when armies are on the move and battles are planned and implemented.

This did not mean that they were not called upon to be brave. They were and that early on in the war. Of the six companies formed at Kitchener between January and May 1940, five went with the British Expeditionary Force to France (the third company formed at Kitchener, known as the 77th, did not go because of, ironically, an outbreak of German measles[17]). Fred Pelican was in one of the two companies that went to France in January and which established a camp in western France near the city of Rennes. There all five companies eventually settled into a routine of road building, and working in an ordnance depot loading lorries with armaments for the front. The work was very hard, but the French were friendly and there was plenty to do in Rennes including, according to Fred, 'a rather posh brothel'. But this relatively easy existence was brought to an end in May 1940 when the German Army invaded France through Belgium. French defences crumbled and the British Expeditionary Force began a hasty evacuation from Continental Europe.

The chaos of the withdrawal of British forces from France, the courage of the troops, and the extraordinary support of the 'little ships' that crossed the Channel to bring approximately 300,000 soldiers home, have become legendary. The 'Dunkirk spirit' has become part of Britain's sense of itself and these Kitchener men were part of it. The Pioneer Corps companies from the Kitchener Camp were all based well south of the French port of Dunkirk and their much nearer possible evacuation points were the ports of St Malo and Le Havre. Judging by the accounts of the men who were involved in these evacuations further south, they were just as chaotic, improvised and stoical as the one from Dunkirk. They were also later than Dunkirk and the Kitchener men could hear and even, according to one account, see the German advance through northern France.[18] Orders kept changing: at one moment they were in Le Havre and Harfleur waiting for ships to take them to England, at another they were sent back to near Rennes to build a huge bomb-proof army headquarters, which one ex-Pioneer Corps man says they called the 'officers' funkhole'.[19] Fred Pelican remembers that during this period of chaos the officers disappeared for at least a day: 'it seemed as if we were part and parcel of the forgotten brigade'.[20] But the officers had vanished in order to arrange transport to an evacuation point and weapons for the men: 'one rifle each and five rounds of ammunition for every two men'. This was not going to go very far, but at least one man, Heinz Schmoll, 'felt like a real soldier carrying a rifle on the alert'.[21]

However, they were not left long in charge of a weapon. Even before they were finally embarked on an evacuation ship, many of the men were ordered to disarm, much to their fury. Heinz Schmoll described signs of incipient mutiny:

We were told to hand in our rifles and there were angry scenes as the men threw their rifles on a heap. I was extremely upset to be disarmed, since my reason for joining the British Army had been to kill Nazis. I put in an application to my Commanding Officer to be transferred to an internment camp. This unprecedented application was not granted. Perhaps just as well.[22]

Lord Reading remembered a similar type of event, but this time back in England:

On the evacuation of the BEF from France, the five Companies from the Centre which had gone overseas from Sandwich came temporarily back to Westward Ho. Having gone out unarmed, they arrived back armed, every man with a weapon, many with two; and it was a bitter disappointment to them to be required on arrival to hand them back.[23]

These men had already taken a long and arduous journey towards a total shift in identity and loyalty. Not only had they, for the three or four months they were in France, made a considerable logistical contribution to the war effort, many of them had also, on their cross Channel return to England, been subjected to aerial bombardment from which they were lucky to escape. Despite this, the removal of their weapons was an indicator of a deep and continuing mistrust on the part of the British authorities and understandably many men thought it completely and demonstrably unjustified. Trust, as the war progressed and the Battle of Britain began, was to become a major issue, not just for the Pioneer Corps men but also for all other Jewish refugees.

The Kitchener men who had been in France never returned to Kitchener; their future service in the Pioneer Corps, in the early years of the war, was to be based in the west of England, in Devon, particularly in camps at Westward Ho!, Ilfracombe and Weymouth.[24] However the Kitchener Camp itself, constituted both as a refugee camp and as a military camp for 'friendly aliens', continued into the first half of 1940. Some of those who stayed in Sandwich were soldiers: those from the company that had been left behind and those who were still needed at Kitchener. Harry Rossney, for example, who had enlisted in January 1940, was kept there to help with the reorganisation into a fully fledged military camp: his particular skill in sign writing was needed for the new militarised signs. But the bulk of the men who stayed behind were those who, for different reasons, had not joined up. Some were prevented from doing so: there were still some very young men in the camp and if they were below the age of 20 they were simply too young to enlist. Hans Jackson was such a youngster and he was delighted to be kept occupied at the radio 'listening post', where he and his young companions could contribute to the war effort by listening to and translating messages sent between German ships. The doctors and dentists in the camp, of whom there were about seventy, were told not to enlist in the Pioneer Corps – their skills would be more appropriately deployed in the Royal Army Medical Corps. There were also a large number of men who were keen to enlist but, like Philip Franks, failed the medical – often because they had been so mistreated in the concentration camps.

The remainder of the Kitchener men who did not enlist were those who thought, either that in so doing they would lose the opportunity of emigrating, particularly to the USA or Palestine, or that if they did so their families in Greater Germany would be put at special risk. There were about 700 men who had 'visas for early emigration to America' who had not joined up.[25] In total it seems that there were about 1,200 Kitchener men who, for one reason or another, had neither enlisted nor left the camp.[26] They were not, however, at a loose end. Their tasks now were entirely orientated towards servicing the military side of the camp, in particular the provisioning of the Pioneer Corps men.[27] Joint dining facilities between the 'military' and the 'civilian' side remained in place and joint entertainment, still overseen by Phineas but with Coco as theatre manager and star performer, continued. Soldiers and civilians were probably by December living in separate parts of Kitchener but for most purposes, apart from square bashing, the camp was still operating as a single entity.

A couple of months earlier, during the period of October through to November 1939, someone who was familiar to many of the men but new to the Kitchener Camp had first put in an appearance. Julian Layton, whom we last encountered in this story in the Rothschild Palace in Vienna, where he assisted

Dr Benjamin Murmelstein at the IK with the selection of men for Kitchener and fended off the depredations of Adolf Eichmann, was in Sandwich from mid-October 1939 onwards.[28] Unknown to him, Layton's life was about to become even more entwined with the fate of the Kitchener men, and of other Jewish refugees, than it had been when he was active in Berlin and Vienna. That autumn and into the first half of 1940 he stayed at the Bell Hotel, where one of his fellow guests was Lord Reading. Given the financial difficulties of the London Fund it is likely that Layton, a wealthy and generous man, probably financed his early stay there himself and had initially volunteered his services towards the pastoral care of the men, many of whom he already knew from Vienna.[29] However, judging by the letters that Norman Bentwich and his assistant Chaim Raphael increasingly sent him from December 1939 onwards, Layton had by December acquired an official and paid post at Kitchener. But, Layton's most important role vis-à-vis the camp began in January 1940 when he was appointed director of the civilian side of the Kitchener Camp for a period of three months, until the end of March 1940. He replaced Jonas, who had now taken up full military duties on the military side of Kitchener.

Everybody seemed to like and respect Julian Layton. Chaim Raphael, who had been so rude to Mrs Sugden of Broadstairs when she wrote about getting a Mr Levin out of the camp in time for Christmas, wrote to him in a lighthearted way – a sign of a relaxed relationship which had never characterised letters to or from Norman Bentwich. For example, at the end of a long letter to Julian about administrative matters concerning particular Kitchener men, Chaim Raphael cracked a joke:

> *Chaim Raphael:* serious complaint from this man that he has not seen his wife and child for three days, and wants leave to visit them at Oxford. Has enough money for single journey. Told him to stay here until Bentwich's return tomorrow, and then to leave and never darken Woburn House's door again.[30]

Raphael must have felt that Julian Layton would be understanding of his desperation to get back to his family.

The rest of this letter from Raphael to Layton, sent very shortly before Christmas 1939–40, also indicates the real bitterness that had crept into relations between the camp management and the Kitchener men by that time, and how strict the camp regime remained about leave, even in the days just before Christmas:

Dear Layton,

Two cases of leave extension:

PM (603, Hut 8/2) is here, he says, on the recommendation of Dr Heller, to recover his health. His leave expires on Dec 19 and he is still not well. He is staying with friends [the address in Marylebone is given]. I take it under the new dispensation, you have no objection to such cases remaining in London longer. I told him therefore that I would write to ask and that he might stay until the 20th. If there was no extension granted by the Camp by that date, he had to return. Reply direct to him.

DM (2256, Hut 35/1) Staying c/o [address in Holloway given]. Wants extension of leave which expires on the 20th to look round for work and so on. Usual story. I told him that if he hears from you he may stay, otherwise return.

I was nearly stabbed in the back by one of your spiritual children who refused to take no for an answer when I refused to give him any money for fares in London or the return journey. He was one of those who wished he were back in the Concentration Camp, and I agreed with him.

EL (538) This was the man about whom I had a letter asking if, pending the approval of his guarantee, he might spend Xmas with would be guarantor Mrs H.S. [address in Broadstairs given]. I have told Mrs S that she will hear from you or the man. I suppose you will agree.[31]

The management, fearful of the men becoming a 'public charge', were trying to keep the men at the camp so that they could maintain them with the benefit of economies of scale, and, at the same time, obtain their services to support the military side of the camp; the men, on the other hand, wanted to taste the freedom of movement and association that they had thought 'England' represented. The somewhat dismissive tone of this letter was probably also reflected in personal interactions between camp managers and men. This was a potentially volatile situation and so it was to prove.

The men's anger ran deep. Its extent was revealed in a letter which was copied to Julian Layton, dated 1 April 1940.[32] In it the author, who was almost certainly Robert Waley Cohen, described a meeting that had taken place with Lord Reading concerning the difficulty they were having in finding a replacement for Julian who had, at the end of March 1940, formally come to the end of his contract to direct the civilian camp. The letter suggested that Julian had irreplaceable personal skills, demonstrated by the way he had resolved a set of fearsome problems that had arisen when he had taken over the civilian camp in January:

> The Chairman had reminded Lord Reading of the position of disgruntlement at the Camp at the time when Mr Layton took over, when it was clear that we were within measurable distance of a strike and trouble of a first-class order. Lord Reading agreed that it would be to nobody's interest to appoint an inferior man, and that it would be an undue risk to entrust such a man with the very difficult job of running the Kitchener Camp to meet the needs of the Army and the national interests generally.

Given the problems at the camp, it was imperative that Layton be retained in his civilian capacity. He was unique: single-handedly he had turned a very unhappy set of men around:

> The personal position of Mr Layton had been discussed, and Lord Reading had expressed his entire agreement with the Chairman's view of the exceptionally valuable services which Mr Layton had rendered in re-establishing the morale of the Camp and organising the civilian element in such a way as to give every satisfaction to the military units …

Mention of the possibility of a strike suggests a complete breakdown of relations between the 'civilians' at Kitchener and the camp management before Julian took over. It is not clear exactly what had occurred but Chaim Raphael's letter and its implicit lack of care indicates the kind of attitudes to the Kitchener men that had become, by the end of 1939, common currency amongst the Anglo–Jewish gentry who had rescued them. They were furious with these men for not enlisting, the men were furious with the management for not letting them leave the camp.

Julian Layton seems to have been altogether a more caring man. Perhaps, having come from his job in Vienna and, within the Rothschild Palace, having met many of the men's families, particularly their parents or wives, he had a special understanding of their anxieties. Perhaps he ran a more relaxed regime at the Camp, with more easily given leaves and dispensations. Whatever he did it appears to have worked: his services retained for the months of April and into May, the camp seems to have returned to something resembling an even keel.

Suddenly, however, and completely unexpectedly, a drastic change overtook the Kitchener Camp. At the end of May 1940, in the space of twenty-four hours, the entire set up, both the military camp and the civilian camp, was suddenly brought to a very abrupt end. The civilians and the soldiers were marched out of the camp, some to Sandwich railway station, others loaded on to lorries.

The huts were emptied, the dining room and kitchens abandoned, the gate closed for the last time. Only the luggage the men had brought with them from Berlin and Vienna was left behind. It was, and felt like, an expulsion. Sandwich people who remember this removal have told me how deeply shocking they found it – these were men whom they had got to know and like and had worked with, particularly building local coastal defences. What they found most shocking was that the Kitchener men, who until that moment had been deemed trustworthy and many of whom wore British Army uniform, were marched through Sandwich and transported away under armed guard. Relations had not only soured between the London Fund and the civilian Kitchener Camp men, but also between the British authorities and these 'refugees from Nazi oppression'.

It was the progress of the war that had triggered this expulsion. The sudden fall of France in May–June 1940 caused a major panic in Britain about foreigners, particularly people of German origin. France had fallen so rapidly and so unexpectedly that only one explanation took purchase – there had been in France a 'fifth column' of spies and saboteurs, Nazi infiltrators and informers, who had instigated the crumbling of the French army and the collapse of French national morale. With Britain now on the front line, xenophobia and anti-German sentiment took hold. Churchill, who had replaced Neville Chamberlain as prime minister on 10 May, is reputed to have said, in relation to Germans resident in Britain, 'collar the lot'. Irrespective of the findings of the tribunals that had sat in October and November 1939, this meant *all* aliens were suspect and were potential internees. From 12 May 1940 a wide coastal belt stretching from north-east Scotland to Dorset in south-west England was named as 'protected' and all alien men aged 16 to 60 living in this area became subject to special restrictions and many were subsequently interned. Sandwich, a coastal town with only 25 miles of sea between it and France, was deemed far too vulnerable to German invasion and these one-time Germans at the Kitchener Camp had to leave.

They were to depart in two different directions: the Pioneer Corps men were still regarded as trustworthy to some extent and retained their status as soldiers. They were taken to makeshift army camps well away from the south-east, and located in south-west England. Lord Reading, Jonas and Phineas went with them, and eventually they were joined there by the five Pioneer Corps companies evacuated from France in early June. The civilians, on the other hand, including the men too young to enlist who had been until the day of their removal manning the secret 'listening post' at Kitchener, the doctors and dentists who had been told they should wait until they could join the Royal Army Medical Corps, the men who had tried to enlist but failed the medical – all these men, and their civilian companions who were waiting to leave for the USA and Palestine, were sent northwards and to the other side of England to Liverpool. There they boarded ferries and crossed the Irish sea to the Isle of Man, where internment camps had been prepared in requisitioned hotels and houses. These two new locations for the Kitchener men, the one in Devon in the south-west, the other in the Irish Sea to the north-west of England, reflected different shades of mistrust – but it was mistrust all the same.

There was a caring aspect, though, to this sudden change. Julian Layton, almost certainly funded by the Home Office, accompanied the Kitchener men who were interned on the Isle of Man. It was as though Julian had become a shepherd, and the internees his flock. He settled into yet another hotel, this time in Ramsey, the main town on the Isle of Man. Norman Bentwich wrote to him there on 30 May, very soon after the Sandwich expulsion:

> My dear Julian,
>
> I reproach myself that I didn't get to the Camp before it moved. I have been back now a fortnight from Palestine, but have been terribly busy and am now engaged at the Ministry of Information with Wyndham Deedes in setting up these new emergency information centres. Had I known that the Camp was still there last week-end I could and should have come because I got as far as Miss Essinger's school.[33] It is good to know that you are with the men, and I say it in all simplicity and sincerity – that you are doing a better war job than most of us. I hope I may get the chance of coming to the Isle of Man and having a weekend with the men. Give them all my greeting and tell them to be of good cheer.[34]

Norman was still being polite about the men, and evidently did not share the general scorn that prevailed amongst his colleagues. Not so Lord Reading, who, in a handwritten letter to Julian, indicated how delighted he was to see the back of the Kitchener civilians:

> Dear Layton,
>
> Many thanks for your various letters, which I have not answered before as I did not know in what part of the UK you might be. I certainly do not envy you your present job and the move of that rabble from Sandwich must have taxed all your powers of organisation. I expect they are pretty difficult to handle in present conditions. It cannot be amusing to go from a concentration camp to an internment camp, especially after an interval of liberty. But, sorry though I am for them in many ways, I can't altogether forget that they had their chance

and rejected it. I told them quite plainly last November that, if they did not join the Army, they had only themselves to thank if later on spy-fever raged and they found themselves interned, but they would not believe me. The case of those going to the USA is harder. I wonder if they are going to let them go if they produce the necessary documents …[35]

Julian Layton was an empathetic man who swam against the tide of disillusionment and 'told you so' smugness that prevailed among his Anglo–Jewish colleagues. He was the good shepherd:

Dear Bentwich,

Many thanks for your letter of the 29th of May [*sic*]. I was very glad to read that you appreciate what I have been trying to do on the men's behalf.

It is not all so easy, and I have written long, detailed letters with various suggestions and recommendations to Sir Robert, and I have little doubt he will show them to you, should you so desire.

It is a great contrast here between Richborough, and I am very worried about the food question, as the rations are really on a very meagre side, although the food is not too bad. Whilst I have been buying a lot of bread, margarine, and fruit for the men on their account in the town it has been a little better, but I anticipate in a few day's time they will not have any money left to buy anything with and, unless I have succeeded in the meantime in obtaining various relaxations and concessions, I do not know how to solve this problem.

The kosher people, I must say, have been most reasonable and on their best behaviour but, except from the bread, margarine, and an occasional bit of fish, are not eating anything at all. Could you let me know with whom we ought to get in touch on this point?

I hope you will in the future find time and get the necessary permission to visit the Camp in due course, as our men are very depressed and worried in their new surroundings.

I hope to come to London in the course of the next week or so and have a Committee meeting to discuss the new situation which has arisen, as I do not think any of us think that our work of the Kitchener Camp has completely finished, because this is far from being the case.[36]

His efforts did not go unnoticed; scattered in his papers are a few rather touching 'thank you' notes from Kitchener men. One indicates that by the end of June Julian had somehow managed to get them some pocket money:

Mooragh Camp, Ramsey
24th June, 1940

Dear Mr Layton,

In the name of 41 internees of house 17 may I express our gratitude to you for what you have done for us: to-day we received one shilling pocket money each! It is not only the material help, it is perhaps even more your concern and sympathy for our position and feeling which gives us some hope and spiritual support. We know that you understand the position of our less fortunate fellow-internees, who are not registered with any Bloomsbury House committee.[37]

May I also thank you for the chalk?

Yours sincerely,

Dr Leo Liepmann

The writer of this letter may well have wanted chalk to write on a blackboard. As is now well known the Second World War internment camps, largely occupied by German Jews, became hives of intellectual, musical and educational activity. Some of the men made a positive experience of it all – for example the world-class Amadeus Quartet who first came together on the Isle of Man, or Kurt Schwitters, the artist, who is said to have so appreciated the time and space to paint that he didn't want to be released – but for others it was a massive waste of their time and talents.[38]

The story of the Kitchener Camp had come to an end. There were now two groups of men – of soldiers on the one hand, and internees on the other – who shared a common history and ethnicity and who had travelled together from Greater Germany and lived together as refugees for some time. All of them had been found to be, five months earlier, 'friendly aliens'. In those basic senses they were virtually indistinguishable. Yet, due to differences in age, fitness, levels of anxiety about their families, or because they expected shortly to go to the USA or Palestine, they were now categorised as totally different from each other. In one location, in the Irish Sea, they were behind barbed wire, in the other, in England's 'west country', they were subject to military discipline but otherwise free. It was a sad moment, and the policy of internment – a euphemism for incarceration without trial – both during the Second World War and much later continues, rightly, to be highly controversial. Internment of German–Jewish refugees in the Second World War was an expensive and undiscriminating policy, or, as one of the commentators of the time said, it was 'a lamentable story of muddle and stupidity'.[39]

Most of the Kitchener internees were released within a few months, many to take up their visas to the USA, others because they took the opportunity to join the Pioneer Corps – an opportunity that was made available to them again two months after their internment, in August 1940. If internees enlisted then they were immediately released. In that sense, internment for many of the Kitchener civilians was in reality a punishment for not being able to handle anxiety about loved ones still living in the enemy country.

And this is a reminder that in the midst of all this upset and change one very important aspect of the Kitchener Camp story has tended to disappear. The closure of the Kitchener Camp, the return of the Pioneer Corps companies from France, the internment of aliens – all these events were triggered by the sudden fall of France in May–June 1940. Once France had fallen, almost the whole of western Continental Europe, from the Arctic Circle to the southern coast of the Iberian peninsula, was either occupied by Fascists, or governed by overtly Fascist regimes, or with governments inclined towards Fascism. There was hardly anywhere for the families of these men to go – assuming the unlikely possibility they had the resources to escape from Germany. Only the yawning space on Germany's eastern borders, in particular Nazi-occupied Poland, stood waiting for them. For the husbands, fathers, brothers, sons, who had come to the Kitchener Camp with such hopes that they were the start of their family's migration to Britain, it was too late. Time had run out and the gates to freedom and safety had closed behind them.

Notes

1. Correspondence between Norman Bentwich and a Mr M.F. Moor, September 1939, BWP, File P174/15c.
2. Robert Waley Cohen to Jonas May, 26 October 1939, BWP, File P174/15c.
3. The Council for German Jewry, 'Form of Guarantee', BWP, File P174/14c.
4. F. Lafitte, *The Internment of Aliens*, Penguin Special, London, Allen Lane, 1940, p. 50.
5. Ibid.
6. Robert Waley Cohen to Jonas May, dated 26 October 1939, BWP, File P174/15c.
7. 'Appendix D. No.3 AMPC Training Centre' (Based on a note by Brigadier Lord Reading), in Norman Bentwich, *I Understand the Risks*, op. cit., p. 186.
8. Ibid., p. 184.
9. Norman Bentwich, *I Understand the Risks*, op. cit., p. 34.
10. Coco The Clown, *Behind my Greasepaint*, London, Hutchinson and Co, 1950.
11. Ibid., p. 48.

12. *Coco the Clown, His Life Story told by Himself*, London, Aldine Press. First edition published in 1941. In this book Coco calls himself Nicolai Poliakoff. His surname seems to have been as variable as that of the other Kitchener men.

13. Personal communication from Mrs Judy Pollard of Sandwich whose family have stayed in touch with the King family to the present day.

14. Peter Leighton Langer, *The King's Own Loyal Enemy Aliens: German and Austrian Refugees in Britain's Armed Forces, 1939–45*, London, Vallentine Mitchell, 2006.

15. Fred Pelican, op. cit., p. 43.

16. Norman Bentwich, *I Understand the Risks*, op. cit., pp. 56–57.

17. Norman Bentwich, *I Understand the Risks*, op. cit., p. 36.

18. Interview with Harry Brooks, 2008, author's notes.

19. Account of Heinz Schmoll, quoted in Leighton Langer, op. cit., pp. 14–17.

20. Fred Pelican, op. cit., p. 48.

21. Heinz Schmoll, op. cit.

22. Ibid.

23. Norman Bentwich, *I Understand the Risks*, op. cit., Appendix D, by Lord Reading, p. 187

24. For an account of their lives in Devon, see Helen P. Fry, *Jews in North Devon During the Second World War*, Devon, Halsgrove, 2005.

25. Letter to Alexander Maxwell, permanent under-secretary, Home Office, almost certainly from Robert Waley Cohen, dated 30 January 1940, JLP, 1205/2/10. The number of 700 is much higher than the number of 200 that was given to the Executive Committee of the London Fund in December 1939. There is no explanation of this discrepancy.

26. 'The number of men on the Camp roll today is 1572. Some are always on leave from time to time, and some are away on account of sickness. It is reckoned that usually about 1200 men sleep in the Camp. That is, of course, exclusive of the men who are enlisted in the AMPC.', Norman Bentwich to E.N. Cooper, Home Office, March 13 1940, BWP, File P174/20a.

27. 'the service for the Military who are billeted in the Camp is not separated from the general work – the principle of the Camp being that everybody in it shares in the work as a whole.', Ibid.

28. Bentwich wrote to Julian Layton at the Bell Hotel on 11 October 1939, BWP, File P174/15c.

29. It is unfortunate that the papers that I have found pertaining to Julian Layton are relatively thin (certainly compared to the Bentwich papers) (see the Julian Layton Papers, 1936–1993, Document collection 1205, Wiener Library) and that the interview of him, undertaken by the Imperial War Museum (Accession no 004382/03) while very interesting concentrates

more on his Australian experience. A full account of his efforts to rescue refugees in Vienna would have been invaluable for this story, as would his account of his activities in relation to the Kitchener men, which were considerable, post the outbreak of war.

30. Chaim Raphael, working from Woburn House, to Julian Layton at the Bell Hotel, 18 December 1939, BWP, File P174/15c.

31. Ibid.

32. Document 1205/2/14, JLP.

33. This was a school, founded in Germany by Miss Essinger and her sister, which, because it took large numbers of Jewish children, moved to England in 1933. It was located at Bunce Court, Faversham, about 20 miles from Sandwich. Having taken a large number of *Kindertransport* children in 1939, it too was very suddenly removed from its Kent location to North West England at about the same time as the Kitchener Camp was closed down.

34. Bentwich to Julian Layton, 30 May 1940, BWP, File P174/19.

35. Lord Reading to Julian Layton, written from Westward Ho! Camp, 1 June 1940, JLP, 1205/2/21.

36. BWP, File P174/20b.

37. This is presumably a reference to internees who had been living independently before their arrest and who had no support from the Jewish agencies. Evidently Julian Layton had also been working on their behalf.

38. Jennifer Taylor, 'Internment', Chapter 5, in Marian Malet and Anthony Grenville (eds), *Changing Countries, the experience and achievement of German-speaking exiles from Hitler in Britain from 1933 to today*, London, Libris, 2002.

39. Lafitte, op. cit., p. 9.

14

IDENTITY AND DEATH

The Kitchener Camp, as a rescue operation, was now over. But there were ripples beyond and down the generations – and a number of loose ends.

One immediate loose end was the luggage left behind when the men were expelled from Sandwich. This luggage was of a significance well beyond its intrinsic value. Mothers and wives would have packed family photos, farewell letters, mementos of children to help the men remember the past, linen, pots and pans, tools of their trades, religious artefacts, to help them prepare for the future. As the men were dispersed to Liverpool and Devon in May 1940, they would have been aware that not only were they now moving further away from their families, but they were also separating from the material objects which they had once shared with them and which embodied and represented a family life they were in immediate danger of losing.

Soon after the men left the Kitchener Camp, the luggage store was broken open and its contents plundered. The news of this vandalism must have taken a while to get through to the men, because it was not till late December 1940 that Meyer Stephany wrote to Alexander Maxwell, permanent under-secretary at the Home Office, to complain:

With the outbreak of war and the enlistment of about 1,000 men in the AMPC, the luggage belonging to those men who had enlisted was separated from the rest, and kept in a separate locked hut adjacent to the Haig Camp. In May 1940 the number whose baggage remained in the original store in the Kitchener Camp was roughly 1,000. On the 26 May orders were suddenly received for Kitchener Camp to be evacuated the same day and all of the [civilian] men in the Camp were transferred to the Isle of Man where they were interned [...] arrangements were made to leave the Camp, including the luggage huts, in the care of a civilian caretaker from Sandwich. Shortly afterwards the camp was forcibly occupied by the military. A number of sheds where some hundreds of bicycles belonging to the transmigrants had been stored were broken open, and the bicycles were broken up and destroyed. Further, the luggage hut was broken open, quantities of the luggage were stolen, and other packages were broken open and the contents pilfered. It is perhaps relevant to state that some men of the Forces were caught in the act of stealing the luggage. Efforts have been made by the Committee which was responsible for running the Camp to sort out the luggage which was left, and trace its rightful owners; but the condition in which the hut was found with cases and luggage broken open and articles of clothing strewn all over the place has rendered the task impossible ...[1]

Sir Alexander replied promptly. He would ask his colleagues to look into 'the question of compensation', although he imagined 'that it will be fraught with difficulties'.[2] It was not till two years later, in October 1942, that Norman Bentwich, writing to Ernest Joseph, noted with pleasure that 'I see that the question of the compensation for the lost baggage of the men in the Camp is coming before the Council this week. The Government are offering £9,000 which seems generous enough.'[3] It was generous – a Spitfire plane, so essential in the Battle of Britain, is said to have cost, in 1940 values, £5,000 so this was nearly the cost of two Spitfires. However, given the high sentimental value of the lost items it is likely the men found it inadequate. It is perhaps the men's descendants who have the most regret for the disappearance of the objects that came from that lost German–Jewish world.[4]

It was, not surprisingly, Norman Bentwich who continued to tie up the Kitchener loose ends – although Kitchener matters played a relatively minor role in his otherwise very busy life. Of an age where he might have been expected to take things a little easy, he was determined to contribute his considerable energy to the war effort. He lived in London during the Blitz, and he and his wife Helen became local ARP wardens and would sometimes stand together on the heights of Hampstead Heath (which he called the 'ceiling' of London) and watch that great city, particularly the East End, burn. Helen was a London County Councillor and for a while Norman worked for the Ministry of Information in the same building as her. They both became involved with the people who slept every night in the bomb shelters and Norman attempted, in his optimistic and enlightened way, to introduce improving lecture series for the many thousands of Londoners sheltering in the dimly lit passages and platforms of the London underground.[5] The Blitz brought strange encounters: in October 1940 he noted, in a letter to a one time Kitchener man now based in Devon, 'I am constantly coming in touch with the Kitchener Camp men, and one or two companies of the men in the Pioneer Corps are working in London as pioneers, clearing the debris from the air raids. I hope to meet them soon.'[6]

It was during this period of 1940/41 that the Kitchener men continued to write to Norman, almost always asking for help and usually he replied with thought and sensitivity. For example, he was particularly concerned with the family of the Blumenthals: the husband had been a Kitchener man and Norman and Helen had employed Mrs Blumenthal as their housekeeper in their little cottage in Sandwich. It seems Mr Blumenthal was in danger at one point of being sent to an internment camp in Australia, even though he and his wife had visas for the USA. Norman, who had got so cross with his colleagues when they put in special pleas for men during the lifetime of the camp, was certainly not averse to special pleading of his own when it came to this couple of whom he was clearly fond.[7] He was still worrying away about them in 1941, hoping that the Overseas Settlement Department at Bloomsbury House would manage to get them to the USA, although, as usual he was deeply torn, expressing his desire for *both* orderly queuing *and* special treatment: 'I know that cases have to be taken in due order. But I hope it may be possible for you to arrange their passage fairly soon.'[8] He also stayed in touch with Walter Marmorek, the camp architect, (aka 'Marmalade'), writing him a sad letter when the Kitchener Camp was itself bombed in July 1940:

> Mr Ernest Joseph was down at the Kitchener Camp last week, in connection with an enquiry about the stores taken over by the Army. He told me that the Camp had been bombed and the cinema building and the class rooms had both been partially wrecked. The whole place is empty except for the care-taker, and he was not hurt, although he was blown out of May's office. It is sad to think of all your beautiful work being destroyed by the Nazis. We haven't been to Sandwich since Easter. But the town, I am told, has not been damaged …[9]

Sandwich, that charming and intact medieval town, was in fact hardly damaged in the Second World War, although some bombs did fall; fortunately no one was killed.

Other members of the one-time camp management were further afield in the early part of the war, mostly in Devon. Jonas and Phineas were both now lieutenants in the Pioneer Corps, and Phineas was just as energetic in his pursuit of entertainments as he had been in Sandwich, organising concerts and theatrical performances for the people of Ilfracombe and its hinterland. Coco the Clown and his daughter Helen were the frequent stars of the theatrical performances, and the Pioneer Corps orchestra, conducted by a Sergeant Strietzel and led by a Private Aronowitz, performed music from the Viennese operettas. Once again the local populace flocked to these events – to such an extent that extra performances of the 1940 Christmas panto, Cinderella, had to be put on. The Ugly Sisters were a particular hit.[10] Phineas spent the latter part of the war in Egypt and from there he sent his new wife Vivienne a series of delightful cartoons, outlining the travails of daily life in wartime.[11] He also wrote her touching letters some of which were later published in a collection of 'Last Letters Home'.[12] War did not dull his capacity or his desire to communicate and entertain.

Also in Devon were other members of the camp staff, among them Walter Marmorek, the architect, and Poldi Kuh, who had brought the boys from the Berlin training camp to Kitchener in its early days. There they consolidated their friendship and Poldi, whose wife had come with him from Berlin, became a father for the first time.[13] These men were 'bedding down' into a new nationality, and founding families with a British identity. Many other men began a similar journey towards a stable Britishness. Harry Rossney worked, in the early 1940s, in the quartermaster's store of the Ilfracombe Pioneer Corps Training Camp. It was there that Harry began to encounter what he calls, in his memoir, 'English pioneers' of the same lowly rank as himself, and as he says, very directly, 'I took a liking to the English.' He also began to feel at ease with himself for the first time in his young life and he too began to develop a British identity:

> Ilfracombe was a turning point in my early life. The establishment of an identity had always been problematic right from the start, being the younger son of a mixed marriage landed me in no-man's-land. Neither a 'properly recognised Jew', nor a Christian. Six years of intensely pervasive Nazi propaganda added to a feeling of being different, unwanted and inferior. Being a foreign refugee in England made me grateful to be alive, but enhanced the clouds of doubt and insecurity which had hung above my head for so long. After Ilfracombe my attitude changed for the better.[14]

Fred Pelican returned from his military service in France to a Pioneer Corps camp in South Wales where, in the second half of 1940, he was engaged in forestry. Fred did not share Harry's worries about his identity and how the British saw him. He was very secure in his Jewish identity despite, and perhaps because of, his dreadful experiences in Dachau. As for the British, he had, while at Kitchener, encountered Mrs Joyce Piercy with whom he had developed a very comfortable friendship. In January 1941, when Fred was moved to London to help clean up after the nightly bombing raids, he discovered life in a diverse capital city; he took to going to Blooms, the Jewish restaurant in the East End, and a Lyons Corner House in the West End, which had become a popular meeting place for the 'refugee fraternity'. He developed a passionate love of Britain: 'The nation as a whole had my full admiration: war or peace, this was the greatest country on earth, I can repeat it a thousand times.'[15] Not surprisingly it was not long before Fred met an English Jewish girl, Gladys, whom he married in November 1941. He too was about to establish a strong British–Jewish identity.

In contrast, finding a British identity was not so easy for the internees. After all, Britain had incarcerated them, despite having found them to be 'friendly' aliens when the war had first started. They had a right to feel alienated. Moreover, many of the internees had decided not to enlist when first given the opportunity precisely because they expected to migrate to another country and acquire that nation's citizenship. As internees in Britain they were in a no-man's-land. Fritz Mansbacher, the one time Dovercourt boy who had spent three months at the Kitchener Camp, was partially in that position – he had always hoped to go to the USA – and he had also been too young to enlist. But until the morning of his arrest he had been making a very successful go at settling down in Britain. He had won a scholarship for technical training at Essex Technical College, and from September 1939 he had held down a good job as a mechanic in a garage owned by a Mr Norman in a village near Cambridge. He also lived with the Normans, and they grew very fond of him. When the local police had phoned Mr Norman (a part-time constable), at the end of May 1940, to tell him to 'bring in his boarder', Mr Norman had assumed there had been a mistake and they 'would be back from the Cambridge police station in an hour'. Fritz, much more accustomed to the twists and turns of a nation state, particularly in relation to Jews, had had a better grasp of what was happening and had immediately packed a bag. At the police station he was arrested and when he eventually arrived on the Isle of Man, he was spitting tacks. As he says in his memoir, it was 'a personal insult'.

His attachment to Britain had been loosened and, despite having made many British friends (he was clearly a very likeable young man), he became less and less inclined to stay. When the opportunity arose to leave, he grasped it, and was transported to Canada – as an internee – six weeks after his initial arrest. There he mouldered away in internment camps for a further nineteen months. Although some of his colleagues in Canada were persuaded to join the Pioneer Corps and thus return to Britain, Fritz decided not to do so. His heart was set on American citizenship; there was distant family in the United States and he knew that his mother, (still, as he thought, in Lübeck) was keen to join them. He did eventually become an American citizen, married a German Holocaust survivor, and, with a daughter and a son, they established an American family.

At some point Fritz changed his first name to Peter. His memoir, written from a Chicago suburb in 1988, indicates a man happy in his very active retirement. In the late 1980s, Mr Norman, his one-time boss in Over, near Cambridge, finally managed to trace Peter whom he had been looking for for many years. Mr Norman parcelled up his teddy bear and some old family photos and sent them back to Peter in the USA. A year later Peter came to England and spent three days with Mr Norman, and there they went over the letters they had sent each other over the years and which had always come back 'Return to Sender'.[16]

Of course not all internees turned away from a British identity. For most, internment was a brief and awkward sojourn but not a permanently damaging one in relation to Britishness. Hans Jackson was one of the Kitchener men whose experience of internment was particularly gruelling and unpleasant and yet this did not put him off. He was interned straight from Kitchener – he also was too young to enlist – and taken to the Isle of Man. There, as he told me in an interview, he was 'frightened out of my wits'; there was something about the close proximity of so many much older men that really alarmed him. The regime of the internment camp was a stark contrast with the Kitchener Camp, which he had positively enjoyed particularly when he became part of the team listening in to German short-wave messages. When, after a month, an opportunity arose to transfer to an internment camp in Australia, he, with four other young men, decided to go. Anything would be better than the Isle of Man. They left Liverpool on 10 July 1940 aboard the SS *Dunera* and found themselves among 2,542 other 'enemy aliens', the vast majority of whom were Jewish refugees. It was then that Hans and his friends discovered they had made the wrong decision. It turned out to be a very cruel journey and deliberately so: all the men were confined in the ship's hold for the entire fifty-seven days of the voyage with seven lavatories between them; some of the British NCOs on board routinely beat them, and their luggage was either thrown overboard or stolen.[17]

The 'Dunera Affair', as it came to be known, had consequences: questions were asked in the British Parliament, three British officers and men responsible for these appalling events were court martialled, and eventually some compensation was arranged for the loss of the luggage. Maybe Hans was impressed by this display of British justice even in the midst of a world war. Possibly more important, the familiar figure of Julian Layton, by now a major in the Pioneer Corps and seconded to the Home Office, arrived in Australia, in early 1941, to, once more, act as a good shepherd and advocate for the internees. It was Julian's responsibility, first to negotiate with the Australian authorities for the men's release either into the Australian Army or into the British Pioneer Corps, and then to find some means of getting the men who wanted to return to Britain on to a ship going to the UK. That Julian Layton managed to find berths on ships while there was a war on was one of his many quiet successes. Hans Jackson was one of 400 men who returned on the first ship Julian could commandeer; the SS *Stirling Castle* reached Liverpool, after a very risky voyage, in November 1941. Hans had, thereafter, 'a wonderful war' finishing up based in Scotland where, post-war, he founded a successful printing business and acquired a Glasgow accent that fused attractively with his Germanic English. Julian Layton was to remain in Australia and take responsibility for the welfare of the rump of the internees for almost the entire war until January 1945.

The story of the Pioneer Corps, and the way in which many of these refugee soldiers eventually, in 1942 and 1943, were encouraged to join the combatant parts of the British Armed Services, has been told elsewhere.[18] Some of them were quite exceptionally brave and joined Special Operations Executive, which entailed being dropped behind enemy lines for sabotage and espionage purposes. Some who have featured in this story undertook other essential activities. Walter Marmorek, for example, joined the Royal Engineers and spent time in North Africa and Italy, where he was rapidly promoted to the rank of major; Harry Rossney was sent, reluctantly it has to be said, to a Graves Registration Unit in northern France after the Normandy landings, and given the task of marking the names of the dead. As he says in his memoir 'someone had to do it'.[19] Fred Pelican remained with the Pioneer Corps for the whole of his war, landing in Normandy on D-Day 'plus five' and he worked with the 21st Army Corps as they moved through France and thence to liberated Holland.

When peace in Europe was finally achieved in May 1945 the work of these refugee soldiers did not end. Indeed, for large numbers of them the hardest part of the war and its aftermath was, in a sense, still to come. The Allies were determined to uncover, in its full horror, the nature of the Third Reich and to ensure that the new German government was free of Nazis. The refugee soldiers were perfectly placed to play a major part in these processes: their facility with the German language and their familiarity with German customs were invaluable assets when it came to uncovering the enormity of what had happened in Germany and the occupied East. A very large majority of them were immediately engaged in the work of the post-war War Crimes Commission, and in the process of denazification of German governance. As a result, the men heard at first hand, sometimes saw with their own eyes, the consequences of the Third Reich for the Jews of Europe. Fred Pelican, for example, in the course of his work in the denazification process, visited Displaced Persons camps that largely contained concentration camp survivors, acted as an interpreter in interviews with suspected Nazi war criminals, and personally interviewed members of the SS who were suspected war criminals. Throughout that process he kept absolutely quiet about his German–Jewish origins, and of his deep concerns about the whereabouts and fate of his own mother. His memoirs make little of the strain he must have been under (until he comes to his emotional response to news that his mother had, amazingly, survived Auschwitz). But for all the German refugees involved it was, all day and every day in their regular working lives, a time when they had to face the immediate consequences of their own rescue, and the fact that so many others had *not* been saved. We get a flavour of what they went through on a daily basis in an interview with Julian Layton undertaken decades later, in the 1980s, by the Imperial War Museum. Julian of course was not someone who had been rescued; rather he had been involved in the selection of those who were to be rescued and he therefore had a very full understanding of the limits to the rescue operations mounted before the war. As the concentration camps were liberated, he was sent, by the then Home Secretary, to Germany in order to write a report, with an American counterpart, of what he saw. He told the interviewer that he 'spent ten days in Belsen and visited many of the other concentration camps and it was the most ghastly few weeks that I've ever spent in my life. In fact it left such a deep impression on me that I've never been back to Germany since.' As he says these words, his voice grows hoarse and he appears to break down.[20]

Knowledge of what had happened to European Jewry as a whole came both before the war was over, with the liberation of the concentration camps, and once peace had come, when individuals who had survived were moved to so-called 'Displaced Persons' camps. In contrast, knowledge of what had happened to particular individuals was slow and depended on the work of the international Red Cross, which, post-war, worked to reunite Holocaust survivors with other surviving family members. Most of those who had been rescued before the war, like the Kitchener men, expected the worst; hardly anyone had heard from their families left in Nazi-occupied Europe since 1942, when the Final Solution had started. Fred Dunstan assumed from 1943 onwards that his parents were dead, but only received confirmation from the Red Cross in 1946.[21] Philip Franks heard from the Red Cross eighteen months after the war's end that his mother had been taken to the 'showcase' Theresienstadt ghetto and thence to Auschwitz in November 1943.[22] Fritz Mansbacher knew early on in the war that his father had died from multiple sclerosis – his mother had been able to let him know. He received his last letter from her in November 1941. In 1944, via a roundabout route, he was informed that his mother, his aunt and his cousin were living in Theresienstadt; he immediately sent his mother a food parcel via the Jewish agency in New York City. It was only in 1946 that he heard that his mother had been transported from Theresienstadt to Auschwitz, and immediately gassed there, two months before he had sent the food parcel. For Fred Pelican, the news that his mother was still alive came many months after the liberation of the concentration camps and long after he had given up hope of finding her again.

Of the other individuals who have been mentioned in this story we also, through the availability of the records of Holocaust victims, know what happened to them. In 1981, a sister of Alfred and Kurt Jacobi, the young brothers from Göttingen who had fought so hard – and failed – to get to Kitchener, completed a 'page of testimony' for each member of the family she had lost. These pages are kept on the Central Database for Shoah Victims' Names, held at the Holocaust Memorial, Yad Vashem, in Israel. There are pages for Alfred and Kurt and their mother Frieda, all of whom were last heard of in Theresienstadt. Alfred and Kurt's brother Hugo had managed to get to Holland but was rounded up there, their sister-in-law Edith was taken on a transport from Hannover. Of the men who ran the Jewish agencies in Berlin and Vienna, Dr Paul Eppstein, who had been so angry with the Jacobi brothers when they tried to make their own way to Kitchener, was shot, the day before Yom Kippur, in 1944; Otto Hirsch, the director of the Berlin RV who had been in London so very often in the months before the outbreak of war, was taken to Mauthausen concentration camp in May 1941 and died there three weeks later, probably as a result of torture.[23] Dr Loewenherz and Dr Murmelstein, both of the IK, the Jewish agency in Vienna, survived the war in the Theresienstadt ghetto; in the post-war period they were heavily criticised for having co-operated with the Nazis in the transport, from Theresienstadt, of Jews to 'the East'.

This story contains such a mixture of elements: approximately 4,000 lives were saved by the Kitchener Camp rescue (if we include the men's wives and children who also got away), and yet, knowing that, we also know the consequences for the many who failed to be selected. Even worse, of the 3,500 men who were directly rescued to Kitchener hundreds lost their very nearest and dearest. Their personal 'race against time' failed, and failed in such awful circumstances. For years I have had in my possession the list of 582 children that was sent to Norman Bentwich by the Kitchener Camp Social Department on 4 October 1939.[24] The list of these children, whose fathers were in the Kitchener Camp, was put together by a Dr Plaut, the director of the Social Department, in the hope that Norman Bentwich could persuade the British government to allow the children to enter Britain even after the Second World War had begun. Some of the children, as Dr Plaut indicated in his covering letter, already had visas to come on a *Kindertransport*, others were already in 'neutral' countries such as Holland and Belgium. Most were still in Germany and Austria. On this list the children's names are given, their dates of birth, and their last known address. There are large families of siblings, single children, brothers and sisters, at least two sets of twins, babies – even babies so young that they must have been born just as their fathers were coming to Kitchener or after their fathers had arrived. Over the years I have had this list in my possession, I have only been able to search for the children in short sharp bursts – any more and the lists of names of people who were murdered begin to make me feel very distressed. The Shoah database, containing up to 3 million names, is an amalgam of a number of sources and, despite its size, it is well known that there are a great many Holocaust victims who are not included.

It has not been difficult, indeed in many respects it has been too easy, to access the information I have sought, including information about what happened to these children's mothers. The Gestapo and the SS, as they set about the systematic murder of European Jewry, kept meticulous records, particularly of those sent to the larger death camps such as Auschwitz. It is striking how accurate the Nazi information was, including and especially the child's date of birth. Sometimes on the database there is, in addition to the SS record, a 'Page of Testimony', submitted by someone who knew the child, often with a little photo, a note of who the parents were, the relationship of the submitter to the child. Very occasionally the submitter of such a page is the father, and that father has an address in the UK. When I have encountered a page submitted by a father it has been a particular shock. These moments of revelation – the single page, the block capitals of the North London address of the father, the black-and-white photo of a girl or boy, coupled with the knowledge of the full context of this tragedy – have been, for me, really distressing. How much worse for those for whom the loss of a particular child was direct and personal?

Of the 582 children left behind by the Kitchener men, I know, with absolute certainty, that 293 perished in the Holocaust; and in the vast majority of those cases, their mothers went with them.

Notes

1. Meyer Stephany to Sir Alexander Maxwell, Home Office, 17 December 1940, CBF Archives, 91/64.
2. Alexander Maxwell to Meyer Stephany, CBF Secretary, 20 December 1940, CBF Archives, 91/66.
3. This letter was noted by the author when she was given access to the Bentwich papers before they were catalogued. Hence there is no File number, other than P174. The letter is dated 12 October 1942 and largely concerns the whereabouts of a missing cello which had been loaned by a member of the Anglo–Jewish community to the Kitchener Camp orchestra.
4. Edmund de Waal's best selling book, *Hare with the Amber Eyes*, London, Chatto and Windus, 2010, demonstrates exquisitely the freighting of such objects with meaning for generations of descendants.
5. Norman Bentwich, *Wanderer in War*, London, Victor Gollancz, 1946.
6. BWP, File P174/21c.
7. BWP, File P174/19.
8. BWP, File P174/12b. They did get to the USA in the end. Mrs Blumenthal wrote a Page of Testimony for her father Louis Rowelsky, who perished in the Holocaust, from an address in California.
9. Norman Bentwich to Walter Marmorek, 31 July 1940, BWP, File P174/20b.
10. Newspaper cutting from a local Ilfracombe paper, undated, Collection relating to service of Lt. Phineas L. May, 22 (41) [May], IWM Department of Documents.
11. Copies of these postcards are held in the Wiener Library.
12. Tamasin Day-Lewis, *Last Letters Home*, Basingstoke, Macmillan, 1995.

13. Walter Marmorek wrote a deeply affectionate obituary for 'Captain Poldi Kew' in 1974, *The Ex-Service Man*, No. 345, April 1974, London, The Ex-Service (1943) Association.

14. Harry Rossney, *Grey Dawns*, op. cit., p. 37.

15. Fred Pelican, op. cit., pp. 58–9.

16. Peter Mansbacher, op. cit.

17. There is a growing literature on 'the Dunera affair'. See, for example, Paul Bartrop, *The Dunera Affair: A Documentary Resource Book*, Melbourne: Jewish Museum of Australia/Schwartz and Wilkinson, 1990.

18. See for example, Peter Leighton Langer, op. cit.; Helen Fry, *The King's Most Loyal Enemy Aliens, Germans who fought for Britain in the Second World War*, Stroud, Sutton Publishing, 2007; Norman Bentwich, *I Understand the Risks*, op. cit.

19. Helen Fry, ibid., p. 210.

20. Julian Layton interview, IWM Sound Archives, Accession number 004382/03.

21. Fred Dunstan interview, IWM Sound Archives, op. cit.

22. Interview with Philip Franks, IWM Sound Archives, op. cit.

23. At least one of his children got to England. His daughter was the author's nanny.

24. BWP, P174/15a.

15

FORGETTING AND REMEMBRANCE

At the end of the Second World War, the Kitchener Camp was vacated. Just as after the First World War, the residential huts, the railway lines, the water towers, began, once again, to deteriorate and the weeds began to creep over the site. As the people of Britain worked to renew their country after the devastating war, and cope with the daily grind of the post-war austerity that had come in its wake, detailed memories of what had happened began to slip to the back of their minds. For those who had lost loved ones in the Holocaust, many memories became, literally, unspeakable and, as many children of survivors know, silence prevailed.

It is not known how many Kitchener men remained in Britain after the war. Norman Bentwich, in one of his three post-war books on his refugee experiences, claims that the great majority became British citizens, and this is probably true although he cites no hard evidence.[1] Before the outbreak of war, there is evidence that the number who actually left Kitchener as originally intended was remarkably low. Robert Waley Cohen wrote a report to the American Joint Distribution Committee at the end of August 1939 saying that up till that point 'about 20 men had left direct from the Camp for countries overseas', although in typical optimistic Waley Cohen fashion he added that he expected that in the next few months, 600 to 700 would depart to the USA or Australia.[2] It was after the war that men were able to leave Britain in safety and there is no doubt that many did. In the course of writing this book I have received emails from the descendants of Kitchener men living in the United States, Canada, Australia, Israel; there are personal memories on the internet from Sweden and it is highly likely there are descendants in some of the countries of Latin America. Certainly the nearest the Kitchener Camp came to fulfilling its role as a *transit* camp was after the war, and definitely not before.

Of those many who stayed in Britain, most were scattered across Britain and into Continental Europe by the war and then returned, not to Sandwich, but to places such as North West London where there were well established and large Jewish communities. But 'a few, a very few', as Norman Bentwich put it, 'found their permanent homes in the County of Kent, having taken to themselves English wives'.[3] One of those who returned to Kent after the war was Philip Franks. While at the Kitchener Camp Philip had made very good friends with some miners at Betteshanger colliery – quite possibly at the 'social' to which the men had been invited in June 1939. Philip kept in touch with these new friends throughout the war and when, post-war, they invited him to a Kentish wedding, he decided to stay in the area. For a while he worked as a miner himself at Betteshanger colliery, and then, when he met his wife, who worked 'on the buses', he settled in Deal. Eventually he had to stop mining for health reasons, and over the next forty years he built up a successful business in East Kent as a jobbing builder.[4] It is perfectly possible that Norman and Helen employed him to mend the windows and paint the weatherboarding of their little Sandwich weekend cottage. Also in Deal there is still, in 2013, a family who, during the war, changed their name to 'Layton' after Julian Layton; the Laytons of Deal were founded when a young Kitchener man spotted a charming schoolgirl at Sandwich station, and fell in love. Post-war, he became a local garage mechanic and eventually a garage owner in Deal. Again, it is perfectly possible that Norman and Helen knew him and used his services when they drove down to Sandwich to stay in their cottage.

The men who became British citizens – eventually in 1947 – did not form an association of ex-Kitchener men. Perhaps the memories of such a mixed experience were too painful. But there have been a number of associations for Jews who were soldiers in the Second World War, and, particularly for the old soldiers of the Pioneer Corps, there was often a Kitchener link.[5] Harry Rossney, for many years, held an informal meeting in the Imperial Café in the Golders Green Road (in the heart of the North West London Jewish community) once a month; even now old soldiers still 'meet again' for companionship and reminiscence. It is largely through this group that I have met, and interviewed, the very few Kitchener men who were still alive when I started this project.

Their stories, as they have told them, have tended to be dominated by their childhoods in Germany and Austria, their experience of the Third Reich, their arrival in Britain, their experience of war and their subsequent lives in post-war Britain. The place of the Kitchener Camp in their often well-rehearsed narratives has been relatively very minor – it was, I began to realise, an experience that on the whole they had forgotten or, perhaps, preferred to forget. However there are material objects that most have kept, usually documents of registration on their arrival in the UK and photos of themselves, with companions, in the

Kitchener Camp. In addition, a few of these men, or their descendants, have in their possession a single-issue magazine, published in October 1939, by the Kitchener Camp Committee. This magazine, entitled '*Some victims of the Nazi terror: the reward of the Salvors*', contains striking and modernist photographs of men at the camp, often grouped on the page around headings, such as 'New Found Freedom', 'They Find Happiness in their New Work', 'Where Every Man Has a Job'. In all the photos the sun is shining and in some of them a man is photographed with his shirt off, holding some heavy implement above his head. There is a eugenic tone to these photos, with one caption beside a photo of a half naked man saying 'Fine specimens of manhood are to be found everywhere in the Camp. Brave fellows with spirits that no cruelty or adversity can break'. The magazine, of which 50,000 were printed, was probably devised and paid for by Robert Waley Cohen with a view to persuading the American–Jewish communities to provide further funds for the Kitchener Camp, although it is not clear whether this actually happened. Copies seem also to have been given to the Kitchener men, as a souvenir. It is, in the present era where this propaganda style has become associated with totalitarianism, a somewhat incongruous memorial to a rescue to liberty.[6]

In the course of these interviews I have been struck by the similarity of these men's trajectories into Britishness. Usually they have married an English woman, not necessarily Jewish, and often they have had a career working in their own business, often a business, as with Philip Franks and Mr Layton of Deal, based on the craft skills they had originally acquired in Greater Germany. None of the men I have met in the course of this research has been, in any obvious way, very well off. As I have stepped over the thresholds of fairly modest houses in North London and in the Manchester and Sheffield suburbs, 'comfortable' has always been the word that has come to mind; given the context and the history, that has been a particularly warming thought. At the end of Fred Pelican's book there is a charming epilogue written by his wife Gladys, whom he had met at a Lyons Corner House all those years before in 1941. She describes how Fred, immediately post-war, started a 'small building company' with a friend, and how later on he established a small lino and carpet shop in North London, which he later expanded into larger premises; he also opened a branch in East London. Her final paragraph sums up a life that in many ways reflects the British lives of the other Kitchener men that I have met:

> At sixty-five years of age, he retired, and we live in our nice house in the secluded area of Woodford Green. Right through our married life, Fred has attained whatever he set out to do. He was a long-standing member of the London Chamber of Commerce, the Hackney Chamber of Commerce, the Federation of Master Builders, Vice-President of our Ex-Service Association,

and a high-ranking officer of an ancient and honourable institution. In his retirement, he follows his love of writing and his lifelong hobby of philately. For one who came to this country in 1939 with practically nothing and a limited knowledge of English, I am extremely proud to say he has been a gem, and, above all, my loving husband.[7]

In 1945, the town of Sandwich had begun the slow process of post-war renewal. In this it was helped by the arrival of two large enterprises, one of which purchased the Kitchener Camp for its own purposes in 1947.[8] Petbow Engineering wanted the residential huts of the camp, both to house its workers during the acute housing shortage of bombed out Britain, and to use the remaining huts as industrial premises. Pfizer, the global pharmaceutical company, developed an enormous site immediately adjacent to Petbow, and to this day the buildings of state-of-the-art biochemistry laboratories feature on the Sandwich skyline. Many newcomers, with no knowledge of Sandwich during the war, began to move into the town. The buildings of Petbow (which now exists under another name) and Pfizer (which has also moved on such that the much reduced site is now called 'Discovery Park') have also obliterated the Kitchener Camp itself. When descendants of Kitchener men come visiting there is hardly anything to show them: only one small hut smothered in ivy, and some larger buildings, which may have housed the concert hall and the cinema – all on the other side of the road from the site of the main camp. Not only have the memories begun to fade and the people who remembered died or moved away, but also the material foundation of those memories has almost completely disappeared.

Nevertheless, it remains a surprising feature of the Kitchener Camp rescue that it has been so comprehensively forgotten. It was, after all, the 'other' rescue, alongside the *Kindertransport*, intended to dovetail with that more famous rescue, and organised in exactly the same way. Moreover, the collective rescue of 3,500 men, and their location in a single place, is a significant event. But it is only the *Kindertransport* that has become embedded in the British national psyche: that story is part of the British narrative on British identity, taken to indicate more than just tolerance of strangers – rather, positive kindness and generosity.[9] A play about the *Kindertransport* features in the curriculum of national school examinations, there is a well known statue of the *Kinder* placed outside Liverpool Street station in London, and every year there seems to be a reason for a member of the British royal family to meet the *Kinder* who are still alive. The distinguishing feature of the *Kindertransport* was, of course, that it was for children and it is certainly this element that draws the attention of the public and commentators alike; the vulnerability and innocence of children make their persecution even more shocking. Their plight can also be a powerful political tool. As David Cesarani, one of Britain's historians of the Holocaust, has put it,

'[The *Kindertransport*] shows that racial discrimination and ideologies which lead to mass murder do not draw the line at the persecution of innocent children. Their plight can be the trigger that finally stirs bystanders to action, but such help too often comes too late and benefits too few.'[10] Moreover it is the presence of these children, captured in the many and widely available photos of their arrival in Britain, that has maintained the presence of the *Kindertransport* in the British sense of themselves to the present day.

Both the Kitchener and the *Kindertransport* rescues had the pain of loss embedded within them. While the pain of the *Kinder* has in itself been used as a platform to instil empathy for the 'other' amongst British schoolchildren, the complicated fact that many adult men also lost their loved ones has perhaps been a reason for wanting to forget. As we have seen, the Kitchener Camp was frequently not a happy place and it is not surprising that many men preferred not to talk of their experience in any detail to their descendants.[11] Moreover, there were aspects of Kitchener, particularly the confinement and the authoritarianism that took hold during the few months after war broke out, that have served to confuse it with the internment camps that came shortly afterwards. A cursory glance on the Internet produces numerous references to the 'Kitchener internment camp' and I have received emails, particularly from the USA, where descendants claim that their fathers were imprisoned without trial, by the British government, at Kitchener. In these instances, the *fact* that this was a rescue operation mounted by Anglo–Jewry is completely obliterated by the *belief* that it was simply one of a number of internment camps for aliens instituted by the British government.

There is one more set of reasons for the forgetting of the Kitchener Camp. First, it seems to be the case that this rescue does not fit with the dominant popular narrative that has developed over the past few decades concerning the type of German–Jewish refugee who was able to find refuge in Britain. The popular narrative tends to assume that the German refugees who reached Britain were very well resourced, well networked and above all, cultured and intellectual.[12] The idea, often quoted, that the Pioneer Corps 'turned intellectuals into navvies' reflects that view. There is a large element of truth to this – it is certainly the case, as always of migrant streams, that it was the better off, the professional and the well networked who predominantly got away to Britain. Moreover there is evidence that it was actually Home Office policy, encouraged by Anglo–Jewry, to make certain that only people of the middle class immigrated.[13] But it is also an awkward and complicating truth that the Kitchener Camp rescue was a counterbalance to that tendency – the men who came to Sandwich were indeed talented and many had intellectual interests, but they were predominantly men who in Germany had been the other Jews – the 'small merchants, intinerant traders, shopkeepers, tailors, artisans and industrial workers'.[14] Moreover, they could not have come without the full and targeted support of the Anglo–Jewish establishment.

This in turn does not fit with the professional narrative that has developed, amongst historians, concerning the role of Anglo–Jewry in the rescue of German Jews during the Third Reich. From the 1990s onwards, British historians have criticised the Anglo–Jewish establishment of the 1930s for weakness, ambivalence, general reluctance, to promote the immigration to Britain of German–Jewish refugees. They have argued that this was because the Anglo–Jewish grandees were terrified that a large influx of refugees would provoke anti-Semitism. Given that so many members of these grand Jewish families were well integrated into the British establishment, they had a great deal to lose.[15] There are indeed some shocking examples in the minutes of ministerial meetings of the time, where British Jews argued that German–Jewish immigration should be reduced or even stopped altogether (one such is quoted in Chapter 2) but *Kristallnacht* really does seem to have been a turning point, both in the policies adopted by the Anglo–Jewish establishment, and in the sympathy of the British people for the plight of German Jewry. British historians have so far ignored the presence of the Kitchener Camp, partially, no doubt, because the Bentwich papers, deposited at the Hebrew University of Jerusalem, have only recently become available (I was the first person to consult them), but the fact of this rescue is also an awkward complication in an argument that seeks to suggest that the Anglo–Jewish establishment did not do a great deal for German Jewry as a whole. The story told here indicates that, for this rescue (and for the *Kindertransport*) they did a huge amount, both in terms of extraordinary financial contribution often from their personal coffers,[16] and, particularly in the case of Norman Bentwich, in terms of time and emotional commitment. They were rewarded by the fact that the evidence from Sandwich indicates there was no consequential upsurge in anti-Semitism – if anything quite the reverse.

The people who did try to keep the memory of the Kitchener rescue were the Bentwiches. Both Norman and Helen Bentwich wrote post-war books which contain chapters on the Kitchener Camp.[17] In Norman's case it is fair to say that they are not full histories. They are engagingly written personal reminiscences. Even though he could have consulted his voluminous personal papers on the Kitchener Camp rescue (which he bequeathed to the Central Archive of the History of the Jewish people at the Hebrew University, Jerusalem) he seems to have used only his appointments diary to jog his memory, combined with an occasional foray into the minutes of the Executive Committee of the Council for German Jewry. His chapters have a connection with the evidence as it has emerged here, but they are very partial accounts and are often vague, or even demonstrably inaccurate. To take a simple example, he forgot the maximum age of the men in Kitchener, always referring to it as 40 years of age,[18] when in fact it was 45. Numbers are often not given; he preferred to use the words 'many' and 'the majority', and where numbers are given they usually bear only a limited relation to those that are mentioned in the archive documents. He also saw the Kitchener Camp through distinctly rose-coloured spectacles, describing a happy community run on co-operative lines, which was 'a hive of industry and goodwill'.[19] There were times, of course, when this was the case, but, as I have suggested in this story, there was also irksome authoritarianism, confinement and surveillance. Communal living was by no means easy or pleasant and Norman had received a number of letters from the men telling him that, but when it came to writing his memoirs he chose to forget them. Above all, for the men, there was the strain of separation – but Bentwich never mentions this either, even though his correspondence of the time was full of letters concerning wives and children who had been left in Greater Germany. A typical example of his rosy view of the camp occurs in *They Found Refuge*:

> The life of the camp attracted the attention of politicians, civil servants and publicists in England. It symbolized the contrast between the freedoms of the English asylum and the brutal tyranny of Nazi Europe. It was known to its inmates as Anglo-Saxon-Hausen, in contrast to the notorious Sachsen-Hausen concentration camp in Germany from which many were delivered.[20]

He was such an endearingly 'glass half full' man, but the reference to 'Anglo-Saxon-Hausen' can only have been a profound misreading of a piece of gallows humour circulating among the Kitchener men.

Helen Bentwich also did her best to keep the memory of the Kitchener Camp, in a book she published privately, in the same year (1971) that Norman died and which she dedicated to his memory.[21] Her *History of Sandwich in Kent* is also modelled on Norman's style of historical writing – just as with his books, there is no bibliography (a fact for which she apologises) but she contrasts herself with him in stating that she is 'an amateur historian'.[22] Now more than forty years since it was written, her book remains the most recent work on the general history of Sandwich and has become the standard reference for the local town guides. Like Norman she presents a very positive picture of the camp, and like him she presents numbers with an air of certainty. However, Helen Bentwich's numbers are usually wrong, even wildly wrong. For example, she claims that about 'a quarter [of the Kitchener men] were Christian non-aryans' and that altogether '[the Kitchener men's] numbers rose to some five thousand'. In fact the highest number of 'Christian non-aryans' resident in the Kitchener Camp was probably 100,[23] and, at its peak, the total number of residents in the camp, including the approximately 200 wives who were there briefly at the outbreak of war, was in the region of 3,800. Of course the Bentwiches wanted to present the Kitchener

Camp in the best possible light. They, and particularly Norman, had devoted so much time and energy to its inception, to its management, and to its aftermath. Through their efforts, if we include the wives and children who were able to join their men, about 4,000 Jews were saved from the Holocaust. This was in itself an extraordinary achievement and it is does not need any further inflation.

The camp itself influenced the Bentwiches' lives to the very end, since, for nearly thirty years, they continued to come to their little cottage in Sandwich for weekends and holidays. In the summer, Norman, still in his eighties a man of enormous energy, could be seen taking an early morning swim in Sandwich Bay every day. It was after his death, in 1971, that the Association of Jewish Refugees, together with Helen Bentwich and Walter Marmorek, decided that there should be a memorial to the Kitchener Camp (or as Norman consistently called it in his memoirs, the 'Richborough Transit Camp') somewhere in Sandwich. They chose to place the memorial on the inner arch of the Sandwich Barbican, at the spot where the Kitchener men would regularly enter the town. The wording on the memorial plaque was, without a doubt, devised by Helen, and it was therefore, in certain respects, somewhat misleading, particularly in respect to the number of men rescued and with respect to the fact that the word 'Jews' does not occur – presumably because Helen thought, wrongly, that so many of the men were converted Jews who had become Christians. On 20 June 1971, Julian Layton stood in the archway and drew the little curtain that unveiled the plaque while the Mayor of Sandwich, Helen Bentwich, Walter Marmorek and other erstwhile members of the Kitchener staff and the camp looked on.

The plaque, recently refurbished by the Town Council at the urging of Walter Marmorek, is still there in 2014, although those who wish to read it have to dodge the traffic coming through the narrow arch of the Barbican. It says:

> This plaque is to commemorate the
> RICHBOROUGH TRANSIT CAMP
> 1939–40 where 5,000 men found refuge
> from Nazi persecution on the Continent.
> During the Second World War most of them
> volunteered to fight for the Allied cause.
>
> Erected in gratitude to the citizens of
> Sandwich and East Kent
> who, as in the past, welcomed the refugees.

As, hopefully, this book has shown, the story of the Kitchener Camp was somewhat more complex than the plaque implies. Certain statements on the plaque are close to the truth: the Kitchener Camp rescue, in terms of the lives it saved, was a very considerable success and the welcome of the people of Sandwich and its hinterland helped to make life in the camp easier. Very many of the men who had been rescued, probably the majority, served in the British armed services during the war. However, the peculiarly rapid passage of time in 1939, and the existence of an absolutely vicious and anti-Semitic regime in Continental Europe, means that the rescue was also tinged with unimaginable sadness. This book is another memorial – to the men of the Kitchener Camp, to the family members they lost, and to the people of Sandwich.

Notes

1.   Norman Bentwich, *They Found Refuge*, p. 114, op. cit. 'The veterans of the camp are, indeed, found in all parts of the world, in Israel, the United States, Australia, Canada and the South American countries. But the large majority are British citizens.'
2.   Robert Waley Cohen, 'Report on the Kitchener Camp', 22 August 1939, JDC archives. It is possible that hundreds of men did leave the camp for the USA between September 1939 and May 1940 but it seems very unlikely given the trouble about funding the fares. Some Kitchener men will have left for the USA from internment camps. The 300–400 men originally expected to re-emigrate to Palestine did not materialise due to the British government's refusal to grant immigration certificates to Palestine – see Bentwich to Miss S.J. Warner, 29 January 1940, BWP, File P174/21b.
3.   Norman Bentwich, *They Found Refuge*, op. cit., p. 114.
4.   Philip Franks interview, op. cit.
5.   See for example, the Association of Jewish Ex-Service Men (AJEX), and the Royal Pioneer Corps Association websites.
6.   A complete copy of the magazine is held in the Sandwich Guildhall archives. Copies of the magazine and the *Kitchener Camp Review* are available from the Sandwich Guildhall website.
7.   Gladys Pelican, 'Epilogue', in Fred Pelican, op. cit., p. 204.
8.   I am grateful to James Bird, one time CEO of Petbow Engineering, for this information.
9.   See for example, Mark Jonathan Harris and Deborah Oppenheimer, *Into the Arms of Strangers, stories of the Kindertransport*, London, Bloomsbury, 2000 and the Warner Brothers film of the same name; Samuels, D. *Kindertransport*, London, Nick Hern books, 2009.
10.   Harris and Oppenheimer, ibid., 'Introduction' by David Cesarani, p. 19.
11.   Conversation with Peter Posaner, son of a Kitchener man, July 2013.

12. See for example, Daniel Snowman, *The Hitler Emigres, the cultural impact on Britain of refugees from Nazism*, London, Chatto and Windus, n.d.

13. Geoffrey Alderman, 'The Holocaust: Why did Anglo–Jewry stand idly by?', Graduate School of Jewish Studies, Touro College, 2001.

14. Cesarani, op. cit., p. 3.

15. For an overarching discussion of these historians' critiques, from a counter point of view, see Pamela Shatzkes, *Holocaust and Rescue, Impotent or Indifferent? Anglo–Jewry 1938–1945*, Introduction. The main protagonists in this debate are, in alphabetical order, Geoffrey Alderman, Richard Bolchover, David Cesarani, Tony Kushner, Louise London, all of them distinguished historians who argue, with varying degrees of vehemence, that Anglo–Jewry could and should have done more. Shatzkes argues against these critiques, suggesting they are overdrawn and misread Anglo–Jewry's motives and context. She does mention the Kitchener rescue, as part of the response to the 'watershed' moment of *Kristallnacht*, but devotes only one paragraph to it. A fuller discussion of its nature would have been grist to her mill.

16. Amy Zahl Gottlieb, *Men of Vision, Anglo–Jewry's Aid to victims of the Nazi regime, 1933–1945*, London, Weidenfeld and Nicholson, 1998. Gottlieb was the archivist of the Central British Fund and her book is based on the CBF archives. Her contribution to the history of this period is particularly useful for an understanding of the financial implications for the CBF of the policies pursued by Anglo–Jewry. She also produces evidence of the leadership's personal generosity. As the title of her book implies, she is not critical of the Anglo–Jewish establishment.

17. Norman Bentwich, *I Understand the Risks*, op. cit., 1950; Norman Bentwich, *They Found Refuge*, op. cit., 1956; Norman Bentwich, *My 77 Years*, op. cit., 1961; Helen C. Bentwich, *A History of Sandwich in Kent*, Deal, T.F. Pain and Sons, 1971.

18. *I Understand the Risks*, op. cit., p. 28.

19. Bentwich, *They Found Refuge*, op. cit., p104.

20. Ibid., p. 105.

21. Helen C. Bentwich, op. cit.

22. Ibid., Preface. Of course the present author is also an amateur historian.

23. Letter from Bertha Bracey, General Secretary of the Society of Friends German Emergency Committee, which took responsibility for the selection and funding of Christian non-aryans in the camp, dated 24 April 1939, BWP, File P174/13b. In the same file a letter from Bentwich to Bertha Bracey refers to 'the small group of non-Aryan Christians in the camp', letter dated 29 November, 1939.

APPENDIX:
A LETTER TO
THE TIMES

The following letter was published in *The Times*, 1 November 1939:

THE DARK AGE

GERMAN WITNESSES IN ENGLAND

A LETTER FROM THE TRIBUNALS

The following letter, in which cross-heads have been inserted, has been addressed to the Editor by Sir George Bonner and five fellow barristers who have been determining the status of refugees from Germany. It shows that much of what they have heard in evidence bears out the stories of Nazi brutality told in yesterday's White Paper.

Sir, We the undersigned were appointed by the Home Office to act as 'tribunals' at Richborough Camp in Kent to consider the cases of some 3,600 aliens whose status was changed by the declaration of war from that of 'refugee' to 'enemy alien'. They are all Jews by race or have Jewish blood in their veins. Among their number are some who profess the Protestant, the Roman Catholic, or other religions. In view of the difficulties placed in their way it is a matter of surprise that so many succeeded in getting away from Germany. Before passports were returned (they had been confiscated as a preliminary) and leave to depart given, evidence had to be forthcoming of authority to settle in some other country. The following requirements had then to be satisfied:

1. The passport had to be produced with a 'visa'. A large number of refugees got over this difficulty by selecting Shanghai as their ultimate destination. As a free port no visa, in this case, was necessary. The Government exploited this desire and even arranged for, or provided, sea transport. In the event the price of tickets soared, payment had to be made to the Government, and ultimately as to half in foreign currencies.
2. A receipt was required showing that all taxes had been paid, and also a receipt for the due proportion of the fine imposed on Jews after the death of the German Military Attaché in Paris.
3. An official certificate to the effect that his business, if any, had been sold and handed over to an Aryan.
4. A receipt for duty paid on clothes and furniture proposed to be taken away. In the later months this amounted to as much as 100 per cent.

In some cases, where passports were not returned, the German refugee was compelled to purchase from the 'Gestapo' a Greek passport, and, fortified with this, after other requirements had been satisfied, was allowed to depart. The cost of this fraudulent document was 3,000 marks (approximately £250).

ALLEGATIONS PROVED
In the course of our investigations, from which the facts stated here have emerged, there has been so much corroborative evidence of gross ill-treatment that we think it right to make public some of the facts proved to our satisfaction. Constituted as separate Tribunals, we have selected cases proved before one or more of the Tribunals, and have only accepted such allegations as are corroborated and, in our opinion, proved.

The witnesses told their stories with obvious reluctance. They were afraid, in the event of identification, of reprisals that might follow against their relatives still in Germany. Further, before leaving a concentration camp each man was warned against ever saying what he had suffered or seen or was told. 'We have our spies everywhere.'

The suffering of these unfortunate people took many forms. We feel that the most lasting injuries are intangible and will be measured for the rest of their lives in shattered nerves and broken physique. One professional man, advised to try to forget what he had suffered, replied, 'I can never do that. I dream so often about the concentration camp.'

A distressing feature of a number of these cases is the inevitable breaking up and parting of families. We were told by husbands of wives and children still in Germany, with very little hope of ever being reunited. The man was arrested, or given a stated time in which to leave Germany, while the rest of the family had to remain. Since then, some have been able to remove their families to other countries – namely, France, the U.S.A., Chile, Bolivia, Palestine, and many to England. A large number, however, when asked about their families, give the answer, 'I don't know how, or where, they are living.'

THE BOX OF ASHES

We heard of cases where the arrest of a father was followed in a few days by the notification that he was ill in prison or in a concentration camp, the locality of which was not specified. A report followed later that he had died. In due course a box purporting to contain his remains was brought to the house with a demand for 500 marks – 'the expense of cremation'. No particulars as to the cause of death were forthcoming, nor was there any certainty as to the identity of the remains. In one case a widow who had undergone this terrible experience was arrested six months later on a charge of 'making propaganda with her husband's ashes'. She was released, we were told, later, and the witness added, 'one eye was gone, she was an old hag, and was half dead until she died of her injuries'.

It was unlawful for a Jew to own property. We had innumerable cases where, deprived of his business, the Jew was not allowed thereafter to earn a living. A typical case was that of a general store where the shop or shops were closed and the stock sold at some totally inadequate figure, arrived at by the authorities, to a party man. The purchase price, if paid at all, was then, by the incidence of fines or confiscation, reduced to a vanishing point, and the victim, after any payment made for clothes, was allowed to bring out of the country a maximum of 10 marks.

A Jew was fortunate if he was able to escape without detention in a prison or a concentration camp. The accounts of journeys by rail are almost unbelievable. As many as 10 to 15 men were accommodated in compartments provided for eight. When travelling in trucks or wagons there were as many as 40 to 50 in one wagon. On journeys which were taken from May to December, 1938, and which, at different times, varied in duration from 14 to 16 hours, they were given no water or food. Every one of these men had heard rifle shots on the train or had seen men shot down. It was a common occurrence for bodies to be removed when the train stopped at stations. On one specific journey, of which there was abundant evidence, three men in one wagon were shot and their bodies thrown out of the window because they complained of the heat. On this journey we are satisfied that at least seven men were murdered on the way.

TORTURES IN CAMP

On arrival at the concentration camp, young and old had to run between ranks of Black Guards, who beat them on the shoulders with sticks or prodded them with bayonets. Meanwhile, they are blinded and bewildered by a searchlight directed in their faces. We were told of old men falling down and being kicked on the ground. They were then carried away. Striking was common and uncontrolled. Such weapons as sticks, stones, shovels, bayonets, rifle butts, whips, and, in some cases, even knucklebusters, were used. Victims often confirmed their statements by reference to scars, to crippled limbs, or missing teeth.

One man stated that, at a particular camp, he was thrown down, beaten, and stoned. His right leg and three ribs were broken, and after his leg had been set he was forced to walk with the leg in splints. Others told of an old man of 80 who had both legs broken and then died.

Another was told by a guard to strike with a spade a friend of his who had formerly been a judge. In his judicial capacity the latter had sentenced two Nazis to death for a criminal offence. The witness refused to do it. He was immediately bayoneted in the arm and had to remain in hospital. Soon after the judge died in camp.

There were so-called 'hospitals' in the concentration camps, and evidence was given as to the conditions prevailing there. One witness, a professional man, employed as a ward attendant, summed up the position. He saw many patients lying either on straw or bare boards suffering from severe injuries, such as broken limbs or head wounds. Others were suffering from exposure or from internal injuries caused by being trampled upon and kicked. He was positive that, in the three months during which he was so employed, there were over 300 deaths from the injuries he described. No medical attendance and no serum was provided by the authorities, and the suffering were attended to by other internees.

A doctor who had worked for six months in a concentration camp put the mortality rate during this period at 10 per cent. Of these 15 per cent had died from injuries and the remainder mostly from pneumonia or diphtheria. It was impossible to provide proper treatment for the latter.

It was a common occurrence for patients to be sent back to work while still suffering. A doctor of considerable standing in his own profession told of a patient, under his care in camp, who was so treated. Unable to do his allotted task, the sick man was made to carry in front of him a board on which were painted the words: 'This man doesn't want to work.' Thereafter, whenever he passed a guard, he was struck. The doctor stated that at last he collapsed on the ground, where he could be seen from the hospital windows, and in three or four days he died where he lay.

SOME PUNISHMENTS

Punishments (other than blows, which were commonplace) for talking or eating while at work or because the task was not being done to the satisfaction of the guard took various forms, of which the following are examples. They are by no means exhaustive.

1. On one occasion in January of this year practically the whole camp were compelled to stand for one night and part of the next day in night attire or in the thinnest of garments in the open air. We were told by several witnesses that in consequence of this exposure many men had died, some putting the number as high as 30.

2. In one hut 150 men were kept without light or fire for a month. The windows were boarded up, and they were allowed out for one hour in the 24. We were told, and had no difficulty in believing, that the conditions became indescribable and the effect on the men terrible.

3. A punishment common to every camp was one in which the hands were bound behind the back and the victim was then suspended from the branch of a tree by the wrists. The pain was said to be excruciating, and the period of punishment, two hours, was generally cut short by unconsciousness.

4. The water punishment took the form of having to stand at attention, with the chin pointing upwards. A spray of water was then played on the victim. As long as the chin was kept up the victim was compelled to swallow, in the act of breathing, large quantities of water. As soon as he lowered his head either from exhaustion or discomfort he was struck on the chin by a sentry. Many men account for the loss of teeth in this way and, in the case of one man, a long scar on the chin, it was stated, was due to a blow from a rifle butt in the circumstances indicated above.

5. We were told of men being compelled to crawl naked along paths of broken granite. Their hand and knees were lacerated and they became exhausted through loss of blood.

    Men were put to death in circumstances so horrible as to be almost unbelievable. Evidence was given before one of the Tribunals of a specific case where a man was seen being taken into an empty room between two 'blackshirts'. His cries for mercy were heard by men in the passage and in the adjoining room. Later he was found hanging from a beam. It was 'officially' reported that he had committed suicide.

    The men from whom we have heard these accounts represent every class – doctors, lawyers, rabbis, merchants, skilled mechanics, clerks, &c. There were few of the labouring class. The majority were well educated and obviously of considerable ability – many can speak and understand English.

We think we are justified in holding very strong views as to the brutalities which we are satisfied were inflicted on a large number of our fellow human beings for no other reason than that they were, by the accident of birth, non-Aryan. We find it hard to believe that a Government which permitted the treatment to which we have referred, or those who inflicted it, can any longer claim to be civilized.

Yours, &c.,

GEORGE A. BONNER, formerly King's Remembrancer and Senior Master of the Supreme Court, King's Bench Division.

TRISTRAM BERESFORD, Recorder of Folkestone

TREVOR HUNTER, Chancellor of the Diocese of Swansea and Brecon, and a Judge of the County Court.

W.BLAKE ODGERS, Recorder of Southampton

F.E.SUGDEN, Barrister-at-Law.

JOHN H.THORPE, Recorder of Blackburn.

October 31.

SELECT
BIBLIOGRAPHY

Unpublished Documentary and Sound Sources:

1) Bentwich papers, referred to in text as 'BWP', Norman Bentwich Collection – P174, The Central Archives for the History of the Jewish People, Jerusalem (CAHJP), Hebrew University of Jerusalem.

2) Central British Fund for World Jewish Relief, referred to in the text as 'CBF Archives', held in microfiche form at the Wiener Library, London, MF Doc 27.

3) Julian Layton papers, referred to in text as 'JLP', Wiener Library, London, Document collection, 1205.

4) Phineas May's Kitchener Camp diary, Wiener Library, London, Document 644/1.

5) Typescript memoirs of Peter Mansbacher, former Kitchener Camp resident, Wiener Library, London, Document 644/8.

6) The Kitchener Camp Review: 'the journal of the Kitchener Camp for refugees at Richborough, near Sandwich written by and for them', Wiener Library, London, Two bound volumes: March–September 1939, Document 644/3; October–November 1939, Document 644/4.

7) Board of Deputies of British Jews: Defence Committee Papers, Wiener Library, London, Document collection 1658.

8) Board of Deputies of British Jews: Collection ACC 3122, London Metropolitan Archives.

9) Imperial War Museum sound archives, referred to in the text as 'IWM Sound Archives', various recorded interviews, Accession numbers in footnotes in the text.

10) Imperial War Museum archives, Kitchener Camp documents, Second World War, documents 8180.

11) Imperial War Museum archives, Private papers of H.H. Rossney, documents 15292.

12) Imperial War Museum archives, Collection of letters, photographs and newscuttings relating to the service of Phineas L. May as entertainments officer in No. 3. Pioneer Corps Training Centre during the Second World War, document 90/103.

13) National Archives: Papers pertaining to German–Jewish refugees and the Richborough or Kitchener Camp, from The Prime Minister's Office (PREM); Colonial Office (CO); Home Office (HO). Papers pertaining to Captain Robert Gordon Canning from the Security Service (KV 2).

14) Records of the New York Office of the American Jewish Joint Distribution Committee, 1933–1944, held at the Joint Distribution Committee Archives, Jerusalem.

15) Uncatalogued documents held at Sandwich Guildhall archives, including 'Work and Training at the Kitchener Camp' and 'Some Victims of the Nazi Terror – the reward of the salvors'.

Newspapers

The Times
News Chronicle
Jewish Chronicle
East Kent Mercury

Kentish Gazette
The Blackshirt
Action

Published Works (Selected)

Robert Benewick, *Political Violence and Public Order, a study of British Fascism*, Allen
  Lane, the Penguin Press, 1969.
Helen Bentwich, *A History of Sandwich in Kent*, Pain and Sons, 1971.
Norman Bentwich, *Wanderer in War*, Victor Gollancz, 1946.
Norman Bentwich, *I Understand the Risks*, Victor Gollancz, 1950.
Norman Bentwich, *They Found Refuge*, Cresset Press, 1956.
Norman Bentwich, *My 77 Years*, The Jewish Publication Society of America, 1961.
Michael Berenbaum and Abraham J. Peck (eds), *The Holocaust and History*, Indiana
  University Press, 1998.
Chaim Bermant, *The Cousinhood*, Eyre and Spottiswoode, 1971.
Michael Burleigh, *The Third Reich, A New History*, Pan Macmillan, 2001.
David Cesarani, *Eichmann, His Life and Crimes*, Heinemann, 2004.
David Cesarani and Paul Levine (eds), *'Bystanders' to the Holocaust, a re-evaluation*,
  Frank Cass, 2002.
Saul Friedlander, *The Years of Persecution*, Phoenix, 2007.
Helen Fry, *Jews in North Devon During the Second World War*, Halsgrove, 2005.
Helen Fry, *The King's Most Loyal Enemy Aliens*, Sutton Publishing, 2007.
Amy Zahl Gottlieb, *Men of Vision*, Weidenfeld and Nicolson, 1998.
Julie Gottlieb, *Feminine Fascism: Women in Britain's Fascist Movement, 1923–1945*, I.B.
  Tauris, 2000.
Mark Jonathan Harris and Deborah Oppenheimer, *Into the Arms of Strangers*,
  Bloomsbury, 2000.
Robert Henriques, *Sir Robert Waley Cohen, 1877–1952*, Secker and Warburg, 1966.
Sharman Kadish, *'A Good Jew and a Good Englishman', The Jewish Lads' Brigade and
  Girls' Brigade 1895–1995*, Vallentine Mitchell, 1995.
Tony Kushner, *The Persistence of Prejudice: Antisemitism in British Society During the
  Second World War*, Manchester University Press, 1989.
Tony Kushner, *The Holocaust and the Liberal Imagination*, Blackwell, 1994.
Peter Leighton-Langer, *The King's Own Loyal Enemy Aliens*, Vallentine Mitchell,
  2006.
Francois Lafitte, *The Internment of Aliens*, Penguin, 1940.
Louise London, *Whitehall and the Jews 1933–1948*, Cambridge University Press,
  2000.

Marian Malet and Anthony Grenville, *Changing Countries,* Libris, 2002.

Fred Pelican, *From Dachau to Dunkirk,*Vallentine Mitchell, 1993.

Martin Pugh, *'Hurrah for the Blackshirts!': Fascists and Fascism in Britain between the Wars,* Jonathan Cape, 2005.

A.W. Brian Simpson, *In the Highest Degree Odious,* Clarendon Press, 1992.

Daniel Snowman, *The Hitler Emigrés*, Chatto and Windus, undated.

Pamela Shatzkes, *Holocaust and Rescue,*Vallentine Mitchell, 2004.

Bernard Wasserstein, *Britain and the Jews of Europe, 1939–1945*, Oxford University Press, 1979.

INDEX